Your Guide to Japan

By Amy Crabtree

First edition published 2020. Updated 2021.

ISBN 978-1-5272-6428-1

Writing, design, illustration, production and editing: Amy Crabtree.
The majority of the photos are taken by Amy Crabtree;
Stock photos are used where necessary.

cakeswithfaces.co.uk

Contents

LANGUAGE

MONEY

FOOD

SURVIVAL GUIDE

SHOPPING

MEMORIES

I first went to Japan in 2010 and must have left a little bit of my heart there, because I always want to go back. I love Tokyo and the exciting, modern side of Japan, but I'm also fascinated by the elegance of traditional Japanese symbolism and philosophies.

My interest in Japanese culture started through anime. I went to an anime club, where we watched new episodes each week and ate Kitkats.

From there my friend showed me the book *Fruits*, and I discovered colourful Harajuku fashion, with decora girls encrusted in rainbow hairclips, plastic jewellery and puffy skirts. The kawaii design style mirrored so much of what I liked in graphic art. I discovered Japanese food, took sushi lessons, started a Japanese audio course, listened to Japanese bands and finally planned my own trip, which turned out to be the first of many.

Whatever brings you to Japan and whichever of the many sides of Japanese culture got you hooked, I hope this book will help you discover Japan and have the adventure you've been dreaming of.

TAG ME IN YOUR PICS!

I always love seeing your photos - remember to tag Cakes with Faces in your pics from Japan, and you can follow my adventures on YouTube:

 @cakeswithfaces

 @cakeswithfaces

 facebook.com
/cakeswithfaces

 youtube.com
/cakeswithfaces

ABOUT THIS BOOK

Often I find that travel guides aren't that helpful, and don't include the things I want to see. So I set out to make one that's genuinely useful.

What it doesn't include:

- Lists of hotels - There are hotel booking sites for that. There are so many hotels in Tokyo that it wouldn't make sense to limit you to a list of hotels. Instead there's guidance on how to choose a hotel that suits you, and recommendations for areas to stay.
- Specific restaurants - Food in Japan is excellent. There's really no need to only go to recommended places to find good sushi or ramen - there are so many amazing places. Part of the joy is discovering them yourself. Japan's not the sort of place where you have to stick to a list to find somewhere good! (Having said that, as a vegetarian it can be tricky, so there's a list of my recommendations on my website!). Here, I'll explain the different types of Japanese food and let you know what to expect, so you can decide which you want to try.

What it includes:

- Help with booking your trip - Travelling independently allows you to do exactly what you want to, on your own schedule. I'll guide you through the process of booking flights, hotels and all the other things you need to sort out.
- Practical information - Standard travel guides offer very little help with practical issues, like how to get around and how to do things if you don't speak Japanese. I'll show you what to expect, and help out with all the things I wanted to know before I first went.
- Things to do - Places I've been and places I'd like to go. The book's focussed on Tokyo, because that's where most people go (and there's enough to do for a whole trip). There's also a section on other areas of Japan, if you fancy travelling around, or for your second/third/tenth trip! Kyoto and Osaka aren't the only places worth going to; there are so many places that we as foreigners don't hear about, beyond the popular destinations!

Lots of places from the book are featured in my videos if you want to see more of what they're like: YouTube.com/cakeswithfaces

UPDATES

Prices are correct at the time of publication. Details can change, and sometimes places even shut down (as I discovered after a good half hour searching for the Captain Jack Sparrow cake shop in the alleyways of Nakano). If you're making a special trip to a particular place, please do a quick search beforehand make sure it's going to be open.

If you come across anything that's incorrect or needs updating, please let me know via the contact form on cakeswithfaces.co.uk.

Updates will be published on cakeswithfaces.co.uk/updates

Why Japan's an Amazing Place

Here are just a few of the things I love about Japan. Everyone has different reasons to fall in love with the country - there are so many - and I'm sure you'll discover even more on your travels.

CULTURE OF RESPECT

Obviously this is a huge generalisation but on the whole, people tend to be friendly and respectful to each other. Perhaps because of the high population density, the culture's built on being polite and considerate, so everyone can get along together easily without bothering each other. While people do tend to be reserved and polite, they're also really welcoming, friendly and helpful.

IT'S A PLEASANT PLACE TO BE

It's hard to put your finger on it, but things in Japan just work. That's not to say everything's perfect (offices still use fax machines, and if you've ever tried making a booking on a Japanese website, it can be an extremely convoluted process). But the trains are on time, there are well-stocked vending machines on every corner and I've seen whole teams of workmen preening one small flower bed. It's extremely clean and there are so many conveniences you wouldn't even think of, that simply make it pleasant to be there.

Left: A helpful panda informing you about the eco-friendly features of a vending machine.

EXCELLENT SERVICE

The Japanese culture of *omotenashi* means looking after your guests and making people feel at ease. Customer service in shops and restaurants is excellent - the staff shout "irasshaimasse!" (welcome) when you enter, and you're well looked after. People pride themselves in performing their jobs well, turning up every day and devoting themselves to doing their best.

FOOD

Japan's known for excellent food, pretty much everywhere. Even cheap food is good. It's part of the reason I always look forward to going back to Japan. And it's so much cheaper than at Japanese restaurants at home. Rather than being fancy or offering a large menu, restaurants focus on providing well-prepared dishes with quality ingredients.

KAWAII STYLE

As a designer, I love how there are cute characters to spot everywhere. Kawaii mascots give a friendly face to businesses; anything can be personified with a cheerful smile, and cute characters remind you to be mindful of others on the train.

There are also so many colourful and fun things in the shops: a huge variety of clothes, stationery, kitchenware, household bits and pieces and cute character merch that you won't find anywhere else.

SO MANY PLACES TO DISCOVER

There's an amazing variety of places in Japan. The length of the country spans such a range of climates and different landscapes, with over 6,000 islands. It constantly surprises me when I discover a stunning-looking place that we never hear about. It's definitely a land of contrasts - and my list of places to visit never ends!

Glossary

bento
Japanese word for a lunchbox.
A bento box is a lunch in a box with different compartments.

bullet train
Fastest intercity train - also known as the shinkansen.

cover charge
A bit like an entry fee to a bar, paid per person with your first drink.

Edo period
Period of Japan's history: 1603 - 1868.

ema
Wooden boards at a shrine that people write their wishes on.

fukubukuro
Lucky bags full of mystery items from shops, available in the January sales.

gachapon
Capsule toys that you buy from machines - see p128.

IC card
Cards that you can use to pay for trains - see p56.

hiragana
Japanese "alphabet" of phonetic characters.

Honshu
The main island of Japan.

Hokkaido
Japan's northern island - it's wintry and snowy!

izakaya
A Japanese pub/bar

JR Pass / Japan Rail Pass
Discount train pass for foreigners - see p64.

kaitenzushi
Conveyor belt sushi restaurant.

kakigori
Shaved ice with syrup; a summer treat.

kanji
The most complex Japanese "alphabet", with thousands of pictogram characters.

katakana
Japanese "alphabet" of phonetic characters, used for foreign terms.

Kansai
Region of Japan's main island Honshu, containing Osaka and Kyoto.

kawaii
Cute, adorable or lovely.

konbini
Japanese word for convenience store.

Kyushu
Southernmost of the four main islands of Japan.

maki
Sushi roll - monomaki are single filling rolls and futomaki have multiple fillings.

matsuri
A Japanese festival.

metro / subway
In Tokyo and many other cities there are overground and underground trains. Technically in Tokyo there's the Toei Subway and Tokyo Metro. To keep it simple, in this book the terms metro and subway refer to all underground trains.

nigiri
Sushi consisting of a small, shaped ball of rice with a topping.

Okinawa
Southernmost group of islands in Japan - warm and tropical!

omikuji
Fortunes at temples and shrines.

omiyage
Japanese word for souvenirs.

onigiri
Rice ball (usually triangular) with fillings - the equivalent of a sandwich.

onsen
Natural hot spring bath - see p132.

prefecture
Japan's divided into 47 prefectures, like counties.

purikura
Photo booths where you decorate your picture with stickers and doodles.

ramen
Noodles in broth - not the same as instant ramen you might have had at home!

rotenburo
Outdoor, communal hot spring bath.

ryokan
Traditional Japanese hotel.

shinkansen
Japanese name for the bullet train.

sake
Alcoholic drink made from rice. It can be drunk warm or cold.

Shikoku
One of Japan's four main islands.

Showa era
Period between 1926 and 1989.

soba
Noodles made of buckwheat - healthier than regular noodles.

Suica / Pasmo
Cards for paying for trains. Both are types of IC cards - see p56.

Tohoku
Northern region of Japan's main island.

udon
Thick, chewy noodles.

yukata
Lightweight, summer kimono.

鉄板焼
雅
(旧ほて) 2F

曽根崎の お地蔵さん
ごて地蔵
つきあたり

神通り

Booking Your Trip

Independent Travel vs Tours

I've always preferred to plan my own trip as I like the independence, plus planning's half the fun!

You can book the flights and hotel yourself online, compare options, pick what suits you best, and plan your itinerary to see exactly what you want.

Don't worry about the language barrier - it won't stop you exploring by yourself; you really don't need a guide to help you navigate.

TOUR COMPANIES

If you'd prefer to go on an organised tour, these companies specialise in Japan:

Inside Japan
insidejapantours.com

Japan Journeys
japanjourneys.co.uk

The Dragon Trip
thedragontrip.com

INDEPENDENT

- Tailor your itinerary - see and do exactly what you're interested in. Indulge your niche interests and go beyond the mainstream tourist attractions.
- Flexibility - do what you feel like each day.
- Start and finish your days when you want to.
- Spend as long as you like getting to know each area.
- Cheaper - you're not paying for a guide.
- More planning and research - but I'll help you along the way with this book and my videos!

TOUR

- Pay for the services of a guide and tour company.
- Easier - you don't have to do as much planning.
- See a "best of" Japan.
- Have experiences that might be tricky to organise yourself.
- Meet other people if you're travelling alone.
- Fixed itinerary.
- Visit a lot of different areas - but remember that if you're visiting a different city every day, you'll be spending lots of time travelling, with limited time to explore each location.

IS IT DIFFICULT TO TRAVEL INDEPENDENTLY?

Before I went to Japan, I was worried about how difficult it might be to get around and understand everything. However, most things turned out to be easier and more accessible than I thought. Not everything's in Japanese - there's actually lots of English on signs and packaging, etc. This book will help show you what to expect, what the food's like, how to take the train and everything you need to know. You can watch my videos to see what it's like in Japan, and if there's anything you're unsure about, you can always ask in the comments.

内

Booking Checklist

- ☐ FLIGHTS
- ☐ HOTEL
- ☐ TRAVEL INSURANCE
- ☐ JR PASS (if you need one - details on p64 in the Travel section)
- ☐ YEN
- ☐ POCKET WIFI
- ☐ AIRPORT PARKING
  Or transport to the airport / airport hotel
- ☐ GET EXCITED
  You're going to Japan!

VISA

There are 68 countries (including the UK) that can visit Japan for up to 90 days on a standard tourist visa. You don't need to do anything in advance. They'll give you a slip of paper to fill in on the plane and hand in at passport control. Citizens of most Latin American, African, Asian and former Soviet Union countries need to apply for a visa from an embassy or consulate. As of 2021 an electronic visa system is in development. Check the requirements on visasjapan.com

PASSPORT

Your passport needs to be valid for the duration of your stay. There isn't any requirement for additional validity after your departure.

DEPARTURE TAX

In 2019 Japan introduced a Departure Tax (International Tourist Tax) of 1000 yen per person when you leave Japan. This is collected by your airline, as part of the fees and taxes when you book your flight.

INJECTIONS

- For most people doing normal touristy things, you don't need any vaccinations.
- If you have medical conditions, check with your doctor just to make sure.
- Going for more than a month? You might need a Japanese Encephalitis vaccine, depending when/where you're going. Check with your doctor.
- Going caving or working with bats? You might need a rabies innoculation.

Some over-the-counter medicines aren't allowed in Japan, including Vicks and medicines containing codeine or pseudoephedrine. Check online if you're not sure. Regular paracetomol/ibuprofen headache tablets are fine.

Flights

The first thing to do is book is your flights, which will probably be the most expensive part of your trip.

DIRECT VS INDIRECT

Direct flights go non-stop from your starting point to Japan, and indirect flights have one or more stopovers at airports along the way.

I used to always fly direct because I worried about missing connections and baggage getting lost! However more recently I've flown indirect. I find it more tiring and it takes longer, but it can be more convenient to fly from a local, regional airport (and the airport parking's cheaper).

DIRECT FLIGHTS

- More expensive
- Fast - get there in the shortest amount of time
- No hassle with transfers, missing connections or worrying about whether your luggage will make it to your destination.

Fly direct from the UK to Japan with ANA, JAL and British Airways.

INDIRECT FLIGHTS

- Cheaper
- Watch out for lengthy or multiple stopovers.
- You can fly from a regional airport, which might be more convenient.
- Your route doesn't have to start/ finish in Tokyo; you can fly to/ from regional airports in Japan (open jaw).

OPEN JAW / MULTI CITY FLIGHTS / STOPOVERS

If you're planning on travelling around Japan, you don't have to fly in and out of Tokyo.

Open jaw flights arrive at one city and depart from another, so for example you could fly into Osaka and leave from Tokyo.

Look out for offers with free stopovers, that include an internal flight within Japan.

DEPARTURE TAX

There's now a tax of 1000 yen for everyone leaving Japan, to pay for infrastructure for the increased levels of tourism. It's bundled as part of the airport taxes when you book your flight, so you don't need to worry about paying it separately.

Right: First glimpse of Tokyo from the plane

Haneda vs Narita

There are two airports in Tokyo:

- **Haneda Airport**
  Closer to the city (only 15-30 mins)
- **Narita Airport**
  1 hour by train

Haneda's preferable if there's a choice, but neither is a problem. I'd always choose whichever has the best flight fares.

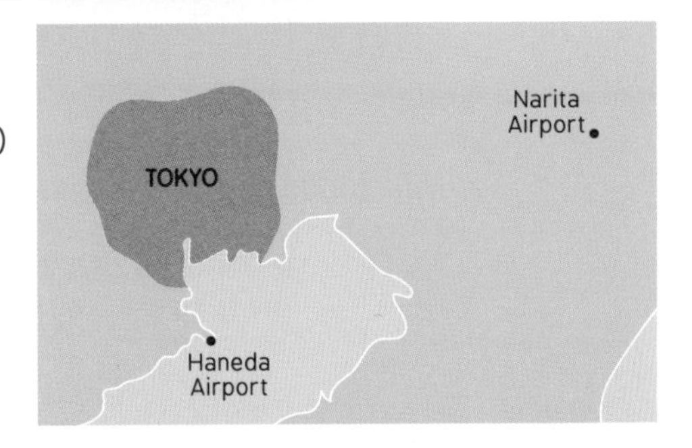

HOW TO GET FROM THE AIRPORT

Both airports are accessible by train. See p60-61 in the Getting Around section for details.

Right: A final (delicious!) taste of Japan at Haneda's departure lounge. The food options at both airports are excellent.

Booking Flights

1

CHECK COMPARISON SITES eg Skyscanner or Google Flights
They compare prices from different airlines so you can find the cheapest ones. Not all airlines are included so there might be some you need to check separately. When choosing an airline, also consider how reliable they are and how good they are in terms of comfort and service - it's a long flight. Compare prices for direct/indirect flights to help you decide. Also check prices if you book directly with Japanese airlines (ANA and JAL).

2

USE INCOGNITO MODE
Some airlines are sneaky and increase the prices if they know you're interested, to make you panic-book, so switch on incognito or private browsing mode whenever you're looking at fares.

3

COMPARE DATES
Fares vary by the day and time of year, so try different dates and days of the week to find the cheapest time to go. On some airlines' websites, if you follow the booking procedure there'll be a useful calendar showing the cheapest dates for that month.

Don't get caught out by the time difference! The day you arrive might be the day after you board your flight.

For indirect flights, double-check the stopover times in case they're too long or don't work for you.

4

SIGN UP TO AIRLINES' MAILING LISTS
You'll be the first to know about sales and offers, so you can grab them straight away when they're announced, before the cheapest tickets are booked up.

5

WHEN YOU'RE READY TO BOOK
You can either book directly on the airline's website, or through sites like Expedia.

Remember to check cashback sites. It's free to sign up and you get cashback if you follow the link from their site when you book. Even a small percentage of cashback on the cost of flights will be a good amount of money back.

After you've booked, get travel insurance as soon as possible. You'll be covered for cancellation from the start date of the policy.

Your Flight Details

OUTBOUND

DATE: TIME:

AIRLINE: FLIGHT NO:

FROM:

TO:

WHICH TERMINAL?

ARRIVAL TIME: (This might be the following day - check before booking your hotel!)

WAY BACK

DATE: TIME:

AIRLINE: FLIGHT NO:

FROM:

TO:

WHICH TERMINAL?

ARRIVAL TIME:

Types of Accommodation

HOTELS

The majority of hotels you'll see online (especially in the city) are standard hotels with western style rooms.

Rooms are small so don't expect much space, especially in Tokyo. Everywhere I've stayed has been impeccably clean, with excellent service. Breakfast isn't usually included.

Business hotels from chains like The B Hotels, Dormy Inn and Sunroute are plain but tend to have good locations and rates.

Most rooms have standard beds. Only a few have futons; if you book through a hotel site like Expedia it'll say if it's a Japanese style room.

RYOKAN

Traditional Japanese inns, with tatami mat floors and futons. Futons are really comfortable, like sleeping in a cloud; I really like them!

There are more ryokan outside the city, especially in onsen towns, where many of them have a natural hot spring shared bath, which can be indoors or outdoors. An outdoor open-air bath's called a *rotenburo*; some are in a closed courtyard, while some are surrounded by nature, or with a view.

You get a yukata to wear, while you explore the garden and enjoy a traditional Japanese meal.

Ryokans are more pricey than standard hotels because of the extra services they offer. They're a relaxing retreat, so it's fine to stay for just a night or two rather than your whole trip.

You can search for ryokans on Expedia on expedia.com/aa/ryokans

Left: Futons make small rooms seem more spacious. I think it's fun to sleep on the floor, and they're so fluffy and cosy!

CAPSULE HOTELS

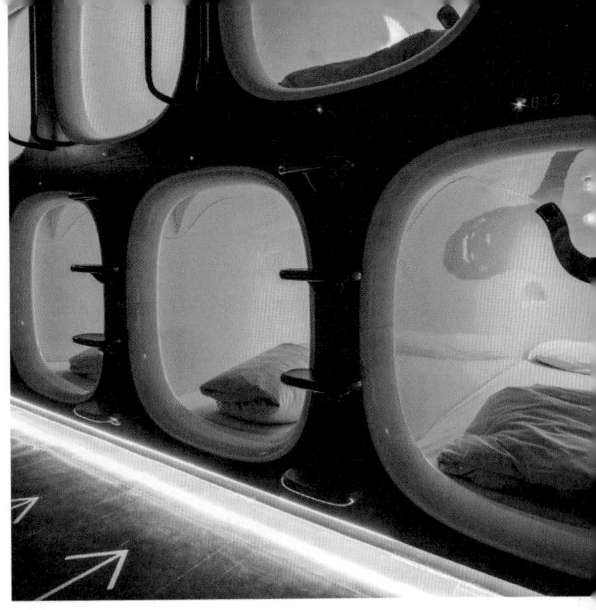

Another cheaper option and a unique experience. You sleep in a small compartment, with a locker for your belongings. Bathrooms are communal, with shower rooms, and there are separate floors for men and women. You can book them on hotel websites. *9 Hours* in Shinjuku/ Narita Airport is particularly futuristic-looking. There's also a chain called *First Cabin* that's slightly more spacious.

HOSTELS

The cheapest option if you're on a budget. Sleep in a shared dorm (some have private rooms too). Sometimes they have shared kitchens. A good option if you're travelling alone as you can meet other travellers in the communal lounges. You can book them on hotel websites - find them by searching for the lowest price.

LOVE HOTELS

Hotels for couples to stay the night or just a few hours for a "rest". Sometimes they're themed, with extra facilities like spa baths or even karaoke. You might see them on hotel websites – you can recognise them by the larger rooms and glitzy style! They also usually have a sign outside displaying the prices for "rest" and "stay". Note that once you check in, you're not supposed to leave until you check out.

AIR B&B

Often cheaper than hotels, and an option for groups and families wanting more space and facilities.

However, there are regulations in Japan restricting Airbnb rentals. In 2018 thousands of bookings were cancelled last minute because the properties didn't have the correct registration. Even if they're legal, they're often not looked on favourably by neighbours. Check the reviews and be careful.

APARTMENT HOTEL

If you need more space, an apartment hotel (or apart-hotel) is an alternative to Airbnb. They're good for families and groups. You'll have more space to spread out, and extra facilities like a kitchenette.

Citadines, Flexstay Inn and Mimaru are chains of apartment hotels - and you can also search for "serviced apartments".

Hotels often provide pyjamas and slippers to wear in your room.

Where to Stay in Tokyo

It saves time to stay somewhere central and well-connected, so you can get around easily (plus you save on train fares). Tokyo's huge, so it takes time to get from one side to the other. I like staying in areas with lots of shops and restaurants nearby - but nowhere in central Tokyo feels like the middle of nowhere!

SHINJUKU RECOMMENDED

If you want to be in the middle of everything

My favourite area to stay. It's just like you imagine Tokyo to be! There's so much going on; shops, restaurants, bars and neon lights. A very lively, busy area. However I've never had a problem with noise in my hotel room, but check reviews just in case.

Shinjuku Station (the busiest station in the world!) has lots of train lines so you can get everywhere easily. Plus it's on the Chuo line so you get across to the east side of the city quickly.

Don't be put off by Kabukicho, which some say has a bad reputation as the red light district. There are well-priced hotels and I've stayed there many times - it doesn't feel unsafe even late at night.

SHIBUYA

Similar to Shinjuku

Also an area with lots going on, places to eat, nightlife, arcades and bars on your doorstep. Shinjuku's bigger and slightly better connected.

Shinjuku

SHIMBASHI / TOKYO STATION AREA

Calmer but still well connected

Shimbashi has plenty of places to eat and is always full of salarymen in the evening, out for a drink after work. However it's calmer and less crazy than Shinjuku and Shibuya.

You can walk to Ginza, an upmarket shopping area, and Tsukiji fish market for a sushi breakfast.

Several well-connected stations are within walking distance and you're not far from Tokyo Station if you're taking the shinkansen.

AKASAKA

A central location

While it's not on the Yamanote line, Akasaka is central, making it easy to get to both sides of the city. Look how many lines you can access from Akasuka-Mitsuke and Tameike-sanno Stations!

Akasaka doesn't have a lot going on for tourists, but there are lots of hotels and it's a chilled place to stay.

Shimbashi

CHOOSING A HOTEL

There are so many hotels in Tokyo that there's no need to be limited to a list of recommended places.

Everywhere I've stayed in Japan has been impeccably clean, with excellent service. That doesn't mean everywhere will be, but Japan's a very clean place, so the standard of your hotel room isn't something you really need to worry about.

Look on a hotel comparison site, set your price range and pick somewhere that's close to a station. Have a quick look at the reviews and you won't go too far wrong!

WHAT TO EXPECT

Especially in the city, hotel rooms are small so don't expect much space. There might only be space to walk around the bed, but that's just how it is; you won't be spending much time in your hotel.

Don't worry whether the staff speak English - thousands of tourists visit Tokyo every year so they're prepared for non-Japanese speakers.

WHERE NOT TO STAY

- **EAST OF THE SUMIDA RIVER**
  I'd avoid staying here or near the SkyTree, because it's out of the way. Tokyo's a huge city; getting from one side to the other can easily take 30-40 minutes on the train.
- **ODAIBA**
  A lovely seaside area with views of Tokyo Bay. A great place to visit, but it's not the most convenient place to stay. The railway line to get there (while scenic, going over the Rainbow Bridge) costs a little more than the other lines.

STAY CLOSE TO A STATION

As long as you're close to a metro station, any area's fine, especially if it's on the JR Yamanote Line. The train system's excellent, so it's easy to get around.

I don't think anywhere in central Tokyo would be a bad place to stay or feel like you're out in the sticks. There are vending machines and convenience stores EVERYWHERE so you won't be stuck for late-night snacks or drinks.

Want a city view? Look for tall hotels - some are on top of office blocks!

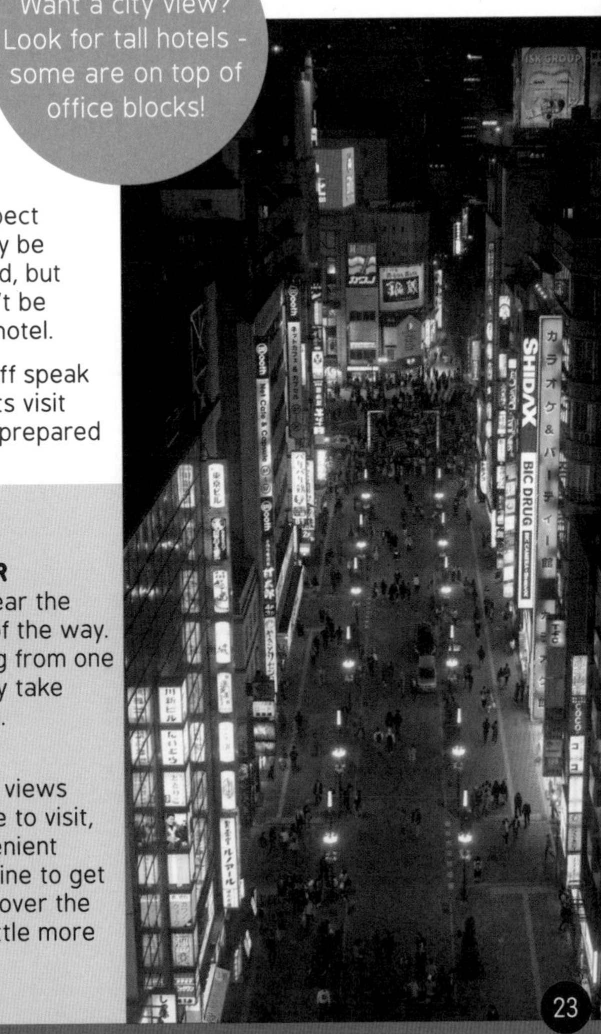

Booking your Hotel

You can book Japanese hotels on regular hotel sites like Expedia and Booking.com, and pay in your own currency with your card as usual.

WHEN TO BOOK

Book early for the largest choice of hotels, especially if you're going at a popular time (eg cherry blossom season). But be aware that most hotels don't take bookings more than 6 months in advance.

ACCOMMODATION TAX

Don't worry about this too much. It only applies in certain areas if your hotel's over a certain price (currently 10,000 yen per person per night in Tokyo), so unless you're booking an expensive hotel it won't apply. It's only 100 or 200 yen per person per night. It should be specified when you book.

GET CASHBACK

Register with a cashback site like Quidco (free to join), then use their link when you're making your booking to get cashback! You could get 10% back on your hotels.

USE A COMPARISON SITE

Sites like Trivago compare rates from different websites. Filter the prices to see what's in your budget, and pick a hotel near a station (you'll be using the train to get around every day, so you'll be doing that walk a lot!). I usually book through sites like Expedia, booking.com or hotels.com – it's just the same as booking a hotel anywhere.

The day you arrive in Japan might be the day after you left your country. So make sure you book the hotel for the correct dates (I've made that mistake!).

COMPARE OPTIONS

HOTEL

AREA

PRICE

NOTES
(Pros, cons, check reviews)

HOTEL

AREA

PRICE

NOTES
(Pros, cons, check reviews)

HOTEL

AREA

PRICE

NOTES
(Pros, cons, check reviews)

Your Hotel Details

HOTEL:

AREA:

CLOSEST STATION:

CHECK-IN TIME:

Most hotels can store your luggage if you arrive before check-in time.

HOW TO GET TO YOUR HOTEL:

Routes for getting from the airport are on p60-61.
There are two airports for Tokyo, so check which one you're arriving at.

NOTES

Where to Go

There's so much to do in Tokyo - I've stayed there for up to two weeks at a time and not run out of things to do. But there's a lot more to see around the country as well! Consider what interests you about Japan, and what sort of things you want to do on your trip.

Should you stay in Tokyo or travel around the country?

STAY IN TOKYO

- There's plenty to see and do. Depending on what you're interested in, you can easily plan a week or two's worth of things to do.
- Experience big city Japan, shopping and modern culture - and there are also shrines, temples and gardens.
- You can still go on day trips in the Tokyo area, for a flavour of Japan outside the city.
- Avoid the expense of a Japan Rail Pass.

TRAVEL AROUND JAPAN

- Most of Japan is nothing like Tokyo!
- More shrines, temples, onsen, old towns and historic Japan.
- If it's your second (or third or fourth!) trip, see more of what Japan has to offer.
- It's easy and comfortable to travel long distances on the bullet train. You'll need a Japan Rail Pass. Or there are internal flights for very long distances.
- Make sure you have enough time to explore each place, so you're not spending your days on the train.
- With the increase in tourism over the last 10 years, well-known destinations like Kyoto have become quite crowded. Consider visiting less popular places for a more unique experience, away from the crowds.
- Japan's a long country that spans different climates, so there's a huge variety of types of places to visit. Relax in the tropical paradise of Okinawa, or explore Hokkaido, the snowy winter wonderland. There are mountains, rural towns and rice fields, rugged coastlines and even sand dunes.

Plan your Route

Which areas and cities do you want to visit? The next step is to plan your route!

The bullet train makes it easy to travel around Japan. For example, it only takes about 2.5 hours from Tokyo to Kyoto/Osaka. While the regular trains are excellent too, if you're travelling longer distances, you'll be able to move around much quicker if you plan your route largely around the bullet train network.

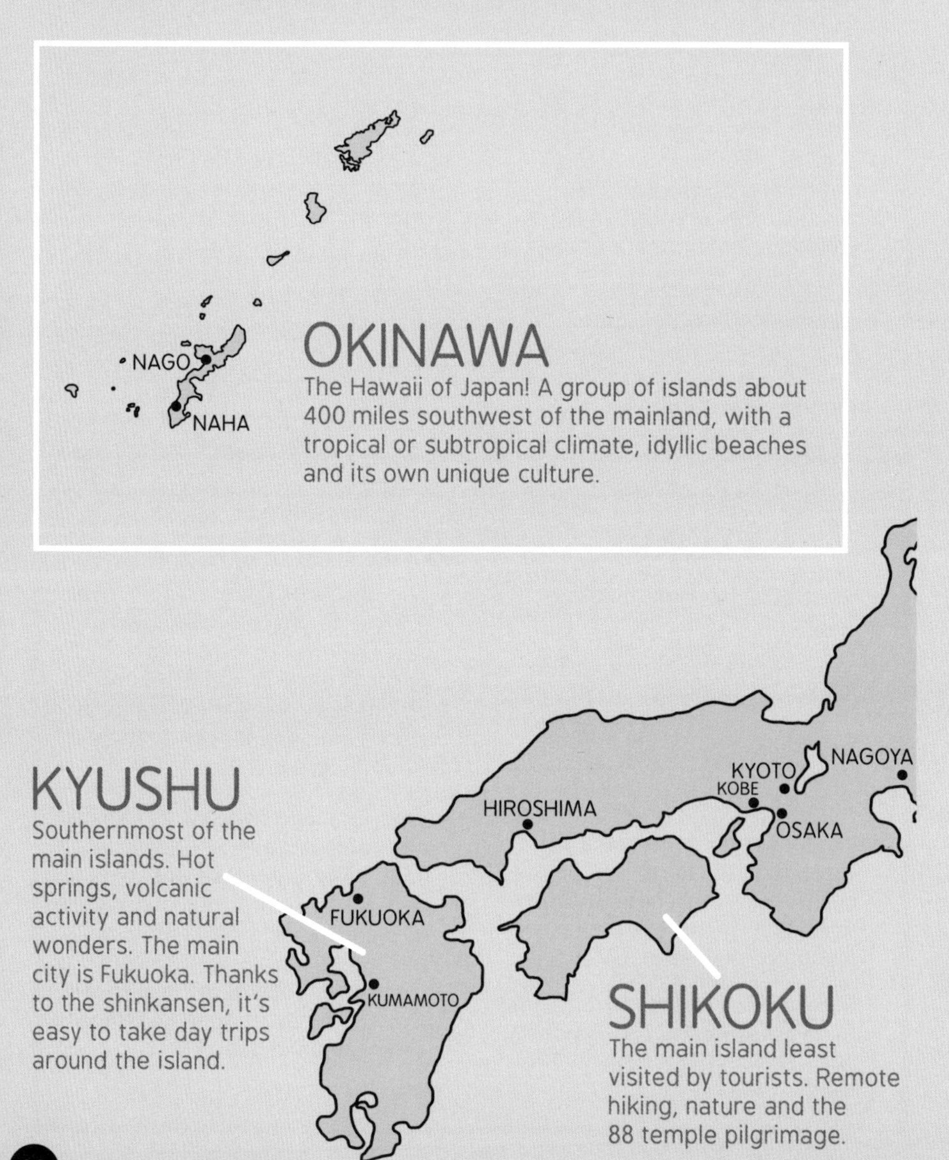

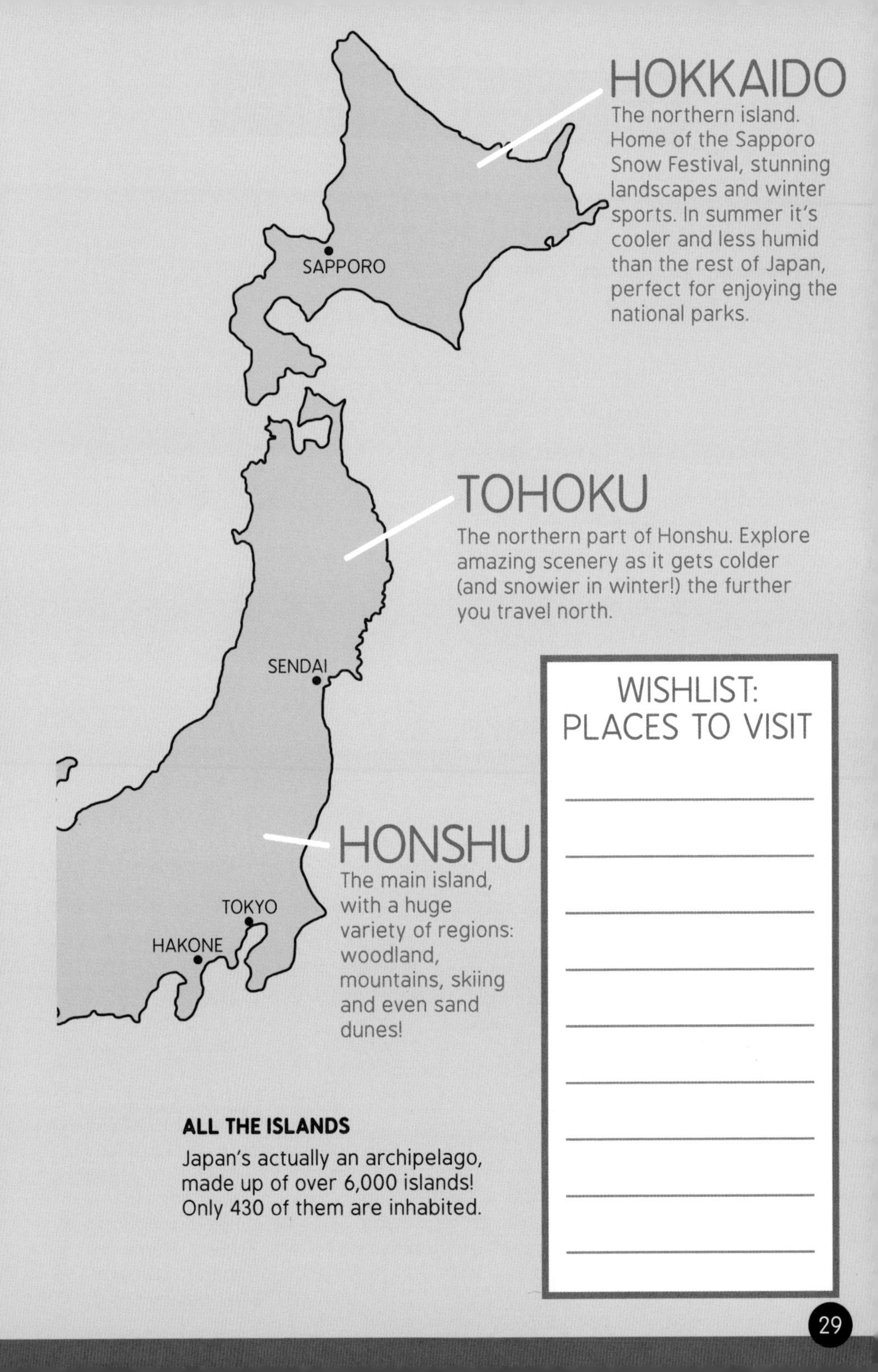
HOKKAIDO
The northern island. Home of the Sapporo Snow Festival, stunning landscapes and winter sports. In summer it's cooler and less humid than the rest of Japan, perfect for enjoying the national parks.
SAPPORO
TOHOKU
The northern part of Honshu. Explore amazing scenery as it gets colder (and snowier in winter!) the further you travel north.
SENDAI
WISHLIST: PLACES TO VISIT
HONSHU
The main island, with a huge variety of regions: woodland, mountains, skiing and even sand dunes!
TOKYO
HAKONE
ALL THE ISLANDS
Japan's actually an archipelago, made up of over 6,000 islands! Only 430 of them are inhabited.

Sample Itineraries

THE GOLDEN ROUTE

The most popular itinerary, covering Japan's "greatest hits".

TOKYO

↓

HAKONE

Visit Mount Fuji and Fuji Five Lakes. It's a hot springs area so you can stay at a traditional Japanese hotel with an onsen (hot spring bath).

↓

KYOTO/OSAKA

Kyoto's the heart of historic Japan, with temples, shrines, traditional gardens and historic streets.

The bustling city of Osaka's only 30 minutes away by train. It's known as the food capital of Japan.

↓

TOKYO

SOMETHING TO CONSIDER

Because it's the most popular route, these places are increasingly busy. Visiting other areas of Japan is a way to have a more unique experience, away from the crowds. Kyoto's not the only place you can see beautiful temples and historic streets. There are so many other amazing places in Japan to discover, beyond these popular areas.

MY ITINERARIES

Here are some of my previous itineraries, in case you find them useful.
There are ideas for things to do in all these places in the "What to do" section.

MY VERSION OF THE GOLDEN ROUTE

Fly into **TOKYO**
Immediately take the bullet train to Kyoto

↓

KYOTO (4 nights)

Day trips to Hiroshima & Miyajima

Bullet train to Tokyo

↓

TOKYO (10 nights)

HOKURIKU ARCH

Another version of the Golden Route is the Hokuriku Arch. Take a more scenic route from Osaka/Kyoto to Tokyo via historic Kanazawa, the Japanese Alps and Nagano.

EXPLORING KYUSHU & TOKYO

I really enjoyed the southern island of Kyushu. It's full of volcanic activity and unique places.

Fly into Fukuoka

FUKUOKA (5 nights)
Day trips around Kyushu

↓

OSAKA (3 nights)

↓

TOKYO (5 nights)

Fly home from Tokyo

JAPAN'S WINTER WONDERLAND

Tokyo and Hokkaido, travelling by bullet train and stopping off along the way. There are lots of other interesting stopovers in Tohoku too.

Tokyo (5 nights)

↓

Hakodate (1 night)
Picturesque coastal town with one of Japan's top night views.

↓

Sapporo (3 nights)
For the Sapporo Snow Festival, with a day trip to Otaru for the snow lantern festival.

↓

Matsushima (1 night)
One of Japan's top scenic views: a bay with over 200 tiny islands.

↓

Fly home from Tokyo

MY RECOMMENDATION

Don't limit yourself to these routes. Read blogs, look online, and find places you find interesting to build your own perfect trip.

Make sure you have enough time to explore and enjoy each place. Don't pack too much in and find yourself constantly on the train. The aim is to have a good time, not see EVERYTHING.

Spring

A popular time to visit Japan, because of the comfortable weather and cherry blossom season.

CHERRY BLOSSOMS (SAKURA)

End March/early April
The most popular time to visit Japan (and therefore also the busiest time!). They don't last long - each year there's a cherry blossom forecast to help you catch them. They start in the south and move north like a wave as the temperature warms up. There are hanami (cherry blossom viewing) parties in parks under the blossoms. You can look up the most popular spots in each town. There are also special sakura-flavoured snacks!

GOLDEN WEEK

A week of bank holidays at the end of April / start of May. Lots of people take the week off work to travel or visit family. There are festivals but it's extremely busy on the trains, at tourist attractions and holiday / day trip destinations.

WEATHER

Springtime's comfortable and warm - a favourite time to visit! It can rain at any time of year so be prepared.

March	Max 14°C	Min 5°C
April	Max 19°C	Min 10°C
May	Max 23°C	Min 15°C

(Average temperatures for Tokyo)

MISSED THE CHERRY BLOSSOMS?

They're not the only seasonal flowers! Flower parks put on special displays throughout the year.

- Ume (plum blossoms) - Late February, before the sakura. They're a brighter pink colour.
- Wisteria - Late April / early May. Walk through beautiful lilac tunnels.

REGIONAL VARIATION

Japan's a long country, so the climate varies between Hokkaido in the north and Kyushu in the south. And the islands of Okinawa are sub-tropical! So you'll need to adjust the temperatures up or down slightly for where you're going.

Summer

Summer's very hot and humid - but there are festivals to enjoy if you can cope with the heat.

TYPHOONS

The peak months for typhoons are August and September. There are around 3 per year in southern Japan, and around 7 or 8 in Okinawa.

Typhoons can be mild, like a windy rainstorm, or they can be more serious, disrupting travel.

RAINY SEASON

Mid June - mid July
1 month earlier in Okinawa

It doesn't rain every day, but you'll definitely get several rainy days during your trip. It varies between light rain and downpours. Hokkaido isn't affected by the rainy season.

FESTIVALS

- Tanabata - 7th July. Decorated with colourful streamers.
- Mitama Matsuri at Yasukuni Shrine, Tokyo, mid July. 20,000 lanterns illuminate the evening.
- Bon / Obon - mid August. Paper lanterns and dancing to honour the spirits of ancestors.
- Fireworks festivals - July and August, all around Japan.

As well as the major festivals, there are lots of smaller ones too so look out for what's on when you're there. Rent a yukata (a lightweight, summer kimono), enjoy the street food and join in!

WEATHER

Summer gets extremely humid and it can be uncomfortable, especially when you're walking around all day. Early June is pleasant if you like hot sunny weather. However it's a risky time: it's just before the rainy season!

June	Max 24°C	Min 18°C
July	Max 29°C	Min 23°C
Aug	Max 31°C	Min 24°C

(Average temperatures for Tokyo)

Autumn

Another popular time to visit; the weather's warm and comfortable, and there are beautiful fall colours.

HALLOWEEN

Although Halloween's western, it's become really popular in Japan - in a very kawaii way. You'll see lots of cute things, displays, photo spots and special edition snacks!

If you're there for Halloween itself, there are Halloween parades and parties. Shibuya crossing is packed, and there's a major parade in Kawasaki.

Earlier in October, there's the Bake-Neko Festival in Kagurazaka (Tokyo) where people dress up as cats!

SEASONAL SPECIALITIES

Look out for chestnut, pumpkin, sweet potato and montblanc flavours. Japan's all about seasonal specialities, so you'll find special edition snacks and drinks throughout the year.

WEATHER

Warm t-shirt weather, staying mild as it gets cooler. Perfect for walking around exploring and hiking.

Sept	Max 27°C	Min 21°C
Oct	Max 22°C	Min 15°C
Nov	Max 17°C	Min 9°C

(Average temperatures for Tokyo)

AUTUMN COLOURS

Autumn leaves in Japan are particularly spectacular, with red maple and yellow gingko. You can look up the most popular viewing spots, or head out to the countryside on a day trip.

They start later than you might think; usually in November.

TYPHOONS

On average only 3 typhoons a year reach the main islands of Japan, usually in the south. In Okinawa, much further south, there are around 7 or 8 per year. August and September are the peak months.

Typhoons involve strong winds and heavy rain. They can be mild, like a bad rainstorm, but occasionally they're more serious, causing transport problems.

Winter

Benefit from the off-season with cheaper flights, and the lowest crowd levels (apart from during winter festivals).

SNOW FESTIVALS

The Sapporo Snow Festival's the most famous, but there are lots of other snow festivals too. They're smaller but less commercial - and just as magical! Search for "snow festival" + the place + the month. They'll be around Tohoku and Hokkaido where it's snowy.

WINTER ILLUMINATIONS

Dazzling displays, with thousands of LEDs. They're not just for Christmas; winter illuminations continue into the new year, even until March. Find them around Tokyo, or head out of town for the largest and most spectacular illuminations at Yomiuriland, Lake Sagamiko and many more.

FUKUBUKURO

Japan's version of January Sales. Look out for fukubukuro (lucky bags) in the shops, where you get a mystery selection of items for a bargain price.

WILL IT SNOW?

Hokkaido and northern Japan get a lot of snow, from late November/December until mid April. There are mountain resorts for skiing and winter sports.

In Tokyo it only snows occasionally. The further north you go, the more likely it is to be snowy.

CHRISTMAS

In Japan Christmas is a day for couples. You'll see interesting translations of the western holiday - like KFC for Christmas dinner!

NEW YEAR

Some attractions, shops and restaurants close for a few days and transport can be busy as people visit family. It's traditional to visit temples and shrines to start the new year.

WEATHER

Winter in Tokyo's fairly mild (although you'll still need a winter coat). It's the least rainy time of year. It gets a lot colder as you go north. In Hokkaido it can even get down to -20°C!

Dec	Max 12°C	Min 4°C
Jan	Max 10°C	Min 2°C
Feb	Max 10°C	Min 2°C

(Average temperatures for Tokyo)

Countdown

6 MONTHS TO GO

- ☐ Book your hotel.
- ☐ Start Japlanning!
- ☐ Keep an eye on the yen rate.
- ☐ Get your travel insurance sorted so you're covered for cancellation.

3 MONTHS TO GO

- ☐ Get your JR Pass if you need one (more on p64).
- ☐ Arrange transport to the airport or parking.
- ☐ Make sure you have comfy shoes for walking and start wearing them in.
- ☐ Check what special events are on during your trip.

1 MONTH TO GO

- ☐ Book tickets for places like Studio Ghibli (p127), TeamLab Borderless (p137) and Tokyo Disney (p152).
- ☐ Book theme cafes.
- ☐ Remember to get your yen if you haven't already (you'll definitely need cash).
- ☐ Book your pocket wifi (p38).
- ☐ Reserve bullet train seats online if you want to.
- ☐ Apply for a visa if you need one. If you're in the UK or one of the other 68 countries that are exempt, you don't need to do anything. Check visasjapan.com for details.

1 WEEK TO GO

- ☐ Check how to find your hotel.
- ☐ Check the weather forecast.
- ☐ Empty your camera's memory cards - you're going to need them!
- ☐ Make sure you have travel plug adapters.
- ☐ Go shopping for toiletries.

DAY BEFORE YOU FLY

- ☐ Charge your camera batteries.
- ☐ Finish packing.

Pocket Wifi

Rent a pocket wifi to use the internet when you're out and about in Japan.

You can connect several phones or tablets, so you can share one device for your group if you'll be travelling around together.

IS IT ESSENTIAL?

It certainly makes it easier to be able to look things up, check opening times, routes and use Google Maps and Google Translate whenever you need to.

I've travelled with and without one. While it's possible to survive in Japan without internet, it makes things a lot easier and I'd always get one now!

If you don't want to rent a pocket wifi, there are free, offline map apps that don't require data (Maps.Me and Ulmon City Maps 2 Go), and most hotels provide free wifi in your room.

SIM CARDS

An alternative is buying a Japanese sim card for your phone. Some people prefer it as it means you don't have to carry an extra box.

However the advantage of a pocket wifi is that you can attach more than one device, so you only need one for everyone in your group, and you can also use it simultaneously with tablets and laptops.

FREE WIFI AROUND JAPAN

Shops, cafes and stations often offer free wifi. However, it can require registration and isn't always available for non-Japanese residents.

AIRBNBS / APARTMENTS

If you're staying in an apartment or Airbnb, sometimes they provide a pocket wifi or a phone for you to use. If it's a phone, be careful about logging in to anything personal or saving passwords on a shared device.

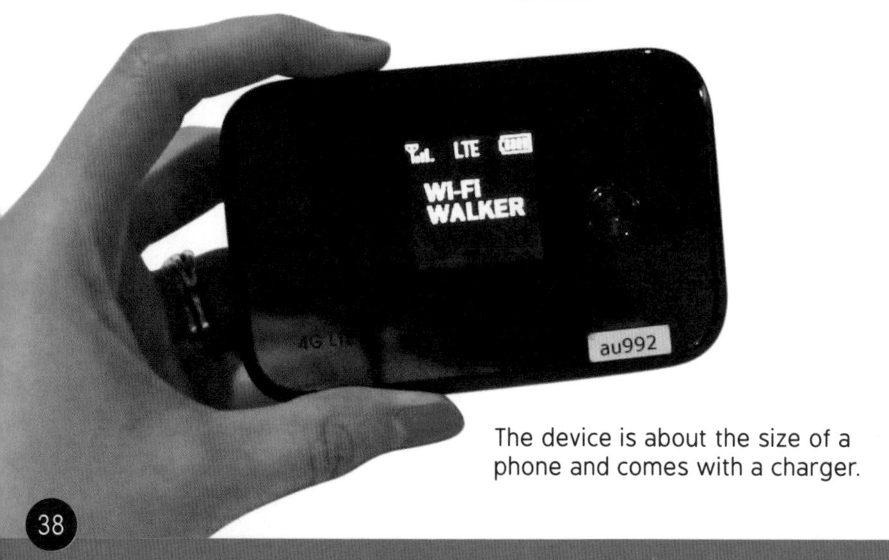

The device is about the size of a phone and comes with a charger.

WHERE TO GET A POCKET WIFI

There are lots of companies that rent pocket wifis. I use japan-rail-pass.co.uk.

While there are cheaper places, I've always found them reliable. My wifi's always been waiting for me, and coverage has been good throughout Japan, even on day trips in the countryside. (Some really remote areas aren't covered, but I haven't come across them yet).

Make your booking online before you travel. You can pick it up at the airport or have it delivered to you in Japan.

PICKING UP YOUR WIFI

You can choose to pick it up at the airport or have it delivered to your hotel. The bonus of picking it up at the airport is that you can use it to help find your hotel! When you book, they'll tell you which counter to get it from. You get the device, charger, a pouch and return envelope.

RETURNING YOUR WIFI

At the end of your trip, post it back in the envelope provided. You'll need to post it in Japan before you leave. There are charges if you forget, so make a note of where your nearest postbox is below!

Saving Up

Work out your budget in the Money section (p208) and colour in the SkyTree as you save up! If you need motivation, think of all the ramen and gachapon you'll buy in Japan!

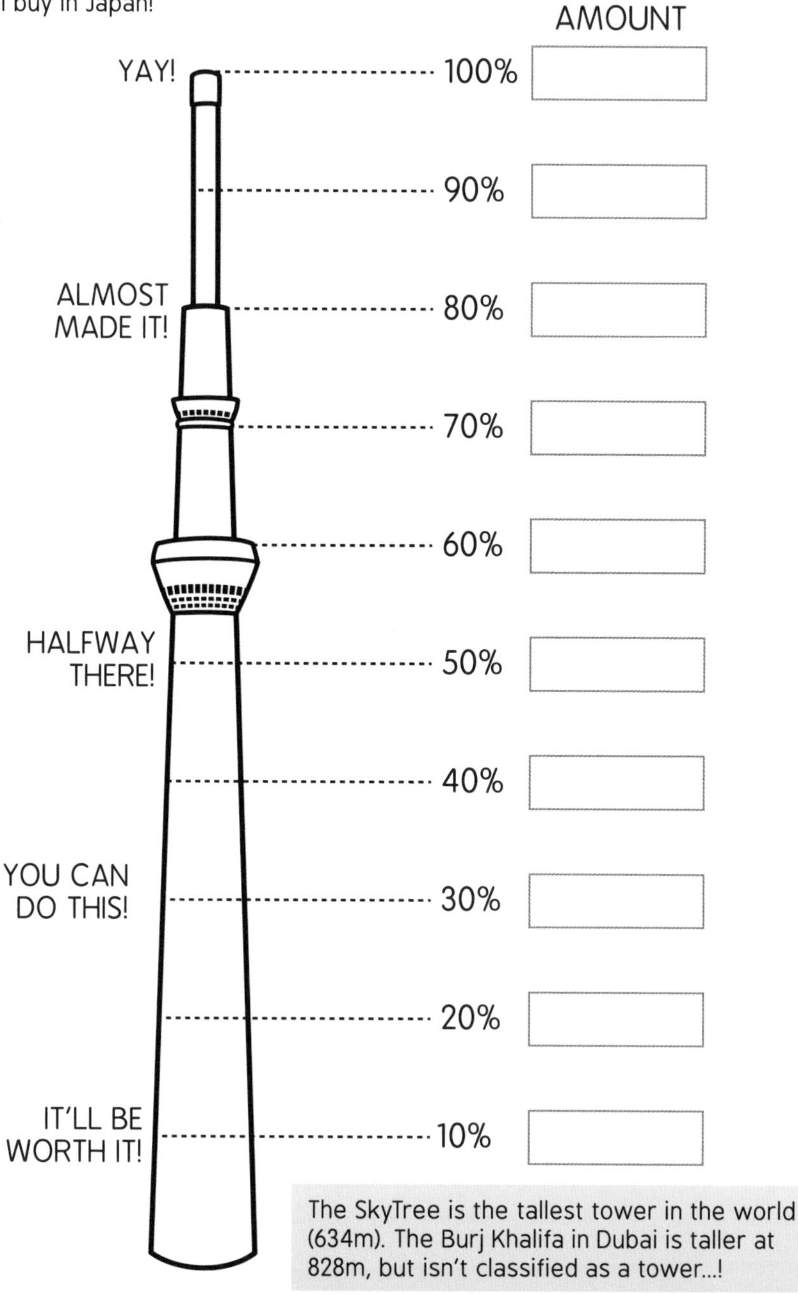

The SkyTree is the tallest tower in the world (634m). The Burj Khalifa in Dubai is taller at 828m, but isn't classified as a tower...!

Tips for a Budget Trip

AIRMILES

Join your airline's loyalty scheme and start collecting airmiles to pay for your flights. It's a long term plan, but it'll be worth it in the end! The long haul flight to Japan will give you lots of airmiles. You can also collect them from supermarket loyalty card schemes, credit cards and online shopping referral sites. When you eventually get your free flights, you'll have to pay the airport taxes, but it's still a big saving.

SALES

Join airlines' mailing lists and wait for sales and offers. Book as soon as you can when the sale's announced for the best choice of dates.

BE FLEXIBLE

Check various dates and find the cheapest time to travel. Flight prices vary by day and time of year. The off-season in winter is cheaper, and certain days of the week will be cheaper too.

FLY INDIRECT

Flying indirect usually saves money. But remember to check how long the stopovers are (the cheapest flights often have long or multiple stopovers).

Japan isn't as expensive as it's perceived to be; The most expensive part is flights & accommodation

ENTRANCE FEES

You'll probably find that a lot of what you're doing is walking around exploring, which doesn't cost anything.

There are lots of free things to do - many temples and shrines don't have admission fees, parks and festivals are free, and you can even get a free view of the city from the Metropolitan Government Building.

TRANSPORT

Walk where you can to save on train fares. Metro stations are often quite close together so if you're only going a stop or two it might be walkable; check Google Maps for distances.

Plan your days so you're not constantly criss-crossing the city - those journeys can add up (and they take time). If you'll be travelling by train a lot on a particular day, it might be cheaper to get a day pass (details on p54 in the Getting Around section).

FOOD

Eating out isn't that expensive in Japan. Even cheap food is excellent, and there are lots of small restaurants where you can get a good meal for less than 1000 yen.

Convenience stores are great for breakfast or lunch - onigiri rice balls, the equivalent of sandwiches, are around 100 yen.

However, there's no need to stick to convenience stores if you're on a budget - and you'd definitely be missing out on a lot of good stuff! At conveyor belt sushi and standing sushi bars, plates are around 100 yen. Ramen, curry rice and other noodle dishes are often less than 1000 yen - and they're excellent quality.

Packing List

CLOTHES

no. of days

- ☐ Comfy shoes
- ☐ Waterproof shoes
- ☐ Underwear
- ☐ Socks
- ☐ Jacket or coat
- ☐ Hoodies
- ☐ T-shirts
- ☐ Jeans/trousers/skirts
- ☐ Dresses
- ☐ Clothes for flight home
- ☐ Gloves/hat/scarf/thermals

TOILETRIES

- ☐ Shampoo
- ☐ Conditioner
- ☐ Dry shampoo
- ☐ Deodorant
- ☐ Toothpaste
- ☐ Toothbrush
- ☐ Antibacterial hand gel
- ☐ Razor
- ☐ Moisturiser
- ☐ Lip balm
- ☐ Make-up
- ☐ Make-up remover
- ☐ Ziplock bag for carry-on liquids

ACCESSORIES

- ☐ Sunglasses
- ☐ Suncream
- ☐ Umbrella
- ☐ Hairbrush
- ☐ Small bag / backpack
- ☐ Contact lenses / glasses case

MEDICAL

Some medication isn't allowed in Japan, including Vicks and some over-the-counter medicines. Check with your doctor if you're not sure.

- ☐ Ibuprofen
- ☐ Plasters
- ☐ Antiseptic cream
- ☐ Any other medication

DOCUMENTS & IMPORTANT THINGS:

- ☐ Passport
- ☐ Yen
- ☐ Credit card for use abroad
- ☐ Debit card for use abroad
- ☐ Purse/wallet
- ☐ Hotel confirmation print-out
- ☐ Flight e-ticket
- ☐ Travel insurance
- ☐ JR Pass
- ☐ Pocket wifi confirmation

ENTERTAINMENT & ELECTRONICS

- ☐ Phone
- ☐ Phone charger
- ☐ Plug converter
- ☐ Portable charger
- ☐ Camera
- ☐ Camera charger
- ☐ Reading book / tablet / entertainment
- ☐ Headphones
- ☐ Memory cards
- ☐ Phrase book
- ☐ Notebook
- ☐ Pen
- ☐ Your Guide to Japan :-)

PACKING TIPS

- If you're planning on going shopping in Japan, pack as light as you can!
- Check if your airline allows two suitcases per person. If they do, pack a medium-sized case inside a larger one, then pack your things inside that. Then you have a spare case for the way back! Or pack an empty holdall or sports bag for your purchases.
- Take a mini suitcase as hand luggage if you need extra room.
- Pack your toiletries in ziplock bags in case they leak.
- A spare plastic bag or two's always useful for dirty clothes.
- Wear your bulkiest clothes and biggest shoes (as long as they're comfy for the plane!).

NOTES

Getting Around

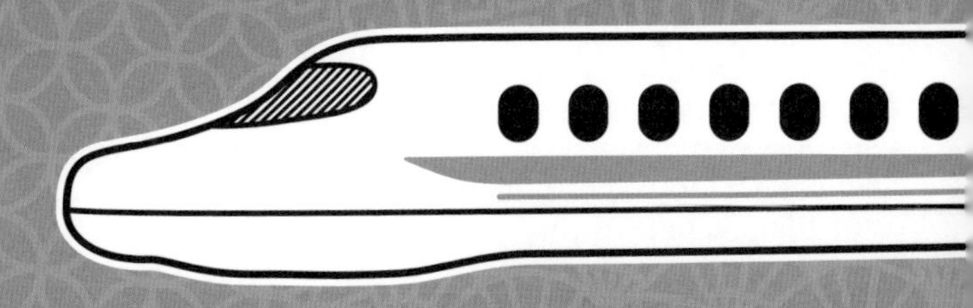

How to get around Tokyo

TRAINS

Tokyo's train system is excellent; both the underground metro and overground railways.

It's clean, efficient, frequent, affordable and definitely the best way to get around the city.

Really this is the only method of transport you need.

WALKING

Tokyo's huge so you can't walk across the whole city, but if you're only going a stop or two on the metro, it's often walkable (less than 20 minutes). For example, if you're going from Shinjuku to Harajuku you can walk through Meiji Jingu shrine. It's a great way to see more of the city and discover surprises along the way!

There's a useful map on Tokyo Cheapo that tells you the walking times between stations: tokyocheapo.com/tokyo-cheapo-walking-subway-map

Even if you're taking the train you can end up walking quite a long way, so make sure you have comfortable shoes and wear them in before your trip!

HOW TO GET FROM THE AIRPORT

Details are on p60-61

BUS

There are buses; in Tokyo you don't need them, because the trains take you everywhere you need to go.

But look how cute the character mascot is! He's called Mikuru, the mascot of Toei buses.

CAR HIRE

You don't need a car in Tokyo; public transport is excellent and you can take day trips outside the city on the train.

If you're travelling around Japan, you'll only need a car if you want to go somewhere remote that doesn't have a station. The bullet train's much faster and more convenient for long distances.

BOAT

There are sightseeing cruises up the Sumida River and across Tokyo Bay to Odaiba.

Look out for the Himiko / Hotaluna, the most futuristic-looking boat I've ever seen - it was designed by an anime artist!

TAXIS

Taxis are quite expensive so avoid taking them if you can, especially from the airport.

You can find them at taxi ranks or by hailing on the street. The doors open automatically and the drivers are very smart, with white gloves! If you don't speak Japanese, it's easiest to write down your destination or show them on your phone. You'll need cash to pay, and there's no tipping.

Map Apps

In Japan not all the streets have names, and addresses are confusing, so forget about them - if there's somewhere you want to go, just search by name or pin it on a map.

GOOGLE MAPS

If you're getting a pocket wifi (details on p38), you can use Google Maps in Japan, just the same as everywhere else.

It's really useful and easy to search for tourist attractions, shops and restaurants in English. You can even use it for directions and to check how long it'll take to get there.

OFFLINE MAPS

If you're not getting a pocket wifi or if you want a back-up, these offline maps apps are free:

- Maps.me
- Ulmon City Maps2Go

Both of these work offline, so you don't need an internet connection or data. Download the maps before you go, and add pins for places you want to visit.

Just like Google Maps, they also show where you are - so you can't get lost!

TIPS FOR FINDING PLACES

Finding particular restaurants or places can sometimes be tricky. Places can be a little hidden away.

- Remember that it might not be on ground level. Sometimes you have to go upstairs or take a shady-looking lift to an upper floor, or go downstairs below ground.
- Look for signs (which can sometimes be tiny!).
- Shops and restaurants might be inside stations. Larger stations have whole underground shopping malls, which can be huge! See if you can find out which section it's in, so you can follow signs to the right place.
- Look up a picture before you go, so you know what you're looking for (especially for restaurants).

What If I Don't Know Japanese?

Before I first went to Japan I was worried that everything would be in Japanese and I wouldn't even be able to tell what was what.

However, it's not like that at all! There's a surprising amount of English. You'll be able to understand all the signs you need in the stations, ticket machines and announcements on the train. Signs and tourist maps on the street are also in English.

If you need to ask for help, some people speak or understand English, but not everyone. However it's amazing how much you can communicate with pointing and gestures!

Some trains even have displays indicating how long it'll take to get to each station. They alternate between Japanese and English.

What if I Get Lost?

You'll definitely get lost - it's virtually impossible to visit Tokyo and not take a wrong turning inside a station at some point! But don't worry about it - you'll be ok. It's all about your attitude - instead of calling it getting lost, think of it as exploring!

- All the signs you need are in English as well as Japanese - including most public maps and signs in stations.
- There are so many metro stations in Tokyo that if you just keep wandering, it won't be long before you come across one, and then you'll know exactly where you are!
- If you lose your way in a station, just go back, look out for signs and you'll find your way.
- If you take the wrong train, just get off and take the return train back - it won't cost you extra.
- People in Japan are generally friendly and helpful. There have been several times when I've been standing looking confused, and someone's come to my rescue!
- You can't really get lost forever if you have Google Maps.

Watch my Getting Lost in Japan video and see what it's like finding somewhere we've never been before!

Accessibility

TRAINS

Stations have multiple exits, many of which have steps as the only option. However, there's usually at least one exit with a lift and/or escalator if you know where to find it. Look for signs, or check the Accessible Japan website (accessible-japan.com) to find out which exit to use.

If you ask at the ticket gate, staff will take you to the platform and fetch a ramp to help you get on the train. They'll even phone ahead to your destination, so someone's waiting to help you get off. Trains have priority seats and areas for wheelchairs.

SHOPS AND RESTAURANTS

Smaller shops and restaurants can be quite cramped, without much space to manoeuvre. Larger shops and establishments, for example in malls and department stores, tend to have lifts, wide aisles and smooth floors.

ATTRACTIONS

Shopping malls and museums are usually barrier-free, with accessible bathrooms. However, at temples, shrines and castles there can be steps, steep slopes or uneven ground. There may still be parts you can enjoy - for example at Fushimi Inari Shrine in Kyoto the main part of the shrine is accessible, but not the whole trail of tori gates up the mountain.

ACCESSIBLE JAPAN

Useful site with information about accessible hotels, restaurants, bathrooms and attractions - including which exits at stations are step-free: *accessible-japan.com*

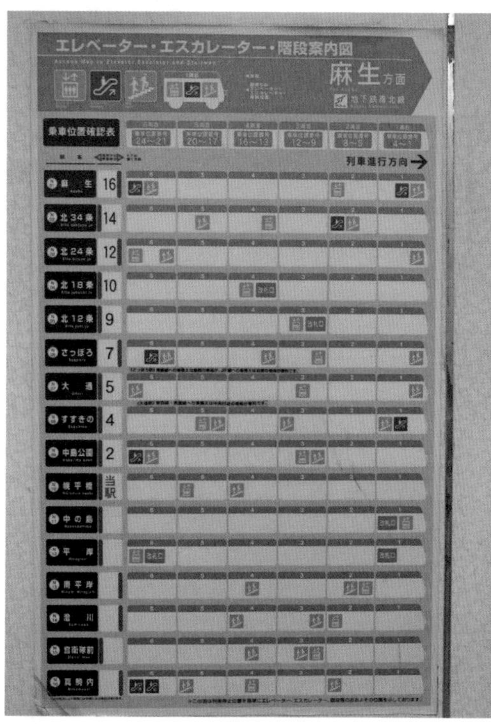

This sign tells you which train carriage is nearest the escalator or lift at each station when you get off.

Trains

Tokyo has an excellent network of underground metro lines and overground trains. They're clean, safe and the best way to get around the city.

IS IT BUSY?

Out of the 50 busiest stations in the world, 45 of them are in Japan! However, it's not really that bad on the trains. We've all seen the videos of people being pushed into carriages, but it's not like that the majority of the time.

If it's busy when you get off the train, wait at the side for a moment for the crowd to clear, then it should be a little calmer.

I'm not a huge fan of crowds, but in Tokyo it's a lot more bearable because of the culture. In general, people are respectful and considerate of others - it's organised so the crowds flow and people don't tend to push in front of you.

Having said that, avoid rush hour if you can, especially when you're travelling with luggage. Once I took the Yamanote Line from Shinjuku (the busiest station in the world) to Shinagawa in the pre-9am rush hour with suitcases. Let's just say it was a memorable experience, but not one I'd recommend!

Cute signs by the doors - don't make the train cry!

Tokyo Train Map

The metro map includes underground and overground trains in central Tokyo. It looks confusing at first, but it's actually not that bad. It takes you everywhere you need to go!

- **Thick, colourful lines** are the underground metro lines. They're run by two different companies (Tokyo Metro and Toei Subway).
- **Black and white stripy line** that goes around the city is the JR Yamanote line. It's very useful!
- **Thin green lines** on the bottom right of the map in the Tokyo bay area are the Yurikamome and Rinkai lines. They take you to Odaiba and Tokyo Disney. The Yurikamome line's a driverless railway.
- **Thin line going east-west** across the city is the JR Chuo and Sobu line. It's very useful but easily missed because it doesn't show up very well on the map! It's a great way to get across the city quickly, from one side to the other. It can save you a lot of time if you're going between Shinjuku and Tokyo Station or Akihabara. Plus, it's a JR line, so it's free if your JR Pass is valid while you're in Tokyo (same for the JR Yamanote line).

TOKYO METRO MAP

You can find the Tokyo metro map on tokyometro.jp/en/subwaymap

Print out a copy to take with you, or save it on your phone.

There are several free apps for trains in Tokyo. I use "Tokyo Rail Map" from Urban-Map. You can search for stations and it'll tell you the quickest way. Note that the official app from Tokyo Subway doesn't include JR lines, so won't always show you the best route!

Tokyo Train Tickets

RECOMMENDED

IC CARD (SUICA OR PASMO)

The easiest way to pay for your trains, and my top recommendation because it's the simplest option.

It's valid for all trains and the metro. Simply top up your card with credit and swipe it as you go through the ticket barriers.

More details on p56.

SINGLE TICKETS

You can get single paper tickets from the machines (they're tiny!). I'd avoid getting them unless you have to - it's a lot of hassle buying a ticket for every trip. However, they're useful if it's your last day and you don't want to top up your IC card.

TIP: AT THE END OF YOUR TRIP

To avoid losing money by topping up your IC card with cash you won't use, here's what to do once you've used up all your credit:

Buy a single ticket from the ticket machine. If you're not sure which to get, just get the cheapest one.

When you get to your destination, go to the Fare Adjustment Machine just before the ticket barriers and pay the correct fare.

DAY PASSES

Several day passes are available, which can save you money if you're taking a lot of trains.

However, be careful to get the right one. The train lines are run by multiple different companies, and most passes don't cover all of them. That's why I recommend a Suica card - it covers all the trains, so you don't have to worry about which lines you'll need that day.

However, if you're on a budget a day pass might save you money, depending on your itinerary. The best is probably:

TOKYO SUBWAY TICKET

- 1, 2 or 3 days.
- Covers all underground lines.
- Doesn't include: JR lines (eg the JR Yamanote line), overground trains or private companies like the train to Odaiba. Basically it includes the thick, colourful lines on the map.
- Buy from the airport, Tokyo Station, Nihonbashi Station or tourist information centres in Tokyo Metro Ueno or Ginza Station.
- It's only for foreigners - so you'll need to show your passport when you buy it.

DAY TRIPS

Often you can use your Suica/Pasmo card for day trips outside the city. But in some cases, special tourist packages are available that'll save you money. I'll mention them as we go along.

TICKET MACHINES

There are ticket machines at all stations.

You can easily change the language to English with the button in the top right of the screen.

Remember that most ticket machines only take cash, and don't accept cards.

IC Cards

An IC card is a rechargable card for trains and buses - just like an Oyster card in London. The two main types in Tokyo are Suica and Pasmo. Trains in Japan are run by several different companies, even within one city, but IC cards are valid for everything (metro and overground). They're definitely the easiest, most hassle-free way to pay for your trains. You can also use them in other areas of Japan.

HOW TO USE AN IC CARD

- Top it up at a ticket machine (instructions on the next page).
- Swipe as you go through the ticket gates, and swipe out again when you leave. That's it!
- Each time you go through the barriers, your balance is displayed so you know when to top up.
- If you run out of credit, the ticket barrier won't let you through. There are ticket machines before the barriers so you can top up.

WHERE ELSE CAN YOU USE IC CARDS?

Some shops, kiosks, vending machines and arcade machines accept IC cards for payment - perfect if you've run out of change!

SUICA AND PASMO - WHAT'S THE DIFFERENCE?

They're exactly the same, just from different companies. Think of them like different types of credit card. They're both valid for all the train lines, and can be used in exactly the same places. Personally I prefer Suica because it has a cute penguin mascot!

OUTSIDE TOKYO

You can use your Suica or Pasmo elsewhere in Japan too - so if you're going to Osaka or Kyoto for example, just swipe in and out like you would in Tokyo. Other cities have their own regional IC cards, but they also accept Suica and Pasmo.

Watch my videos to see how to use IC cards and how to top up:
- *Getting Around Tokyo*
- *How to Take the Train/Metro in Tokyo*

SPECIAL IC CARDS FOR TOURISTS

You can get a regular Suica/Pasmo card, but there are now also versions especially for tourists: the Welcome Suica and Pasmo Passport.

- Valid in all the same places as regular IC cards.
- Expires after 28 days.
- Leftover credit can't be refunded at the end of your trip.

WELCOME SUICA

- No deposit or fee.
- Choose any initial top-up amount (1000 yen upwards).

Where to get it:

- JR East Travel Service Centre at Narita or Haneda Airport
- JR East Travel Service Centre at major JR stations in Tokyo

PASMO PASSPORT

- Costs 2000 yen (1500 yen credit + 500 yen issuing fee).
- Cute design with Sanrio characters.

Where to get it:
21 locations around Tokyo, including:

- Narita Airport (Skyliner and Keisei Information Centre)
- Haneda Airport (Keikyu Tourist Information Centre and Terminal 1-2 information centres)
- Major Tokyo metro stations.

COMING BACK TO JAPAN?

If you'll be returning to Japan, you can get a regular Suica card that won't expire, to use again next time. You'll need to pay a 500 yen deposit. If you return your card when you leave, you can get back any leftover credit.

Where to get it: Any Suica ticket machine (like the one below) at stations on a JR line. Ignore the "My Suica" option - it's designed for people who live in Japan.

If you choose not to keep your IC card for next time, you can return it at any JR ticket office for a refund of the deposit and any remaining credit (minus a small service fee).

HOW TO TOP UP

- Find a ticket machine with a Suica logo.
- Change the language to English (top right of the screen).
- Select "Charge your Suica".
- Select how much you'd like to top up.
- Insert your money.
- Scan your card.

MOBILE APP

Alternatively, on some phones you can use the Suica app. The advantage is you can use a card to top up via Apple/Google Pay. Instructions are on the Gaijinpot blog; search "Gainjinpot mobile IC app" to find it.

Remember: Most ticket machines are cash only

How to Take the Train

1 FOLLOW THE SIGNS

Follow signs to the line you want (they'll be in English).

2 AT THE TICKET BARRIER

Scan your IC card or insert your ticket and go through.

3 FIND YOUR PLATFORM

Check which direction you're travelling and follow the signs.

4 ON THE PLATFORM

Sometimes there's a queue for each carriage, so you don't get in the way of people getting off the train. Just follow what everyone else is doing!

If you get on the wrong train, just get off at the next station and come back. As long as you don't go through the ticket barriers, it won't cost you any extra!

5 AT YOUR DESTINATION

Stations often have multiple exits, so follow the yellow signs to the one you want. Sometimes there's a list of exits for popular attractions.

6 AS YOU EXIT

Scan your IC card or insert your ticket as you go through the ticket barriers.

If your IC card runs out of credit, it won't let you through the barriers. There'll be a ticket machine nearby so you can top up (the button for English is in the top corner of the screen).

GETTING LOST

Some stations are huge, with whole shopping malls and underground tunnels that seem to go on for miles! It's a whole world beneath the city.

You're sure to take a wrong turning at some point, but don't worry too much about getting lost. There are signs everywhere, and they're all in English. Just keep walking and you'll find your way!

TRAIN ETIQUETTE

- No talking on the phone.
- It's ok to play on your phone, but keep it in silent mode (on Japanese phones it's called "Manner Mode"!).
- Don't talk loudly - unless everyone else is.
- No eating - unless you're on a long distance train like the bullet train.
- Be mindful of other people if you have a backpack.
- Keep your bag on your lap, and don't put it on the floor (it's considered dirty).

Displays like this alternate between Japanese and English.

There are two airports for Tokyo; check which one you're arriving at!

How to Get From Haneda Airport

Good news - Haneda Airport's close to the city, so it doesn't take long to get into central Tokyo!

TOKYO MONORAIL

- *Better if Hamamatsucho Station's more convenient.*
- *Covered by JR Pass.*

COST: About 500 yen each way - covered by the JR Pass

HOW LONG DOES IT TAKE? 15 mins

WHERE DOES IT STOP?
Hamamatsucho Station (on the JR Yamanote line, a loop line that runs around Tokyo to most major places)

TICKETS: Discount tickets are available from the ticket machines to anywhere on the Yamanote Line for 500 yen. Suica/Pasmo are also accepted.

Don't get a taxi - it'll cost at least 10 times more than the train!

KEIKYU LINE

- *Better if Shinagawa Station's more convenient or you're taking the bullet train west straight away.*

COST: About 400 yen each way

HOW LONG DOES IT TAKE? 15 mins

WHERE DOES IT STOP? Shinagawa Station (on the JR Yamanote line, a loop line that runs around Tokyo to all major places). Shinagawa's also a bullet train station.

TICKETS: Use your IC card. Or you can get a ticket from the machines at the airport (switch the language to English with the button on the top right of the screen).

How to Get From Narita Airport

NARITA EXPRESS (N'EX)

- *Most comfortable, with space for your luggage.*
- *Just for the airport - so you're not battling against everyday train users.*
- *Covered by JR Pass.*
- *Look out for the SkyTree on the way! And hanging monorail trains at Chiba Station.*

COST: About 4000 yen return

HOW LONG DOES IT TAKE? 1 hour

WHERE DOES IT STOP? Ikebukuro, Shinjuku, Shibuya, Shinagawa and Tokyo Station.

TICKETS: From the JR Travel Service Centre or the JR Ticket Office at the airport. If you're flying home from Narita, get a discounted round trip ticket.

There are other trains that are cheaper than the Narita Express. However, bear in mind that they're regular trains (not just for the airport) so they're not as spacious for your luggage and there'll be everyday commuters, etc. The Narita Express is more relaxed, spacious and comfortable.

KEISEI BUS OR ACCESS NARITA BUS

- *Budget option.*

COST: About 2000 yen return (extra for late nights/ early mornings)

HOW LONG DOES IT TAKE? 90 mins

WHERE DOES IT STOP? Tokyo Station (The Access Narita Bus also stops at Ginza Station)

TICKETS: Book online at keiseibus.co.jp/inbound/tokyoshuttle/en or at the airport at the Keisei Bus Ticket Counter (Floor 1).

Don't get a taxi unless you're rich! Narita's quite far away from the city.

Travelling Outside Tokyo

RECOMMENDED

BULLET TRAIN (SHINKANSEN)

Amazingly fast and comfortable, and the best way to travel long distance. If you'll be travelling a lot, get a Japan Rail Pass and take as many bullet trains as you want! For journeys like Tokyo to Osaka/Kyoto, the bullet train's a great option and only takes about 2.5 hours. There's no need to take an internal flight unless you're travelling the length of the country.

EXPRESS TRAINS

Outside the bullet train network, you can travel long distances on express trains operated by Japan Railways and various private companies. Look up routes, times and prices on Hyperdia.com.

LOCAL TRAINS

If you get a Suica/Pasmo card, it's valid in many other areas of Japan too, on local trains and buses. You can use it wherever you see an "IC card" sign.

Some other cities have their own metro systems, which are similar to the Tokyo metro, but less hectic and with fewer lines (the maps don't look as much like a plate of colourful spaghetti from Harajuku's Kawaii Monster Cafe!).

INTERNAL FLIGHTS

For very long distances like Tokyo to Hokkaido, an internal flight will be quicker than a bullet train.

Look out for airlines offering free stopovers with your international flight, to save money - the first leg of your trip can count as a stopover.

Japanese airlines have special rates for internal flights - check out the JAL Explorer Pass and ANA Experience Japan fare, for internal flights in the 5,000 - 10,000 yen range.

Check Japanese budget airlines for domestic flights too. They have cute names like Peach Aviation and Vanilla Air!

Remember that if you have a JR Pass, it's more cost-effective to take a bullet train, because your trip will be included. Consider breaking up long train rides by staying overnight somewhere along the way. For example, if you're going from Tokyo to Hokkaido there are lots of interesting places along the bullet train line in Tohoku to explore along the way.

COACHES

Highway buses are a budget option for long distance travel. If you can manage to sleep on a coach, you could travel overnight to maximise your time and save a night in a hotel. Some seats on overnight buses even have hoods on the seats for privacy. Check prices and book online on:

- japanbusonline.com
- willerexpress.com

Hiring a Car

SHOULD YOU RENT A CAR?

You really don't need to hire a car in Japan. There's no need to drive in Tokyo, because the metro system's so comprehensive and convenient. And if you're travelling long distance, public transport's still the best option.

The train network throughout Japan is excellent - it runs like clockwork, it's clean and comfortable. For long distances, the bullet train's much faster and easier than driving.

You don't need to hire a car unless you're going somewhere remote that isn't well-connected by train.

Public transport's often cheaper when you consider rental costs, petrol, parking and the numerous toll roads in Japan.

DRIVING LICENCE

The minimum age for driving is 18. You'll need an International Driving Permit (issued in your country). If your country doesn't issue permits, you'll need an official translation of your driving licence.

WHERE TO BOOK

- Compare prices and book on en.tabirai.net
- Japanese rental companies tend to offer better rates than international companies.

TOLLS

There are numerous tolls on motorways, bridges, tunnels and scenic routes, which can be pricey. Expressway passes are available that can save you money.

Joyful Trains

There are a number of novelty and scenic trains around Japan called "Joyful Trains". They have special themes - some with characters, like the *Pokémon With You* train in Tohoku or the *Aso Boy* train in Kyushu, which has a cute dog mascot, fun styling and a ballpond for kids. Some have luxury interiors or large windows and seats facing outwards so you can enjoy the view. The *Toreiyu Tsubasa* in Fukushima even has traditional tatami mats and footbaths!

Many are included in the JR Pass, but you'll need to make a reservation.

Find them on the JR East website by searching for "Joyful Trains" and on the JR Kyushu site in the "JR Kyushu Trains" section.

Japan Rail Pass

The Japan Rail Pass, or JR Pass, is a special rail pass for foreigners. You can go on as many JR trains as you like, including the bullet train. It's perfect for long distance travel and exploring Japan. It's not cheap, but shinkansen tickets are very expensive, so it's actually a really good deal.

WHAT'S COVERED BY THE JR PASS?

While your pass is valid, you can take unlimited trips on:

- **JR trains** - Train lines run by Japan Railways.
- **Shinkansen (bullet trains)** apart from the very fastest services (Nozomi and Mizuho). But you'll still get the full shinkansen experience! The services you can go on are exactly the same trains, running at the same high speeds, they just stop at a few more stations.

The JR railway network is fairly comprehensive throughout Japan, so you can get to most places with a JR Pass. Then use your IC card for any additional trains run by other companies.

WHAT'S NOT COVERED?

- Trains run by other companies eg Seibu, Keikyu, Odakyu, Tobu, etc.
- Underground trains and the Tokyo metro.

HOW DO YOU KNOW IT'S A JR LINE?

The line will have "JR" at the start of the name. For example, the JR Yamanote line and JR Chuo line are run by Japan Railways and are covered by the JR Pass. Train lines tend to be referred to by the operators name eg the Tobu SkyTree line is run by Tobu railways.

Buy it before you go - JR Passes are only for foreigners

DO I NEED A JR PASS?

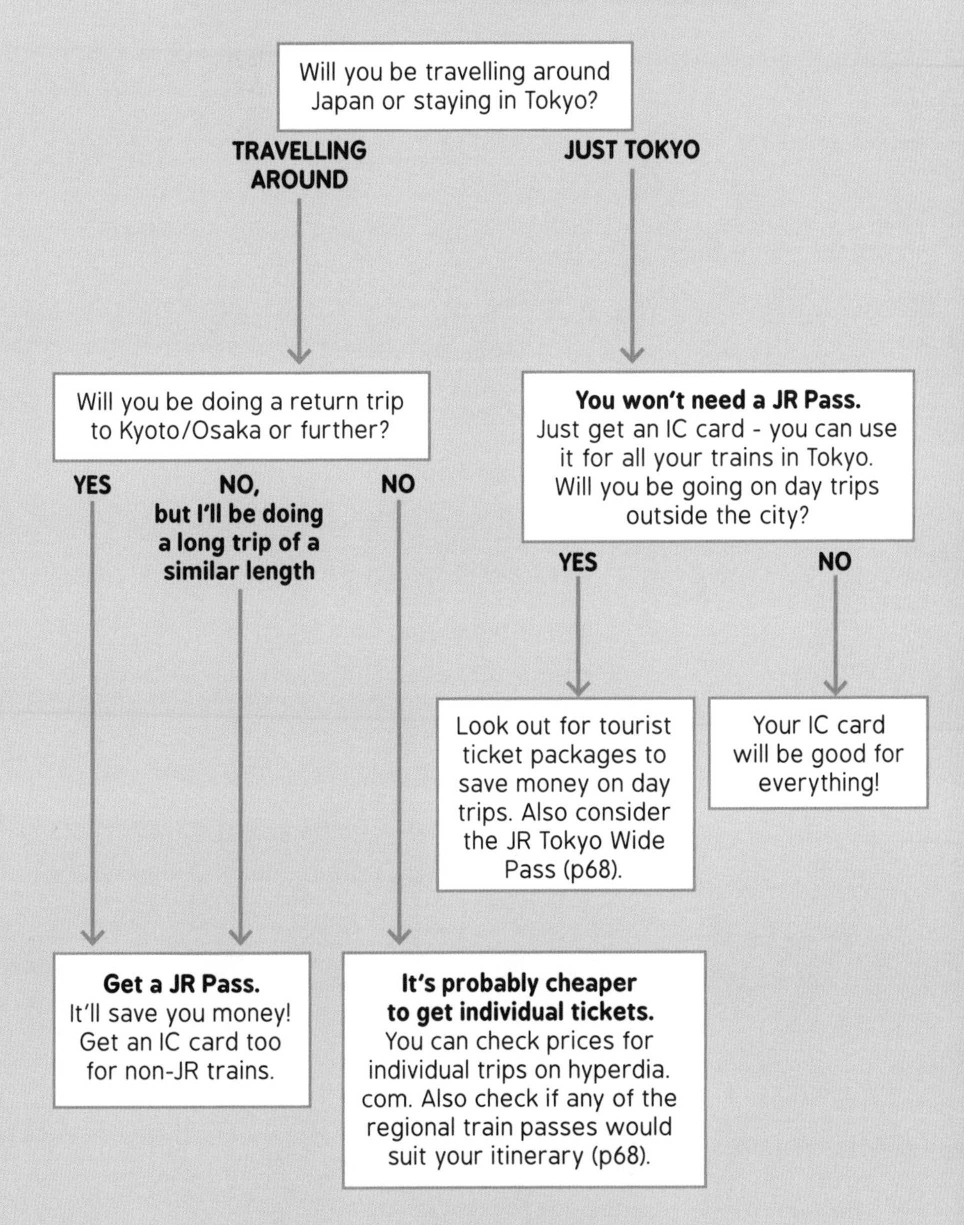

Types of JR Pass

Choose how long you want your pass to be valid for (consecutive days):

7 DAYS | 14 DAYS | 21 DAYS

When you get to Japan, you choose when you want to activate your pass. It doesn't have to be the first day of your trip.

MONEY-SAVING TIP: You might not need a JR Pass for the entire duration of your trip. You'll only need it for the period when you're travelling long distance.

For example, if you're going for 14 days but staying in Tokyo for the first and/or last few days, you might only need a 7 day pass.

Or fly into one city, stay local for the first few days, then activate your pass and travel around, ending up in Tokyo for the last few days.

CHILDREN

Age 5 and under: Travel for free. They can sit in empty seats if the train isn't full, but if it's busy they have to sit on your lap.

Ages 6-11: There are reduced price JR Passes for children. You can get them from the same websites that sell adult passes.

Age 12 and over: Need an adult pass.

GREEN CAR

The Green Car is like first class. The seats are larger and may include a free drink or a hot towel. You can get a special JR Pass that includes the green car. It's less busy at peak times. However, even standard bullet trains are way better than any other train I've been on!

You can now use the automatic ticket gates with a JR Pass - much quicker!

REGIONAL PASSES

The standard JR Pass covers the whole of Japan. There are also regional passes that might suit your trip. Details are on p68 and japan-rail-pass.co.uk

However if your itinerary's based on the popular Golden Route (Tokyo - Kyoto/Osaka), you'll need the full JR Pass for the whole of Japan.

How to Get a JR Pass

Japan Rail Passes are only for foreigners; it's cheaper to purchase before your trip. You can buy it 90 days in advance.

1

DECIDE WHICH PASS TO GET

The options are 7, 14, or 21 days. Choose the length of time you need it for (not necessarily the length of your entire trip).

2

BUY YOUR PASS ONLINE

There are two options:

Buy from an agent: I've always used japan-rail-pass.co.uk - but there are other providers. They'll send you a voucher called an Exchange Order in the post, to swap for the actual pass once you get to Japan. If you lose the Exchange Order you won't be able to get your pass - it's a very valuable piece of paper!

Buy directly from Japan Railways: You can now also buy passes from the official site japanrailpass.net or from a ticket office in Japan. This is an option if you don't have time to wait for an Exchange Order to arrive in the post. You'll also be able to make seat reservations online. However, it costs slightly more than buying from an agent.

3

PICK UP YOUR PASS IN JAPAN

When you get to Japan, swap the exchange order for your JR Pass. They'll send you a list of places where you can exchange it - basically it's at a JR ticket office or travel centre at the airport or at major stations. There'll be someone who speaks English at the counter. It takes a little time to issue the pass, so leave plenty of time in case there's a queue.

When you pick up the pass, choose which date you want it to activate. It doesn't have to be straight away, but it has to be within 30 days.

WHERE TO PICK UP YOUR PASS:

ACTIVATE ON THIS DAY:

Other Rail Passes

These tickets and passes are alternatives to the Japan Rail Pass. They cost less and cover smaller areas.

JR TOKYO WIDE PASS

Unlimited trips on JR lines and the shinkansen within Tokyo and its neighbouring prefectures for 3 days. Good for long distance day trips and overnight trips from Tokyo - but compare with individual ticket prices to make sure it's worth it.

Where can you go? Mount Fuji, the Izu Peninsula, Nikko, Karuizawa, ski resorts and onsen towns like Kinugawa onsen.

Where to buy it: Available from desks at the airport and major JR stations.

More details: Search for "JR East Tokyo Wide Pass".

PLATT KODAMA

Discounted ticket for a single trip on the bullet train on the Tokaido line. It also includes a drink.

You can only travel on the Kodama, which is the slowest service that stops at every station.

If you're doing a return trip, the Flex Ticket (right) is cheaper, for a faster train. The Platt Kodama's only really worth it for a one-way trip, if you're on a budget and have the time.

Where can you go? Anywhere on the Tokaido shinkansen (the line between Tokyo and Osaka).

Where to buy it: From the JR Tokai Tours desk at select stations including Tokyo, Shinagawa, Shinjuku, Kyoto and Shin-Osaka.

More details: JR Tokai Tours website: jrtours.co.jp/kodama/english

SEISHUN 18

Unlimited rides on local and rapid JR trains anywhere in Japan. Not valid on shinkansen or limited express trains. You get 5 tickets, and each is valid for a day. They can shared between people eg one person can travel for 5 days, or 5 people can travel for 1 day. The tickets can be used on any days within a specified period - they don't have to be consecutive days. However it's only available at certain times of year.

Where can you go? Anywhere in Japan - but at a leisurely pace (faster express trains aren't included).

Where to buy it: Ticket offices at JR Stations (known as "Midori no Madoguchi" = green window).

More details: On the JR East website - search for "Seishun 18".

REGIONAL JR PASSES

If you don't need the full JR Pass for the whole of Japan, there are regional versions that can save you money, especially if you're not visiting Tokyo. For example, there are passes for Kyushu, Hokkaido and Kansai (the region around Osaka/Kyoto).

Note: If your itinerary includes Tokyo and Kyoto/Osaka you'll need the full JR Pass, or the Hokuriku Arch Pass, which is only slightly cheaper.

Only a few of the regional passes include Tokyo:

- Nagano and Niigata area
- Tohoku
- Tohoku and south Hokkaido
- Hokuriku Arch Pass

These are also flexible passes, so they don't have to be used on consecutive days like most of the others.

Where to buy them:
Online, then pick up the actual pass when you're in Japan.

More details: japan-rail-pass.co.uk/pass-regional

TOURIST PACKAGES

Special packages are available for some day trip destinations that can save you money, for example:

- Enoshima Kamakura Free Pass
- Nikko
- Hakone and Mount Fuji
- Kawagoe Discount Pass

I'll mention them as we go along, in the Planning What to Do section. You can also find out about them on Japan-Guide.com, and on the train companies' websites.

Where to buy it: The train company's counter at the station. They're for tourists so there'll be English-speaking staff, and leaflets you can point to!

Ticket counter (near the ticket gates)

FLEX TICKET

Special deal for the shinkansen. The ticket includes a round trip on the bullet train, plus an experience/attraction. You can go on any train and return within 7 days.

Flex Tickets are cheaper than the regular train fare, and include an experience coupon for an attraction. You can also go on the Nozomi, the fastest shinkansen, which isn't covered by the Japan Rail Pass. However, you can't reserve a seat, so you'll need to get there early to get a spot in the unreserved carriage.

Where can you go? Kyoto, Osaka, Tokyo, Mishima, Hakone, Nagoya and Koyasan. Your trip can start at any of these places eg if you're staying in Osaka.

Where to buy it: From JR Tokai Tours desk at select stations including Tokyo, Shinagawa, Shinjuku, Kyoto and Shin-Osaka.

More details: JR Tokai Tours website: jrtours.co.jp/en

Shinkansen (Bullet Train)

The shinkansen is a high speed bullet train in Japan. It's a great way to get around the country quickly and travel between cities.

It's fast, safe, clean and always on time - even to the minute!

The shinkansen seems so modern - I think it's amazing it's been around since the sixties (plans first started in the 1930s)!

HOW FAST IS IT?

The shinkansen travels at speeds of up to 200mph (320km/h).

It's fun to open Google Maps and follow your location to see how fast you're going!

WHEN TO TAKE THE SHINKANSEN

The shinkansen is perfect for travelling long distances between cities. You can save lots of time compared to regular trains. It's often cheaper than internal flights (especially with a JR Pass) - and you don't have to get to/from the airport or wait around at check-in.

IS IT EXPENSIVE?

While regular train fares are quite cheap, shinkansen tickets are expensive. In most cases it's worth getting a JR Pass if you're taking the shinkansen, which includes unlimited trips, all around Japan. More details on p64.

WHAT'S IT LIKE?

Travelling on the bullet train is really comfortable. It's clean, on time and a far better experience than any other train I've been on.

The seats are comfortable - if you're travelling long distance you could be on it for a few hours - and there's an impressive amount of leg room. The seats recline and there's a little fold-out table. There are also plugs for charging your phone or tablet, and there are bathrooms between the carriages.

When I'm on the shinkansen I enjoy just looking out the window at the scenery - you're going so fast that it's constantly changing, so you don't get bored.

Look out for Mount Fuji on the line between Tokyo and Osaka/ Kyoto. You can also spot castles, shrines and lots of tree-covered mountains. It's interesting to see how every inch of the country that isn't mountainous is covered with towns or farms. You really get a sense of how densely populated Japan is!

DOS AND DON'TS

Unlike regular trains, it's fine to eat on the shinkansen. Snacks are a must; or get yourself an ekiben as a special treat (more about them in a few pages time!).

Be mindful of other people and don't make too much noise. Put your phone on silent and don't play music out loud. If you need to make a phone call, go into the section between carriages so you're not disturbing other people.

It's fine to walk around if you need to stretch your legs. There's a reasonably spacious rest area where the bathrooms are, between carriages.

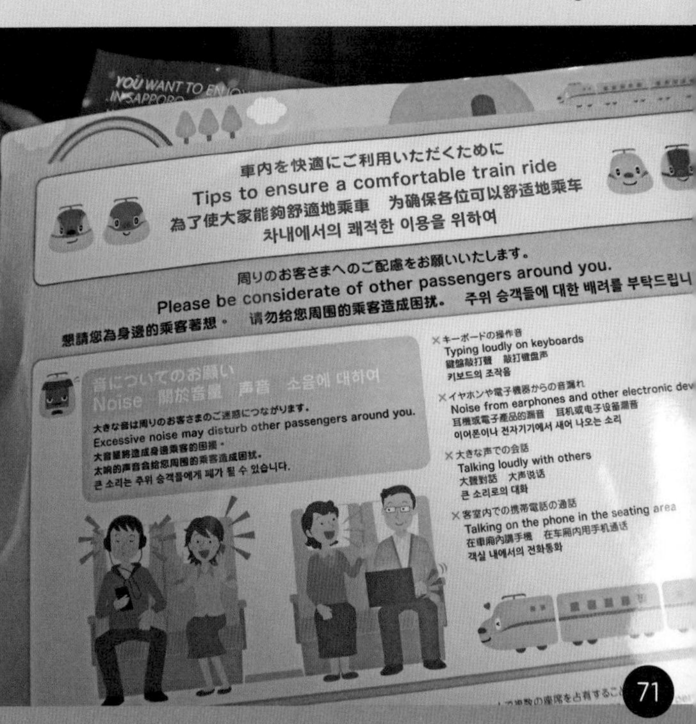

Shinkansen Routes

If you plan your route around Japan with the shinkansen map, you'll be able to travel efficiently and get from place to place without wasting too much time travelling. It's amazingly quick and comfortable to travel long distances.

If you have a JR Pass, you can take as many trips as you like while your pass is valid.

SHINKANSEN TIMETABLES

There are shinkansen timetables online, but don't look at them! They're just confusing.

Instead, search on Hyperdia.com. Enter the starting station, destination and times, and it'll give you all the info you need.

SHINKANSEN STATIONS IN TOKYO

- Tokyo Station
- Shinagawa
- Ueno

ROUTE NAMES

The different lines have names; these are the main ones:

Tokaido Shinkansen
Between Tokyo & Osaka

Sanyo Shinkansen
Between Osaka & Hakata (Fukuoka)

Tohoku Shinkansen
Between Tokyo & Aomori

HOW LONG DOES IT TAKE?

NORTH OF TOKYO

	BY SHINKANSEN	BY CAR
Tokyo to Sendai	1.5 hours	4.5 hours
Tokyo to Aomori	3 hours	8.5 hours
Tokyo to Hakodate	4 hours	13 hours

WEST OF TOKYO

	BY SHINKANSEN	BY CAR
Tokyo to Kanazawa	2.5 hours	6 hours
Tokyo to Osaka/ Kyoto	2.75 hours	6 hours
Osaka to Kyoto	15 mins	45 mins
Osaka to Hiroshima	About 1.5 hours	4 hours
Osaka to Fukuoka (Hakata Station)	2.5 hours	7.5 hours

KYUSHU

	BY SHINKANSEN	BY CAR
Fukuoka to Kagoshima	1.5 hours	3.5 hours
Fukuoka to Kumamoto	40 mins	1.5 hours

JAPAN RAIL PASS (JR PASS)

If you'll be travelling on the shinkansen it's probably worth getting a Japan Rail Pass. It's a special pass for foreigners that lets you go on as many bullet trains as you like, and lots of other trains too. More details on p64, including a chart to work out whether it's worth getting one.

Types of Shinkansen

The shinkansen services have different names, according to how fast they are.

With a JR Pass you can go on **any except Nozomi and Mizuho**, which are the fastest trains. The ones you can go on still reach the same speeds, they just stop at a couple more stations on the way.

IDENTIFYING YOUR TRAIN

Each train has a **name** and **number** eg Sakura 554. The name corresponds to the type of service, like the ones on the opposite page. The number is unique to that train, so it's a good way of finding it at the station. It's shown on your reservation card, signs at the station, on the platform and on Hyperdia.

DEPARTURE BOARDS

Displays at the station show the train name and number, along with the departure time, destination and platform number. They flick between Japanese and English, so if it's all in Japanese, just wait for a few moments!

There are several services on each route, depending on the speed and how many stations they stop at. The names are different on each shinkansen line; these are the ones you're most likely to come across. All of them are covered by the JR Pass, apart from Nozomi and Mizuho.

JR PASS NOT VALID

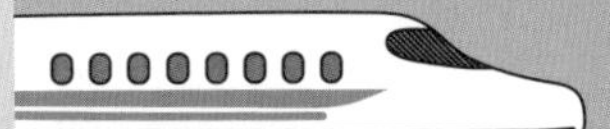

NOZOMI
Wish/Hope

MIZUHO
Harvest

The fastest trains - stopping only at major cities. These are the only shinkansen not covered by the JR Pass.

HAYABUSA
Peregrine Falcon

Fastest of all the shinkansen at over 300km/h! It runs north of Tokyo to Hokkaido. Unlike the other fastest trains, JR Passes are valid on the Hayabusa, but you have to reserve a seat in advance. The Hayabusa also has Gran Class - an extra-luxurious class above the Green Car!

HIKARI
Light

SAKURA
Cherry Blossom

- Stops at major stations.
- Reaches the same speeds as the Nozomi/Mizuho, but stops at a few more stations. The journey time isn't usually too different.

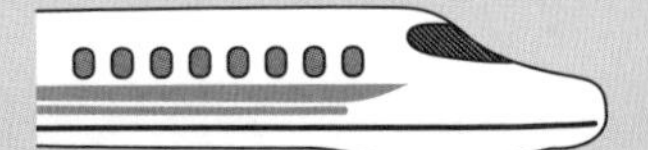

KODAMA
Echo

Stops at all stations, so this service takes the longest - but it's still pretty fast compared to regular trains!

Look out for "Dr Yellow", a special yellow bullet train used to check the tracks. It's a rare sight, said to bring good luck!

How to take the Shinkansen

1 RESERVE YOUR SEAT

With a JR Pass, you can jump on any shinkansen you like (apart from Nozomi and Mizuho). However it's best to reserve a seat (details on p78). If you haven't, don't worry - try for a last minute reservation or sit in the unreserved carriage. Reservations are required if you're going north of Tokyo towards Hokkaido, and for Kagayake trains towards Kanazawa.

2 GET TO THE STATION EARLY

Major stations in Japan can be huge, and it can be quite a walk to get to your train. You'll need time to navigate the station and find the shinkansen section, then get to the right platform. And the bullet train runs like clockwork; if you're a minute late you'll miss it! So make sure you have plenty of time, especially if you're carrying luggage with you. And you're allowed to eat on the shinkansen, so make sure you have time to get snacks!

3 FOLLOW SIGNS TO THE SHINKANSEN

The bullet train has its own section of the station, with separate platforms from the other trains - it's special! When you enter the station, look for signs to the shinkansen like the ones below (they'll be in English). Previously JR Pass holders had to go to the manned ticket gate, but now you can scan your pass at the automatic gates - much quicker!

4 CHECK WHICH PLATFORM TO GO TO

Once you get to the shinkansen area of the station, look for displays telling you which platform you need. You can identify your train by the name and number eg Sakura 546, as well as the departure time and destination. These displays alternate between Japanese and English - so if everything's in Japanese, just wait a moment!

5 QUEUE UP FOR YOUR CARRIAGE

You'll need to sit in your designated carriage and seat. It'll be on your reservation card. There'll be signs showing you where to wait for each carriage. There are even lines on the platform showing you where to queue, so you don't get in the way of people getting off - it's very organised!

FINDING WHERE TO WAIT

Make sure you sit in the correct carriage and seat number. It's very organised, to keep everything running on time - there are even signs on the platform telling you where to wait for each carriage.

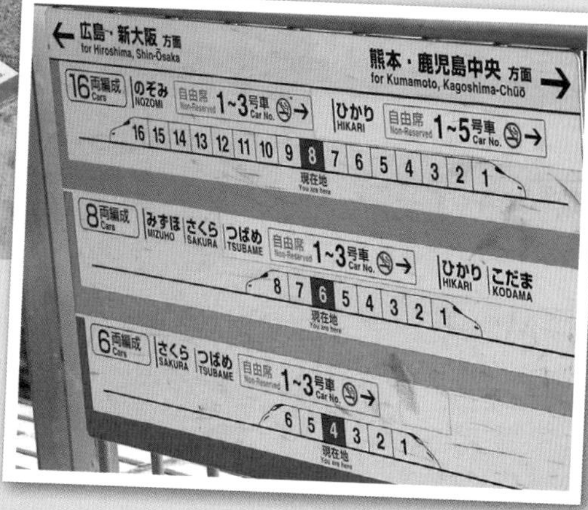

WHERE CAN I PUT MY LUGGAGE?

Smaller bags, like backpacks or mini suitcases (hand luggage size) can go on the overhead racks. There are hooks for handbags and carrier bags. And there's plenty of legroom - you can even put a full-sized suitcase in front of your knees.

There's also a spot for suitcases at the end of each carriage, behind the last seats, but you can only use it if you reserve in advance (below).

BOOKING SPACE FOR YOUR LUGGAGE

The last row of seats in each carriage has a space behind it for suitcases. If you want to use it, you need to reserve the seats at the end of the carriage. If you have oversized baggage, you have to reserve these seats.

To check your suitcases, add up the height, width and depth:

- **Less than 160cm:** Allowed on the train without a reservation. This is the size of *most* checked-in suitcases allowed on airlines without paying an excess baggage fee. If it helps, all of my suitcases fit in this category.
- **160cm - 250cm:** Reservation is required (or there's a fine).
- **Over 250cm:** Not allowed.

If you want to use the luggage spot at the end of the carriage you can reserve online, at the ticket office or the ticket machines. There's no extra charge to reserve. However there's a fine if you have oversized baggage and don't reserve.

You can still bring musical instruments, sports equipment, pushchairs, etc with you, but you'll need to keep them in the space by your seat. If you want to use the space behind the last seat in the carriage, you need to reserve those seats.

How to Reserve Seats

If you have a JR Pass, you can go on as many shinkansen as you like (apart from Nozomi and Mizuho trains). You can just walk through the ticket barriers any time you like, but I'd recommend reserving a seat.

DO I NEED TO RESERVE SEATS?

You don't have to reserve; there are carriages with unreserved seats. However it's best to reserve if you can, especially if it's a popular route or a busy time, to make sure you can sit together.

DOES IT COST ANYTHING?

There's no charge to make a reservation if you have a JR Pass. However, you should only make reservations that you're going to use.

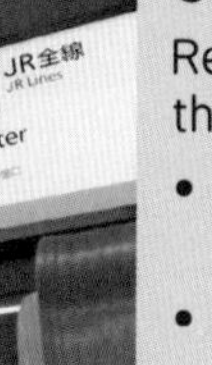

COMPULSORY RESERVATIONS

Reserving a seat is compulsory on these trains:

- Hayabusa - on the line between Tokyo and Hakodate in Hokkaido.
- Kagayake - on the Hokuriku shinkansen between Tokyo and Kanazawa.

IF YOU DON'T HAVE A JR PASS
You can purchase shinkansen tickets from any JR station. Go to the ticket office (Midori no Madouguchi) or buy them from a ticket machine.

WHERE TO RESERVE SEATS

- At a ticket machine at a shinkansen station
- At the ticket office (also known as the Midori no Madoguchi = green window). Leave plenty of time; there's often a designated desk for JR Passes and there can be queues.
- If you bought your pass directly from Japan Railways on japanrailpass.net, you can reserve seats online on japanrailpass-reservation.net, from 30 days before the trip. When you get to Japan you'll need to pick up your reservation cards from a ticket machine or the ticket office.

All of these options are free. You'll get a small card with the train number and departure time, and your carriage and seat number.

WHEN TO RESERVE

It's best to reserve the day or night before if you can.

It doesn't have to be in advance; you can even make your reservation just before taking your train. However, on some occasions when I've left it till last minute, there were no seats available, and I had to wait at the station for the next train.

So it's best to leave more time if you can, especially if you're travelling at a busy time, or if you're in a group and want to sit together.

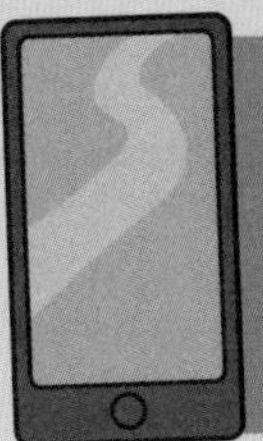

TRAIN TIMES
You can search and check train times on Hyperdia. It's all in English and even tells you which platform you'll need. *hyperdia.com*

Train Times

Hyperdia is a really useful website for looking up train times and checking how long it takes to get from place to place. You can search bullet trains and regular trains, and it's all in English. It even tells you which platform you need!

FROM

TO

DEPARTURE TIME

ARRIVAL TIME

LINE

FROM

TO

DEPARTURE TIME

ARRIVAL TIME

LINE

FROM

TO

DEPARTURE TIME

ARRIVAL TIME

LINE

FROM

TO

DEPARTURE TIME

ARRIVAL TIME

LINE

FROM

TO

DEPARTURE TIME

ARRIVAL TIME

LINE

FROM

TO

DEPARTURE TIME

ARRIVAL TIME

LINE

NOTES

Ekiben

An ekiben is a special treat when you're taking the shinkansen!

Ekiben = eki bento
(station lunchbox)

They're fancy lunchboxes you can only get at shinkansen stations. There are so many different types, with different themes and regional specialities. Some are only available at their local station.

They're wrapped up and look like presents! Some are in special containers, like wooden boxes, and one's even in a ceramic pot that you can keep as a souvenir.

HOW MUCH DO THEY COST?

An ekiben's more expensive that a standard lunchbox - they cost around 1000 - 1500 yen.

WHERE TO FIND EKIBEN

They'll be in the shinkansen section of the station. Follow signs to the shinkansen platforms and you'll come across a shop selling them. Sometimes there's a kiosk on the platform as well.

At Tokyo Station there's a shop called *Ekibenya Matsuri* that sells ekiben from all around Japan.

Planning What to Do

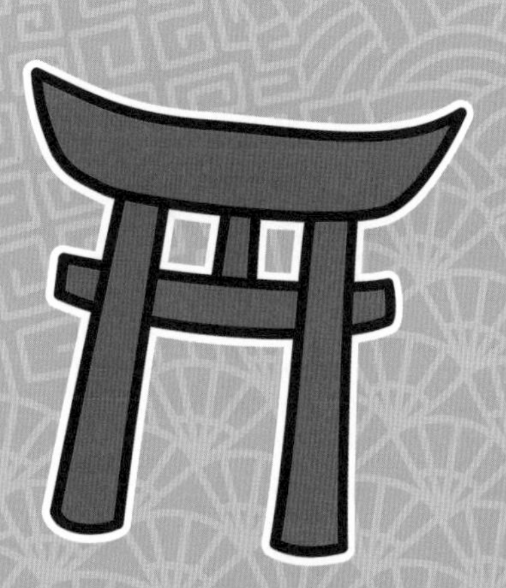

My Tokyo Top 10

There's so much to do in Tokyo; you can easily spend a whole week or more there and not get bored. In no order, here are ten must-do's (in my opinion!):

CITY VIEW

There are several observation decks (p138); whichever you choose, the view's stunning: skyscrapers as far as you can see in every direction. It's the best way to get a sense of the immense scale of the city.

SHIBUYA

Shibuya is full on! It's Tokyo's version of Times Square or Piccadilly Circus. For a classic Shibuya experience, go in the evening, visit Hachiko the dog statue, walk the scramble crossing, go shopping in Shibuya 109, Loft or Tower Records, get some dinner, hang out in arcades, take purikura and do karaoke.

SHINJUKU

If Shibuya is Times Square, Shinjuku is Times Square on every corner, on a much bigger scale. Go in the evening and feel the buzzing atmosphere, with the neon lights of Kabukicho. When you imagine modern Tokyo, this is probably what you're thinking of.

HARAJUKU

The high-energy capital of kawaii and alternative fashion. Browse the shops along crazily busy Takeshita Street, recharge your sugar levels with a Harajuku crepe, get lost strolling through the trendy backstreets, have a picnic and people-watch in Yoyogi Park, then relax in peaceful Meiji Jingu Shrine.

AKIHABARA

If you like anime, schedule at least a day here. Even if you don't, it's a unique place: loud, colourful and covered in anime characters. Wander through games arcades, try the UFO catchers, hunt for gachapon, shop for video games, electronics and anime figures. If you're into figure hunting or collectables, go to Nakano Broadway as well if you have time.

6 ASAKUSA

Visit Senso-ji, the oldest temple in Tokyo. Walk with the crowds along Nakamise-Dori for souvenirs and street food snacks. Stroll through the temple gardens and see a five storey pagoda. Spot glimpses of the SkyTree as you wander through the backstreets and picturesque old alleyways. You can take a boat from here to Odaiba, and the SkyTree's also walkable.

7 ODAIBA

Futuristic Odaiba in Tokyo Bay is more spacious than the rest of the city, with interesting, modern architecture. Enjoy the seaside, unique shopping malls (Venus Fort's just like Caesar's Palace in Las Vegas!), meet the giant Gundam and see robots at Miraikan, the science museum. Don't miss TeamLab Borderless, the digital art museum (which isn't really a museum). And the Trick Art Museum's unique in a completely different way!

8 TEAMLAB BORDERLESS

A unique experience that transcends language. Explore a series of rooms with projection mapping, lights, music and effects to immerse you in an abstract world. I think anyone would enjoy it! Book your ticket in advance - it's very popular.

9 TAKE A DAY TRIP

If you'll be in Tokyo for your whole trip, I'd recommend spending a day outside the city to see a different side of Japan - maybe a breath of nature and the countryside: Mount Fuji /Hakone, Mount Takao or Kamakura.

10 MOST IMPORTANTLY...

Go to places that interest *you* - don't stick to my list, or anyone else's list of "Top 10 Tokyo" attractions if they don't appeal to you. Create your own itinerary filled with what you're interested in. On the following pages there are things to do arranged by theme and area. There's space to make notes from your own research, and links to blogs and YouTube channels I use to plan my trips.

Japan Bucket List

A DARUMA is a Japanese charm associated with goals and wishes. When you set a goal, you colour in one eye, then when you achieve it you colour in the other eye.

Make a list of things you want to do in Japan. Think in terms of experiences you want to have, as well as places to go or things to see; Draw the darumas' first eye when you set your goal and the second one when you achieve it!

Daruma are hollow and weighted at the bottom, so they wobble but don't fall over. This symbolises how there'll be setbacks but you'll recover, and overcome adversity to achieve your goals.

七転び八起き
Nanakorobi yaoki

Seven times down, eight times up

They're based on a monk who's said to have meditated for 9 years. He hadn't moved for so long that his arms and legs fell off, but he carried on, undaunted. At one point he fell asleep and was so annoyed with himself, he cut his eyelids off.

Must-Visit Places

Make a note of places you want to visit, for half days and whole days, to help you plan your itinerary. When you're in Japan you can use this as a menu for what you feel like doing each day.

MUST VISIT - WHOLE DAYS

MAYBE / IF THERE'S TIME

MUST VISIT - HALF DAYS

MAYBE / IF THERE'S TIME

Websites & Blogs

Regular travel guides don't always include the things you want to do, so I do most of my research online. Travel blogs and trip reports are great sources of inspiration - and it's always helpful to hear other peoples' opinions and tips.

JAPLANNING PINTEREST

pinterest.co.uk/cakeswithfaces/japlanning-things-to-do-in-japan

My never-ending list of interesting places and things to do, organised by area. It's messy and more for my own reference really - but it's public if you want to have a look!

JAPAN GUIDE

japan-guide.com

A directory of things to do all around Japan. The most useful part's at the bottom where it tells you how to get around and how to get to each place - which train line and how long it takes. Very reliable for practical information - I check it all the time!

MATCHA

matcha-jp.com

Lots of ideas for things to do and day trip itineraries, with long trip report-style blog posts. I always get stuck in to the related articles and end up with a few more ideas for places to go! The Greater Tokyo section (matcha-jp.com/en/greatertokyo) is good for finding less well known places for your second, third or fourth trip, in Tokyo's suburbs and neighbouring prefectures.

TOKYO CHEAPO

tokyocheapo.com

A huge and excellent site that you'll surely come across at some point if you're searching for Japan info. It's designed with a budget trip in mind, but really the articles are useful for everyone. The events listing's really good for finding matsuri and special events. There's also Japan Cheapo for the rest of Japan.

DIG JAPAN

digjapan.travel/en

Take a look through the "Interests" and "Itinerary" sections and you're sure to find lots of interesting articles and discover less well-known places to go.

GAIJINPOT

travel.gaijinpot.com

Primarily a agency for jobs and moving to or studying in Japan, but their travel blog has lots of interesting things to do, organised into useful categories.

TOKYO CREATIVE

tokyocreative.com/travel
While there isn't that much information about each place, the most useful part is the "Nearby Sights" section. Once you've decided on somewhere you want to go, scroll down the page to see what else is in the area.

IKIMASHO

ikimasho.net
A smaller, more personal blog than the others mentioned here, featuring less well-known places, picturesque backstreets and local areas.
The "A walk around -" and "Postcards from -" features are good.

JAPAN LOVER ME

japanlover.me
For fans of kawaii! Cute things to do from Kaila Ocampo aka Rainbowholic, a scrapbooker and stationery expert living the kawaii lifestyle in Tokyo.

LIVE JAPAN

livejapan.com
All sorts of interesting articles. There are useful area guides with spots tagged on Google Maps.

AND A FEW MORE...

- voyapon.com
- goinjapanesque.com
- en.japantravel.com
- tsunagujapan.com
- zoomingjapan.com

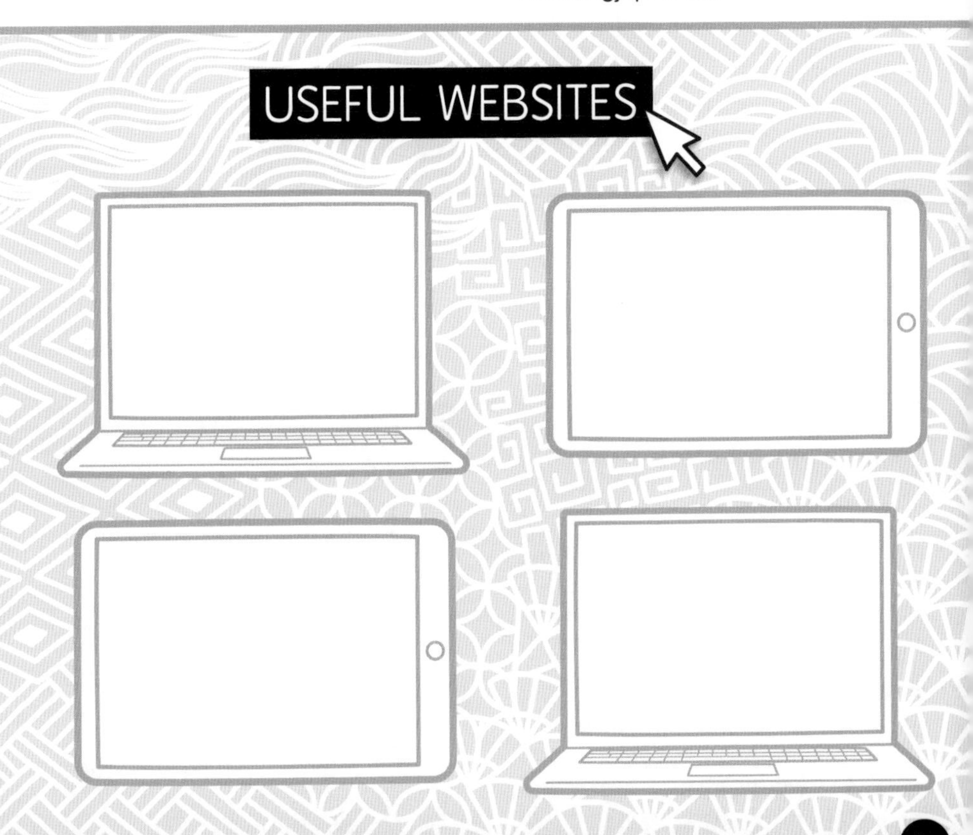

YouTube Channels

I watch a lot of Japan videos - they're a great way of discovering places to go, picking up tips and getting excited for your trip!

CAKES WITH FACES

youtube.com/cakeswithfaces
Of course I had to include my own channel! :-)
Join me on my travels around Japan, plus Japlanning videos to help you plan your trip.

Tell me in the comments that you have my book!

SIMON & MARTINA

youtube.com/simonandmartina
My no. 1 favourite YouTube channel! Informative but also entertaining. I love their sense of fun and upbeat attitude. They're no longer in Japan but there's a great back catalogue with plenty of foodie adventures and restaurant trips - I've discovered lots of places from them!

CURRENTLY HANNAH

youtube.com/currentlyhannah
Beautifully filmed, cinematic travel vlogs and thought-provoking discussion about the travel and tourism industry.

INTERNATIONALLY ME

youtube.com/internationallyme
Top quality travel videos about off the beaten track places that aren't in mainstream guides.

KYDE & ERIC

youtube.com/kydeanderic
Long-form, down-to-earth 45 minute - 1 hour travel vlogs. You're with them every step of the way!

ABROAD IN JAPAN

youtube.com/abroadinjapan
Really well made travel videos - informative and funny. Check the playlists for Journey Across Japan, a vlog series where he cycled the length of the country. The Abroad in Japan podcast is excellent too.

ONLY IN JAPAN

youtube.com/onlyinjapango
Livestreams of walks around Tokyo with interesting insider facts along the way. He also has a channel with feature documentaries (and you might have seen him on NHK World).

PAOLO FROM TOKYO

youtube.com/paolofromtokyo
Informative round-ups about areas, things to do, food and life in Japan. Check the playlists for the "Day in the Life" documentary series.

TOKYO LENS

youtube.com/tokyolens
Discover interesting little hidden spots around Tokyo in the backstreets.

MICAELA

youtube.com/ciaela
One of the few channels to find things to do in Fukuoka and around Kyushu.

SHARLA IN JAPAN

youtube.com/sharlainjapan
Lifestyle vlogs and travel videos, with useful tips for vegans. Check out the back catalogue on her second (original) channel too.

I WILL ALWAYS TRAVEL FOR FOOD

youtube.com/iwillalwaystravelforfood
Quiet tours filmed in first person without narration, just captions. Very calm and relaxing to watch.

RAMBALAC

youtube.com/rambalac
Hour-long walks around areas with no talking, giving you a look at the suburbs and everyday streets as if you're there yourself.

ADD TO THE LIST:

Areas of Tokyo

Tokyo's a huge city; it doesn't have just one city centre - there are several, and distinct areas that are quite different. I always think of the layout of the city in terms of the metro map, which isn't geographically correct, but it's what you look at most when you're navigating.

Here's a very quick guide to some of the main areas - we'll look at each in more detail over the next few pages.

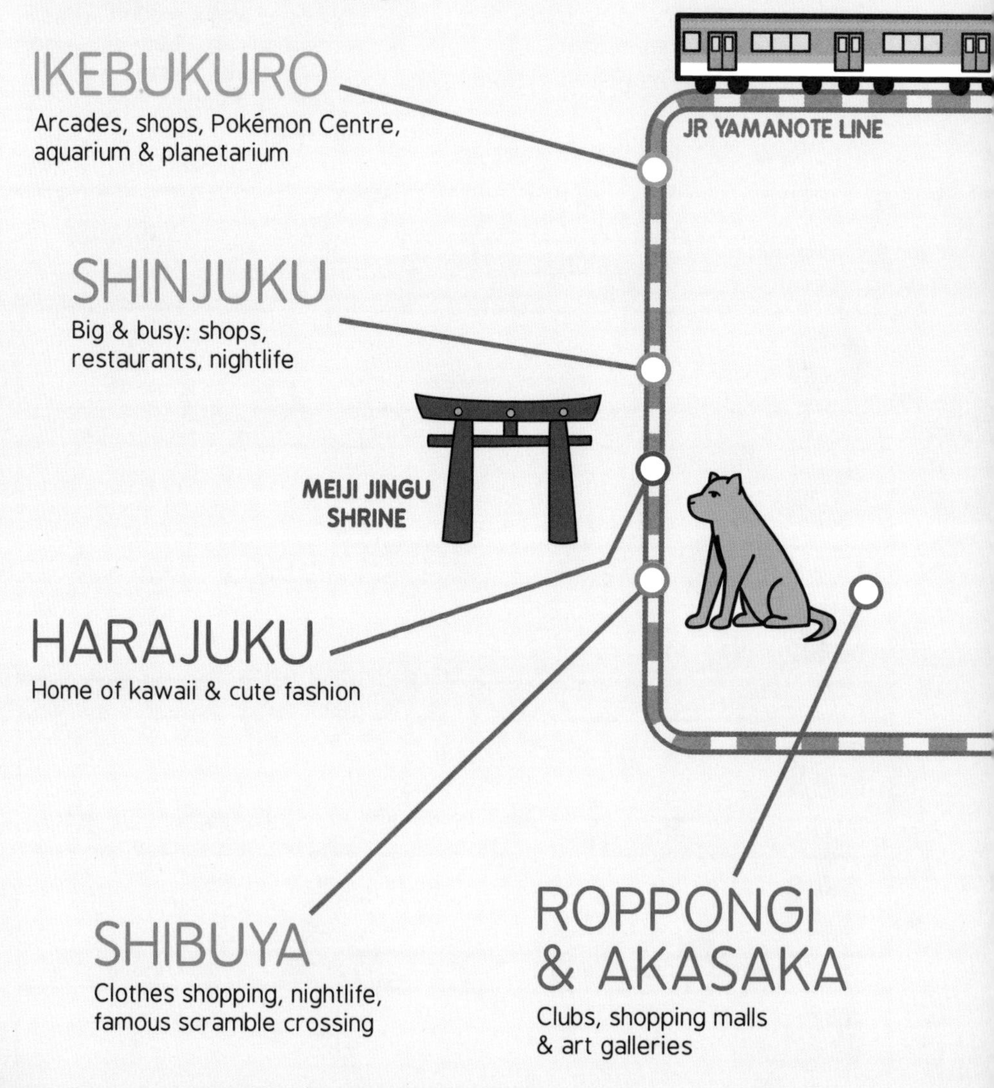

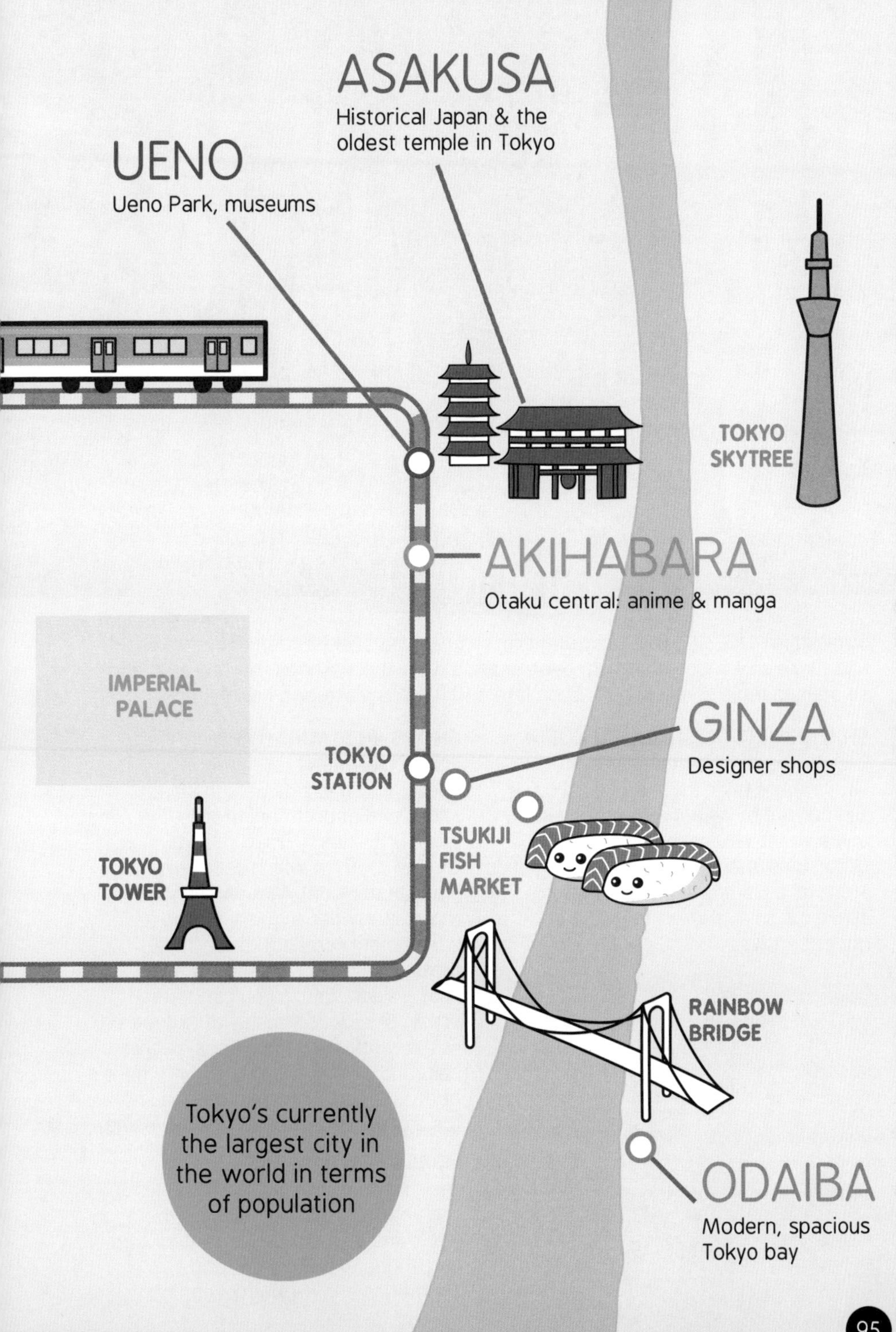
ASAKUSA
Historical Japan & the oldest temple in Tokyo
UENO
Ueno Park, museums
TOKYO SKYTREE
AKIHABARA
Otaku central: anime & manga
IMPERIAL PALACE
GINZA
Designer shops
TOKYO STATION
TSUKIJI FISH MARKET
TOKYO TOWER
RAINBOW BRIDGE
Tokyo's currently the largest city in the world in terms of population
ODAIBA
Modern, spacious Tokyo bay

Shinjuku

Go in the evening, explore the bars, shops and arcades, get some food, go to karaoke and have fun!

Shinjuku is HUGE: it's big, busy and crazy! It has the busiest station in the world, and there's so much going on: neon signs, skyscrapers, shops, restaurants and so many people. Everything's open late and it's busy late into the night.

SHINJUKU PARK (SHINJUKU KOEN)
Escape the city: you can still see skyscrapers over the trees but you're surrounded by lakes, woods, greenery and elegant Japanese gardens.
Grab some snacks from the convenience store or a bakery and have a picnic! There's a small charge to get in but it's not expensive.

SHOPS, RESTAURANTS & ENTERTAINMENT
There are hundreds of high street shops and department stores, including large branches of Tokyu Hands, Don Quijote (both of which sell everything you can think of!), Muji and hundreds more. Many department stores have a basement food hall (depachika), a restaurant floor at the top and a roof garden where you can take a break. Shinjuku's also full of all types of restaurants, karaoke places, pachinko halls and games arcades. Everywhere's open late (including many of the shops); it's a great place to go in the evening.

KOREA TOWN
Just north of Shinjuku is Shin-Okubo, the next train station along, where you'll find lots of Korean restaurants and shops with Korean food, cosmetics and K-pop merch.

KABUKICHO

The red light district - often referred to as the dangerous area of Tokyo. Really it's only unsafe if you go into any dodgy bars. Just ignore the street touts, and it's perfectly safe to walk around the streets. It's an exciting area with neon signs and lots going on - great for photos at night.

TOKYO METROPOLITAN GOVERNMENT BUILDING

Get a free view of Tokyo from the observation deck! It's open during the day and at night. There's an amazing view of the city that never ends: skyscrapers as far as you can see in every direction.

GOLDEN GAI

A network of alleyways with over 200 tiny bars, that used to be a black market. Lots of the bars are themed around the owners' personal obsession, displaying their collection of memorabilia, records or found objects.

MEET GODZILLA!

He's on top of the Hotel Gracery in Kabukicho. At night you might catch him roaring, with lights and smoke. If you stay at the hotel you can go out on the terrace for a close-up view!

OMOIDE YOKOCHO

Aka "Memory Lane" or "Piss Alley", depending how poetic you want to be! The food version of the Golden Gai: small alleyways with tiny restaurants and bars. Some of them only have 6 or 8 seats! They mainly serve izakaya (Japanese pub) food, yakitori and grilled meat.

Shibuya

Walking over the famous scramble crossing and visiting Hachiko the dog statue are classic Tokyo experiences. Shibuya's exciting, colourful and busy, but not quite as extensive as the huge scale of Shinjuku. Apart from shopping there aren't a whole lot of things to do in the daytime, but it's a fun place to go in the evening for bright lights, food, fun in the arcades and karaoke.

SCRAMBLE CROSSING

The most famous image of Shibuya (and possibly the whole of Tokyo) is the mass of zebra crossings in Hachiko Square. It's right by the station. You can get a good view from the bridge connecting Shibuya Station to Mark City shopping centre, and Starbucks in Tsutaya (a books/music store).

SHOPPING

Shibuya's a major shopping destination, especially for young people, with several department stores, Loft (good for souvenirs and gifts - check out the stationery!), Tokyu Hands (household stuff, gadgets and pretty much everything!), Tower Records, a castle-shaped Disney store and lots more.

SHIBUYA 109

The shopping mall of choice among teenage girls for cute fashion. It's an iconic, silver, cylindrical-shaped multi-storey mall, right by the scramble crossing. It was the centre of 'gyaru' culture in the 90s (a western-influenced style with blonde hair, fake eyelashes and suntans).

MAG'S PARK

There's a great view of the scramble crossing from Mag's Park, a rooftop garden at Magnet, the men's version of Shibuya 109. Get a ticket to take unlimited photos from an aerial camera for 100 seconds, from a unique angle looking down at yourself and the crossing.

ARCADES AND PURIKURA
Have fun playing games and trying to win plushies from UFO catchers, then take kawaii pics in purikura photo booths. Follow it up with karaoke for an authentic Shibuya experience.

NONBEI YOKOCHO
Small alleyway near the railway tracks with tiny bars and izakaya (a bit like the Golden Gai in Shinjuku) - also known as "drunkard's alley".

DAIKANYAMA
A fashionable, stylish area with relaxed streets, boutiques and cafes, in contrast to the craziness of central Shibuya.
The main street is Hachiman Dori. Stroll through the backstreets and visit T-Site, a complex centred around Tsutaya bookstore, and Log Road which is built on redeveloped train tracks.

SHIBUYA SKY
Get a view of the scramble crossing from 230m up! It's one of Tokyo's newest observation decks, with a 360° open-air view from the highest point in Shibuya. There's an exciting ride up in the lift with projections and music, as well as a light show at night, interactive digital artwork and a cafe. It's on top of the new Shibuya Scramble Square skyscraper by the station.

NIKU YOKOCHO
A collection of yakitori bars and izakaya specialising in meat dishes (including meat sushi!) in a lively, crowded indoor alleyway. If your group can't agree on one place, you can order delivery from any other restaurant on the same floor. It's on floors 2 and 3; instructions on how to find it are on nikuyokocho.jp/en/access.

HACHIKO SQUARE with the scramble crossing is named after a dog called Hachiko with a heartbreaking story. Every day he followed his owner on the way to work and waited for him faithfully outside Shibuya Station. When the owner passed away, Hachiko continued to wait for him every day, hoping he'd come home. There's a statue of him by the station. And there's also another Hachiko statue, put up 80 years later at Tokyo University, finally reuniting him with his owner.

Harajuku

Go on a weekday, especially if you want to shop. It's very crowded at the weekend.

Kawaii overload at the the home of alternative fashion - loud, cute and colourful. Overdose on cuteness and rainbow snacks, and explore the trendier backstreets. When you've had enough, escape to Yoyogi Park and peaceful Meiji Jingu shrine. If you're into cute fashion you can easily spend a whole day in Harajuku (and you'll probably want to pop back if you have any spending money left over).

TAKESHITA STREET
Start on the main, pedestrianised shopping street - it's busy and crazy! Remember to explore the smaller side streets too. This is the heart of Harajuku, but also the most touristy and crowded. The first time I went, I spent the whole day just on the main street, but there's more to explore in the rest of the area.

BACKSTREETS
Once you get to the end of Takeshita Street, cross over the main road and you're in the backstreets of Harajuku. Most tourists don't make it beyond Takeshita Street; this area's more chilled and trendy, with independent shops and brands you'll recognise from Japanese fashion magazines. It's a bit of a maze - get lost and explore!

YOYOGI PARK

Perfect for picnics and people-watching. The attraction isn't the landscaping, it's how full of life it is. A real city park - and people really use it. If you go at the weekend, you'll see people doing all sorts of things: playing games, sports, walking dogs, musicians and all kinds of clubs and groups.

MEIJI JINGU SHRINE

When the frenetic shops of Harajuku get too much, strolling through the peaceful shade amid the tall trees is the perfect antidote. It's a major shrine where you can often see weddings. Right next to Harajuku Station and Yoyogi Park.

CUTE SNACKS

Refuel and max out your sugar intake with rainbow-coloured sweets and candy, made for Instagram. However, the original snack of Harajuku is crepes. There are literally hundreds of varieties: every combination of cream, fruit, chocolate, custard and ice cream you can think of. It doesn't matter which stand you pick - they're all good!

LAFORET

Find famous lolita brand stores on the basement floor of this otherwise-normal-looking department store.

Then cross the road and get a photo in the mirrored entranceway to Tokyu Plaza Omotesando Harajuku mall - it looks like shattered glass!

KIDDYLAND

Essential Harajuku shop with five floors of cute character merchandise: Hello Kitty, Sumikko Gurashi, Gudetama and lots more you haven't heard of yet!

CAT STREET

The alleyways south-east of Meiji-jingumae Station are more stylish, with creatively-decorated independent boutiques and cafes.

TOGO SHRINE

RECOMMENDED

One of my favourite spots! This beautiful, small shrine is a real hidden gem in the heart of Harajuku; a perfect getaway for a moment of peace. If you're lucky you'll see turtles in the pond, and buy food for the carp. It's hard to believe it's so close to Takeshita Street!

Akihabara

Otaku paradise! The home of anime, manga, electronics and games: loud, vibrant and full-on, with figure shops, merchandise and games arcades.

ANIME SHOPS

There are hundreds of shops where you can buy anime figures, manga, DVDs, cosplay and games. You'll find them easily all the way along the main street. Remember to look upstairs and downstairs - not everything's at street level. The choice is actually quite overwhelming!

If you're looking to buy anime figures, go to Nakano Broadway as well if you have time!

GAMES ARCADES

There are so many multi-storey arcades / game centres in Akihabara (and in other nightlife areas of Tokyo). Play all kinds of video games, try to win prizes from UFO catchers, browse the gachapon capsule toys, and some have purikura photo booths.

KANDA SHRINE

If you need a break, the shrine from season 1 of Love Live is just a short walk away. Check out the anime drawings on the ema boards! And because it's Electric Town, you can get lucky charms (omamori) to attach to your computer and phone to help with IT problems.

GACHAPON

There are gachapon capsule toy machines all around Japan, but in Akihabara you'll see huge banks of them, and more anime-themed gacha.

MAID CAFES

You'll see maids on the street handing out flyers for maid cafes, where you can have kawaii sundaes and omurice with doodles drawn in ketchup by cute maids. There are many, some with themes.

RETRO GAMES

There are several retro games stores where you can buy hardware and games (usually in excellent condition). They're dotted around: look for Super Potato, Friends (hidden away up a shady-looking staircase) and Retro Game Camp. Check that your console's compatible, and remember that most of the games are in Japanese (but they can still be fun!).

ELECTRONICS

Akihabara's also known as "Electric Town". There are stores selling PC and gaming hardware, and all kinds of electronics. Definitely stop by Yodobashi Camera by the station, one of the biggest stores you'll ever see - it sells everything!

A taste of traditional Japan in Tokyo. The crowds can detract from the atmosphere, but it's still beautiful.

Asakusa

The main attraction here is Senso-Ji, the oldest temple in Tokyo. Asakusa's an older, traditional area with great street food.

SENSO-JI

If you only visit one temple in Tokyo, this is the one! As a major tourist spot it's always crowded, so I'd recommend visiting smaller, less popular temples too. It's also more atmospheric in the evening, although the shops will be shut. The red gate at the start is Kaminarimon Gate, which means "thunder and lightning gate"! The street leading up to Senso-Ji (Nakamise Dori) is Tokyo's oldest shopping street, with street food, charms and souvenirs.

Explore the temple complex: there's a five storey pagoda, "omikuji" fortunes, incense for purification and pretty gardens with a small waterfall and koi carp.

RENT A KIMONO

You might see people wearing traditional kimono or yukata and posing for photos. And you can too! Kimono rental places help you get dressed and even style your hair. The choice of patterns is stunning. One rental place is *yae-japan.com/en*

KAPPABASHI

RECOMMENDED

"Kitchen Town" is only a short walk away. So many shops selling plates, tableware, knives and all manner of kitchenware you never knew existed. It's interesting even if you're not into cooking! (And if you are, schedule several hours and start saving up!)

BACKSTREETS & ALLEYWAYS

Once you've explored Senso-Ji, stroll away from the main crowded areas into the backstreets. Wander and enjoy the picturesque, retro alleyways.

ASAKUSA CULTURE TOURIST INFORMATION CENTRE

An interesting building right by Senso-Ji where you can get a free view of the temple, Sumida River and the SkyTree. As a tourist office, there are lots of brochures and they can help with your questions.

TOKYO SKYTREE

There are great views of the SkyTree from Asakusa, contrasting traditional and modern Japan. You can get some great photos from the backstreets around Senso-Ji.

There's a trainline from Asakusa to the SkyTree, but if your feet aren't too worn out you can walk there over the bridge, past the Asahi building with the "golden poop"! It takes about 25 minutes.

Ueno

Ueno is an older and less shiny area of Tokyo. There's a large park that's home to several museums.

UENO PARK

Large park with a lake, temples, shrines, several museums and Ueno Zoo. A good spot for cherry blossom viewing in springtime. Look out for Hanazono Inari Shrine, which has a row of red tori gates like Fushimi Inari, the famous shrine in Kyoto.

NOTE ON UENO ZOO:
Be aware that it's an old-fashioned zoo; some of the enclosures are small, concrete and not a natural environment for the animals.

AMEYA-YOKOCHO

Old-fashioned shopping street alongside the train tracks with kiosks selling food and everyday goods. It used to be a black market. A place to get snacks - and just see what there is!

MUSEUMS IN UENO PARK

- Tokyo National Museum - Oldest and largest museum in Japan, with all sorts of cultural items.
- Shitamachi Museum - See what Tokyo was like in the 1800s and early 1900s.
- National Museum of Nature and Science.
- Tokyo Metropolitan Art Museum.
- National Museum of Western Art.

VISTING SEVERAL MUSEUMS?

It might be worth getting a Grutto Pass, which gives you free/discounted entry to almost 100 museums and galleries (not available in February and March).

Where to get it:
Ticket counters of participating museums/art galleries and some tourist info centres.
www.rekibun.or.jp/en/grutto

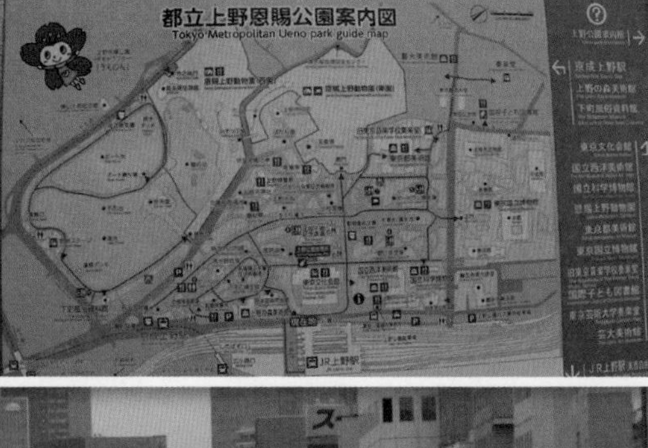

Look out for panda mascots, merchandise and snacks in Ueno, because of the giant pandas at the zoo.

Ikebukuro

From the station, follow signs to Sunshine City

Major shopping area in the north west. There are lots of indoor things to do on a rainy day in Sunshine City, a huge shopping mall with an aquarium, planetarium and the Pokémon Centre. It's also a good area if you like anime - there's Otome Road and some great arcades.

SUNSHINE CITY

Huge shopping mall (built on the site of a former prison!) with several tourist attractions and lots of fun shops. Often there's something going on, like a band, market or some sort of performance. I'd say it's a good, all-round mall with something for everyone - not too high end or fancy.

SHOPPING

There are lots of shops outside in the main shopping area too. By the station there are several large department stores. The first time I went to Ikebukuro I didn't get it at all, but if you follow signs towards Sunshine City, you'll find the main area with the shops and arcades.

LARGEST GACHAPON STORE IN THE WORLD

Find it in Sunshine City mall on floor 3 (in the same building as the aquarium). It has 3000 gachapon machines!

POKÉMON CENTRE

One of the main draws in Ikebukuro is the Pókemon Centre. Really it's just a large shop - with all thé merch, plushies, stationery and homeware you can think of. Be warned: if you're a fan you may spend ALL your money. There's also a takeaway cafe inside.

AQUARIUM

A fun aquarium with penguins, cute fish and basically everything you'd usually expect from an aquarium! You can get combined tickets with the planetarium.

OTOME ROAD

A (much) smaller version of Akihabara, with anime and manga shops supposedly aimed at women - but really it's for everyone! The shops are a bit more dotted around than Akihabara. Instead of maid cafes there are butler cafes. It's to the west of Sunshine City mall.

Look up Animate & K-Books on Google Maps to find the right area.

PLANETARIUM ("MANTEN")

Watch films about the stars on a giant overhead screen. Most of the shows are for entertainment rather than being educational. English audio is available for some shows. For an extra fee there are special cloud-shaped sofas for two people, and grass lawn beds. Combined tickets are available for the aquarium and planetarium (both inside Sunshine City).

SKY CIRCUS

There are lots of observation decks in Tokyo, so Sunshine City made theirs different by adding VR attractions (some for an additional fee). See what it's like being shot from a cannon, or ride a giant rollercoaster over the city.

Perfect for a rainy day - Sunshine City's huge, with lots of indoor things to do.

NAMJATOWN

An indoor theme park, mainly aimed at kids, with mini carnival style games and cute cat characters. There's also a gyoza food hall where you can try different types of gyoza. However the entrance fee's quite high if that's all you're interested in - there are other more authentic places to get gyoza.

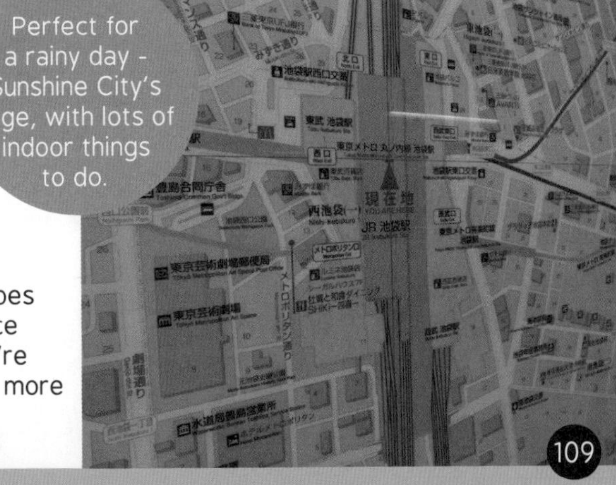

Odaiba

Lots of indoor things for rainy days, but you'd be missing out if you didn't enjoy the seaside too!

Odaiba's an area in Tokyo bay with a completely different feel to the rest of the city. It's more spacious and futuristic, with unusual architecture. There's lots to do, several shopping malls and a lovely seaside area with stunning views of the city.

VENUS FORT

Themed shopping mall with fountains and a fake sky - just like Caesar's Palace in Las Vegas! Worth a look even if you're not interested in the shops.

DECKS TOKYO BEACH

Shopping mall with an island theme that houses Madame Tussauds, Legoland Discovery Centre (only for groups with children), Sega Joypolis (indoor theme park with rides and VR) and a takoyaki museum.

MIRAIKAN RECOMMENDED

Really interesting, modern science museum with robots and a replica of the space station. You can watch a demonstration of Honda's robot Asimo.

SEASIDE PARK (ODAIBA KAIHIN-KOEN)

Sandy beach with a boardwalk and great views of Tokyo Bay. There's no swimming, but on a sunny day it's a lovely place to stroll or sit down with a snack to enjoy the view.

STATUE OF LIBERTY

A mini version! The forced perspective makes it look bigger. Originally a temporary gift from France to celebrate ties between the two countries, it was so popular that it was installed permanently. It's on the waterfront by Aqua City Odaiba mall and the Fuji TV Building.

PALETTE TOWN

The area around Venus Fort (named after an artists paint palette). There's a large ferris wheel with rainbow capsules, TeamLab Borderless and Toyota Megaweb (basically a Toyota showroom turned into a tourist attraction).

 Rainbow Bridge connects Odaiba with the mainland

GIANT GUNDAM

Life size giant unicorn Gundam - it really is huge! Several times a day you can see him move and transform, and in the evening there are projections of anime clips and music. Find him outside Diver City shopping mall.

TRICK ART MUSEUM RECOMMENDED

So much fun! Pose with optical illusions on the walls and go home with literally hundreds of silly photos. Highly recommended! It's inside Decks Tokyo Beach mall on floor 4.

TEAMLAB BORDERLESS (DIGITAL ART MUSEUM) RECOMMENDED

Not a traditional art museum! Explore unique, abstract projection mapping experiences with lights and music. It's beautiful, immersive, atmospheric and fun. There isn't a map - you just wander around and explore. An experience that goes beyond language, really for anyone to enjoy. Book your tickets in advance and avoid weekends as it gets busy.

OEDO ONSEN MONOGATARI

Usually you need to go to the countryside to go to a hot spring bath, but in Odaiba there's an onsen theme park. (Completely non-authentic and not much like a small, traditional onsen). As well as the standard onsen there are mixed areas with foot baths and gardens where you can stroll around in yukata, as well as a food court and matsuri-style carnival games.

RECOMMENDED

BOAT DESIGNED BY AN ANIME ARTIST

The most futuristic boat you've ever seen! Take a trip on Himiko, Hotaluna or Emeraldas - they all look ultra modern and robotic. They run between Shiodome, Odaiba and Asakusa - so you can pair Odaiba with Asakusa or the SkyTree in the same day. The timetable's online to check when they're running: *www.suijobus.co.jp/en*

Ginza / Shimbashi

Ginza is an upmarket shopping district with expensive designer shops. Shimbashi is its less fancy neighbour with lots of places to eat.

DESIGNER SHOPPING

Lots of expensive, designer brands have shops in Ginza, as well as fancy department stores. Even if you're not into designer shopping, there's something about the view of the main street at night, with all the vertical signs lit up.

IMPERIAL PALACE

The large green section in the middle of the Tokyo map is the Imperial Palace, surrounded by a moat. It's just a short walk from Tokyo Station. You're not allowed into the palace itself, but you can catch a glimpse of it over a bridge, and walk around the outer gardens.

ATAGO SHRINE

Small shrine at the top of a long, steep staircase. It's technically a mountain (25.7m high!). Legend has it that a samurai rode up them on a horse to get plum blossoms for the shogun. If you make it to the top, you're granted success in your career, and there's also a koi pond and a cafe with shaved ice.

TSUKIJI FISH MARKET RECOMMENDED

While the commercial market's moved to Odaiba, many of the stalls in the original outer market are still open. Enjoy a breakfast of high quality, fresh sushi and donburi (rice bowls topped with seafood).

TSUKISHIMA

From Tsukiji, cross the river to Tsukishima, an area known for monjayaki (a more liquid version of okonomiyaki), especially along Nishi-Nakadori Street. There's a traditional melon pan bakery, and if you stroll around there are picturesque old buildings, as well as Sumiyoshi Shrine and Tsukuda Park for a walk by the water.

GODZILLA STATUE

Yes, there's a permanent statue of Godzilla in Tokyo (as well as the Godzilla head in Shinjuku)! Search "godzilla statue" on Google Maps and you'll find him near Yurakucho Station. While you're in the area, there are lots of bars and izakaya under the train tracks.

Roppongi

Nightlife district popular with expats and foreigners, with high-end shopping malls and art galleries. Not a must-visit unless you want to visit the galleries or go clubbing. In the evening there are touts trying to get you into their clubs - they can be quite pushy but just ignore them and keep walking.

TOKYO CITY VIEW

Observation deck in Roppongi Hills mall with a 360° view, and an open air deck on the top of the skyscraper.

TOKYO MIDTOWN PARK

Park by Tokyo Midtown with events going on throughout the year, and stunning winter illuminations. There's also a small Japanese garden called Hinokicho Park.

ART GALLERIES

There are three main galleries in the "Roppongi Art Triangle":

- **National Art Centre** - Japan's largest art gallery. There's no permanent collection; all exhibitions are temporary. The building itself is stunning architecture, made of glass.
- **Mori Art Museum** in Roppongi Hills - Contemporary art exhibitions, designed to be accessible for the general public. Some tickets also include entry to the observation deck.
- **Suntory Museum of Art** in Tokyo Midtown - Traditional Japanese art.

MALLS

There are high-end, fancy shopping malls in the glass skyscraper complexes of Tokyo Midtown and Roppongi Hills (look out for the giant spider outside!).

SHRINES

- Hie Shrine - Beautiful hidden shrine with a tunnel of red tori gates.
- Nogi Shrine - A quiet place of calm, dedicated to a general and his wife who committed suicide when the emperor died.

Other Neighbourhoods of Tokyo

Once you've explored the main areas, here are some less well-known districts - recommended for your second or third trip! Rather than specific attractions to visit, these areas are interesting to stroll around and soak up the atmosphere.

YANESEN RECOMMENDED

Picturesque neighbourhood made up of three areas: Yanaka, Sendagi and Nezu. The main street is Yanaka Ginza, but the best part is strolling through the picturesque backstreets. At Yanaka Beer Hall you can relax with a drink in a traditional old wooden building, and at Cafe Nekoemon, also in an old house, you can decorate a lucky cat ornament while enjoying cat-themed snacks. There's also a large graveyard populated by stray cats and beautiful Nezu Shrine, with a trail of red tori gates.

SHIMOKITAZAWA

RECOMMENDED

Could this be the Harajuku of the future? It feels much more laidback and understated, with independent shops, thrift stores, street art, hipster cafes, cosy bars and lots of live music venues. It's an interesting area to stroll around, full of creativity and street art.
Take the Keio line from Shibuya (5 mins) or the Odakyu line from Shinjuku (10 mins) to Shimokitazawa Station.

KICHIJOJI

Home of the Studio Ghibli Museum. Next to it is Inokashira Park, a lovely park with a lake, swan boats, a shrine and a greta place for cherry blossom viewing (hanami) in springtime. Harmonica Alley near the station is a network of narrow alleyways with tiny restaurants and bars.
Take the JR Sobu line from Shinjuku Station to Kichijoji Station (15 mins)

NAKAMEGURO

Trendy neighbourhood in southwest Tokyo with cafes, boutiques and vintage shops. The rows of cherry blossom trees by the canal are really popular in springtime.
Take the metro's Hibiya line (grey) to Nakameguro Station, or the Tokyu Toyoku line from Shibuya (4 mins)

SUGAMO

Known as "Harajuku for grannies", centred around an 800m shopping street called Jizo Dori. Look out for the duck mascot (Sugamo means "ducks nest"). You can stroke the duck's large plushie bottom for luck in marriage and health in old age. There's lots of street food and a market on the 4th, 14th and 24th. Beautiful Rikugien Garden is nearby too.
Sugamo Station's on the JR Yamanote line. Or take a retro tram called the Toden Arakawa line aka Tokyo Sakura Tram (use your IC card or get a day pass), which goes through other less-visited areas of Tokyo.

Left: Inokashira Park in Kichijoji, next to the Studio Ghibli Museum

Kawaii Things to Do in Tokyo

Kawaii means cute, lovely or adorable. While the whole of Japan isn't cute, it's definitely a part of Japanese culture - in fashion, j-pop, design and on all types of products, packaging and signs. Even if it's not your thing, it's interesting to spot all the cute characters and mascots around, making everything more friendly.

HARAJUKU

Kawaii central! The capital of kawaii fashion and rainbow snacks, and the best place to shop for cute, colourful clothes.

WHERE TO GO

- Go on a weekday if you can, especially if you're interested in shopping. It's really crowded at the weekends!
- Start with Takeshita Dori, the main pedestrianised shopping street. (On my first trip I spent a whole day just on this street!). There are a few shops down the side streets too.
- Once you get to the end, cross the road and explore the quieter backstreets of Harajuku. They have a more laidback vibe. This is where you'll find brand shops like 6% Dokidoki, Nile Perch, Candy Stripper, Emily Temple Cute and lots more. And don't miss my favourite sticker shop B-Side Label. The winding alleyways are nice to stroll around, but if you're looking for anywhere in particular you'll need Google Maps!
- Nearby Laforet department store has several official lolita shops and alternative fashion concessions on the basement level.

RAINBOW SNACKS

Along Takeshita Street you'll find cute animal ice cream cones, rainbow candyfloss, lightbulb soda, Harajuku crepes and rainbow cheese toasties - super Instagrammable!

SUPPORT THE SHOPS

As Harajuku's become more touristy, there are more people who come and take photos but don't buy anything except rainbow candyfloss. This has led to Harajuku's original fashion shops closing down, and more touristy shops opening up. Remember to support what you love if you want it to stay!

WILL I SEE PEOPLE DRESSED UP?

Sadly Harajuku's not like the pages of *Fruits* magazine any more. As it's become more touristy, people have taken to posting on Instagram instead - but you might spot a few people dressed up. Remember to ask permission before taking photos. And if you're lucky enough to be there for Harajuku Fashion Walk on the last Sunday of the month, it's extra colourful! Check @harajuku_fw on Twitter for details.

CUTE CAFES

There are hundreds of adorable little cafes in Tokyo so don't stick to this list - go exploring and discover your own! Here are a few that are particularly pink, pastel or kawaii:

- **Q-Pot Cafe**, Harajuku/Aoyama - Perfect for lolita afternoon tea.
- **Cafe RonRon**, Harajuku - Like a conveyor belt sushi bar, but with desserts instead of sushi!
- **Reissue**, Harajuku does 3D latte art - it's pricey but arguably worth it for cute cats or Totoro on your coffee.
- **Hattifnatt**, Kichijoji & Koenji - Looks like a cute little cabin in the woods from the outside, and like a picture book on the inside!
- **All C's Cafe**, Koenji - Sit with teddies and enjoy cute desserts in a charming, cosy cafe.
- **Aoyama Flower Market Tea House**, Aoyama, Kichijoji and Akasaka - A little more sophisticated, combining a florist with a cafe - plants everywhere!
- **2D Cafe**, Shin Okubo - The whole cafe looks like a flat, black and white illustration.
- **Cafe Nekoemon**, Yanaka - Traditional cafe in an old house where you can decorate a lucky cat figurine.
- **Theme cafes** - Look out for limited time pop-ups with character or anime themes (p246). The Alice in Wonderland cafes are particularly kawaii!

CHARACTER STREET

A large row of character merch shops, underground in Tokyo Station, including Sanrio, Moomins and Sumikko Gurashi. There's also Ramen Street (a collection of ramen restaurants) and Sweets Street (Okashiland) - a smaller group of sweets shops. Then head to Daimaru department store to the Kitkat Chocolatory for fancy Kitkats!

How to get there: Inside Tokyo Station, follow signs to First Avenue or Character Street. It's a maze down there so be prepared to get lost!

KIDDYLAND

Character merch shop with Hello Kitty, Sumikko Gurashi, Gudetama and lots of characters popular in Japan that haven't yet crossed over to the west! Their slogan is "For the human smile".

The flagship store is in Harajuku, and there are smaller branches elsewhere too.

MORERU MIGNON (SHIBUYA 109)

At the top of Shibuya 109 there's a haven of cute photo spots: giant cakes and pink doughnuts to pose with! There are also purikura booths and an area to get ready. Once you're done, the rest of the mall's full of cute, pastel fashion stores.
Shibuya 109, floor 7 (right by Shibuya Station). There's also a branch of Moreru Mignon at Ikspiari, the shopping mall at Tokyo Disney.

WEAR A KIMONO

Rent a kimono and take cute photos! The staff can help you put it on and style your hair. Some have photographers for a kawaii photoshoot. There are many rental places; one is Yae Kimono Rental in Asakusa. They have so many cute and pastel-coloured patterns - it's hard to decide which one to pick. There are also kids sizes - super-cute! *yae-japan.com/en*

UNKO MUSEUM

The "poop museum" is dedicated to emoji-style pastel-coloured poop. It's 0% educational and 100% Instagram, with photo backdrops to pose with.
2nd floor of Diver City Tokyo Plaza Mall in Odaiba (Tokyo Teleport or Daiba Station)

CUTE BENTO

On Airbnb experiences there are classes to make a cute character bento lunchbox. If you want to buy bento supplies, check out Loft, Tokyu Hands and Daiso (100 yen store).

YOMIURILAND ILLUMINATIONS

From the end of October until the start of May you can get all starry-eyed amid fields encrusted with LEDs, romantic tunnels of lights, illuminated fountains and slide down a rainbow hill. It's also a theme park so you can go on rides, including cup noodle themed rapids! *30 mins from Shinjuku Station on the Keio or Odakyu line.*

PURIKURA

So much fun, and a perfect souvenir of your trip! They're photo booths with "beauty" features for giant eyes. Copy the poses on screen, then decorate your pictures with stickers and doodles. It's all in Japanese and quite hectic!
Find them in games arcades. Not all arcades have them, but if they do, there'll be a floor upstairs just for purikura. All-male groups might not be allowed.

SANRIO PUROLAND

Hello Kitty's indoor theme park. Really it's aimed at children with gentle rides and shows, but there are lots of cute photo spots, a themed cafe and plenty of merch. There are also Sanrio shops all around Japan; the largest is Sanrio World in Ginza.
Take the JR Chuo line from Shinjuku to Chofu Station (15 min). Change to the Keio line to Keio Tama Center Station (17 min).

KAWAII NAILS

Get your nails done, Harajuku style, with characters, 3D bows, or even tiny pieces of sushi! You'll need time; it can take several hours, and it's not cheap. You might need to book, so pop in at the start of your trip. One that's accessible for foreigners is trunail.jp/en (branches around Tokyo).

CUTE SNACKS

Keep an eye out for adorable snacks all around Japan: Totoro pastries, cat doughnuts, cakes, sweets and kawaii parfaits. Even chains like Mister Donut and Krispy Kreme have cute doughnuts, especially their seasonal ranges.

The cat doughnut below's from Siretoco Doughnuts in Tokyo Station. It's underground, inside the ticket gates on Keiyo Street (the station's huge so it's a kawaii mission to find it!).

MAID CAFES

Immerse yourself in kawaii, with cute dishes served by maids. The most well-known are Maiddreamin' and @Home. At the Heaven's Gate branch of Maiddreamin' you can even dress up in a maid outfit - ask for the 'Moe Change'.
Most are in Akihabara - you'll see maids handing out leaflets.

Historic Japan in Tokyo

IMPERIAL PALACE

Home of the Emperor of Japan. The inner grounds aren't open to the public but you can catch a glimpse of the palace itself (above), and wander around the outer grounds, moat and East Gardens. There are free tours twice a day to see some of the inner areas; tickets are given out at the Kikyomon Gate.
Tokyo Station

RENT A KIMONO

At shrines and temples you'll see people dressed in traditional clothing. Anyone's welcome to rent a kimono or yukata (more lightweight for summer) - choose the pattern you like and they'll help you get ready. Some will do your hair and make-up too.
Lots of outlets around Tokyo, especially in Asakusa eg yae-japan.com

ASAKUSA

Home to Senso-ji, the oldest temple in Tokyo, with a five storey pagoda. While the temple is beautiful, it's always crowded and busy. Leading up to it there's a row of kiosks with street food snacks, souvenirs and good luck charms. Explore the gardens, get your fortune and take pictures with the SkyTree in the background, then explore the backstreets nearby.
Asakusa Station

KOSOAN

Step back in time at a traditional teahouse overlooking a small Japanese garden. Sip matcha and enjoy wagashi (traditional sweets) at low tables, kneeling on tatami mats.
Jiyugaoka Station

GARDENS

Traditional Japanese gardens with arched bridges, ponds and koi carp. Beautiful in autumn with the coloured leaves! Look up Hamarikyu, Rikugien, Koishikawa Korakuen and Kiyosumi Teien. The Hotel New Otani also has a stunning garden that's free (even if you're not a hotel guest).

KAWAGOE

An afternoon trip just outside central Tokyo to Little Edo. Head to the warehouse district around the bell tower and Kurazakuri Street to see dark, old style storehouses,and feast on sweets in Candy Alley.
Kawagoe-shi Station (30 mins from Ikebukuro Station on the Tobu Tojo Line. Get the Kawagoe Discount Pass from the Tobu Railways desk.

KAMAKURA

Take a day trip to "Little Kyoto" for temples, shrines, a bamboo garden and a giant buddha. *1 hour from Shinjuku. Get the Enoshima Kamakura Free Pass from the Odakyu counter at Shinjuku Station*

TEMPLES & SHRINES

There are lots of temples and shrines dotted around that you're sure to come across. Smaller shrines have more atmosphere, especially in the evening, when they take on a mysterious feel. Here are some unusual ones:

- Hie Shrine, Akasaka, has a staircase of red tori gates.
- Toyokawa Inari, Akasake, has lots of fox statues.
- Gotokuji Temple, Setagaya (outside central Tokyo) has a collection of maneki neko lucky cats!

MUSEUMS

These are focussed on Japanese history - there are lots more museums on the next page!

- Tokyo National Museum, Ueno - Tokyo's oldest and largest museum, with swords, sculptures, artwork, samurai armour... a bit of everything!
- Shitamachi Museum, Ueno - See how people used to live, with a small exhibition of old houses and shops.
- Edo Tokyo Museum, Ryogoku (the sumo area) - An indoor recreation of an Edo town. (There's also the Fukugawa Edo Museum, with a reconstruction of a small village). If you'd prefer to see them outside, there's the Edo Tokyo Open-Air Architectural Museum, slightly west of central Tokyo in Koganei Park.

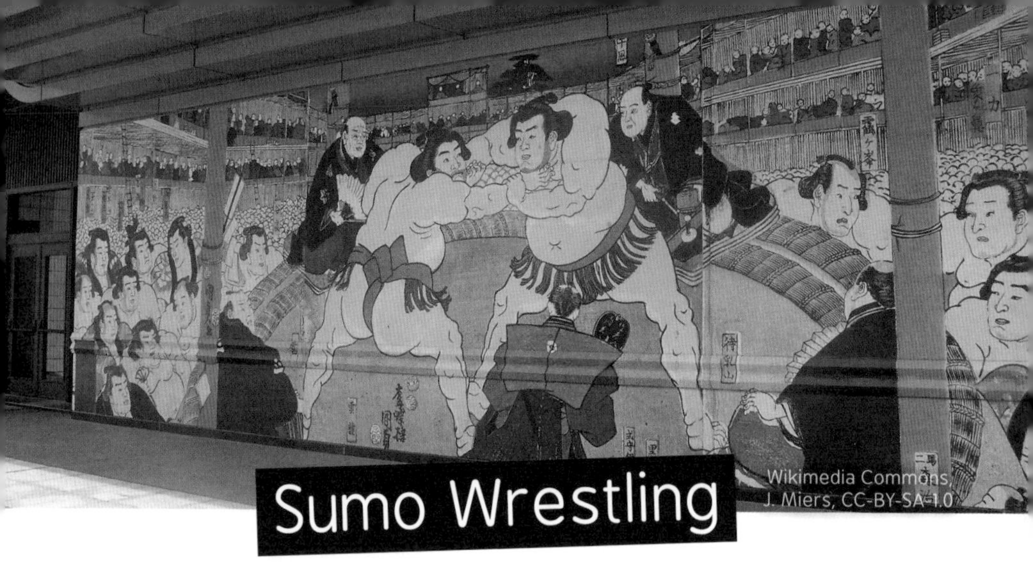

Sumo Wrestling

The sumo area of Tokyo is Ryogoku, on the east bank of the Sumida RIver. Look out for sumo wrestler statues on Kokugikan Street leading up to the stadium - great for photos!

SUMO TOURNAMENTS

Tournaments are held at Kokugikan, the sumo stadium in Ryogoku, and around Japan:

- **Tokyo:** January, May, September
- **Osaka:** March
- **Nagoya:** July
- **Fukuoka:** November

There are also matches between the official tournaments; details are on sumo.or.jp/en

You can get tickets from buysumotickets.com a month before each tournament. A limited number of cheap tickets are also available on the day at the stadium.

VISIT A SUMO STABLE

Sumo stables are where wrestlers live and train. They're private and not open to the public, so if you want to see inside or watch a practice, the best way is to book a tour with a company like Viator, Voyagin, Klook or Magical Trip.

At one stable called *Arashio Beya*, you can watch a morning practice session through the window. Details are on arashio.net/tour_e.html

CHANKO NABE

To grow strong, sumo wrestlers eat chanko nabe, a hotpot with meat, vegetables and seafood prepared by junior wrestlers in the stable. You can try it at several restaurants around Ryogoku. Search on Google Maps for "chanko nabe Ryogoku" to find them. Some even have a sumo ring and live entertainment or demonstrations, like *Kappo Yoshiba*, which was originally a sumo stable.

SUMO MUSEUM

A small museum at the stadium. The reviews aren't great, but it's free. The Edo Tokyo Museum's also very close by if you fancy some history.

EKOIN TEMPLE

This is where tournaments used to be held before the stadium was built. Look out for the cat statues, in honour of the shogun's pet cat.

Museums

There are plenty of museums in Tokyo; this is just a selection. Remember that the amount of English language varies, but there'll still be lots to look at.

TOKYO'S LARGEST MUSEUM

- Tokyo National Museum, Ueno - All kinds of historic and cultural artefacts.

HISTORY

- Shitamachi Museum, Ueno - Reconstructions of old shops and houses.
- Edo Tokyo Museum, Ryogoku - Indoor recreation of an Edo town.
- Samurai Museum, Shinjuku - Weapons, armour, and yes, you can dress up as a samurai!
- Japanese Sword Museum, Ryogoku

SCIENCE

- Miraikan, Odaiba - A modern museum about science, technology and robots (not just for kids!).
- National Museum of Nature and Science, Ueno - Huge, varied exhibits about dinosaurs, nature, evolution, space and technology.

Ueno Park's a good destination to visit several major museums in one day.

ART

- The Art Triangle in Roppongi has three major galleries (details on the Roppongi page).
- Tokyo Metropolitan Art Museum, Ueno Park - Mostly Japanese art with high profile special exhibitions.
- National Museum of Western Art, Ueno Park
- National Museum of Modern Art - Kitanomaru Park, next to the Imperial Palace.
- Sumida Hokusai Museum - Ukiyo-e art by Hokusai, best known for *The Great Wave*.
- Yayoi Kusama Museum, Shinjuku - Spotty modern artworks and infinity rooms. Booking tickets is essential.

GRUTT PASS

Get free or discounted entry to almost 100 museums and galleries for two months. It's not available in February and March. Details are on rekibun.or.jp/en/grutto

OTHER

- Fireworks Museum, Ryogoku - Small, free museum with launchers and posters from fireworks festivals.
- Japan Folk Crafts Museum, Meguro - Textiles, woodwork and painting.
- Parasitological Museum, Meguro - Free museum with a collection of parasites, many from human bodies. (Not for the faint-hearted!).
- Tokyo Metro Museum, Kasai Station, east Tokyo. History of the subway, how it's run and how everything works, with old trains and simulators.

For Anime Fans

AKIHABARA

Otaku central! Here's where you'll find all the anime stores, and lots of arcades (game centres). There are anime posters everywhere, and theme songs blaring out on the streets. There's so much to look round - allow at least a day (and you'll probably want to go back!).
Akihabara Station - Electric Town exit

OTOME ROAD

A collection of anime shops known as Akihabara for women (but they're for anyone really!) and butler cafes like Swallowtail Cafe.
Ikebukuro, near Sunshine City.The shops are a bit dotted around; head towards "Rashinban Ikebukuro", Animate and K-Books on Google Maps.

NAKANO BROADWAY

RECOMMENDED

A mall with all sorts of figures, toys and collectibles - you really can find all sorts! Cheaper than Akihabara for figures. There are great (and cheap) food options in the basement and in the Sun Mall between Nakano Broadway and the station, including standing sushi bars and curry pan. The alleyways beside the Sun Mall are also interesting, especially in the evening.
Nakano Station (JR Chuo line from Shinjuku). Take the north exit and go straight through the Sun Mall to get to Nakano Broadway.

THEME CAFES

Look out for pop-up cafes themed around anime or games. Make a reservation if you can, because they can be really popular.

WHERE TO BUY ANIME FIGURES

- **AKIHABARA** - The most fun place to go figure shopping. The selection is overwhelming! Shop around; prices vary. Remember to check out stores further up the street, away from the station - they often have better prices. Look out for secondhand stores selling figures in glass cabinets (above right). You'll find them easily along the main street.
- **NAKANO BROADWAY** - If you have time, I'd recommend going to Nakano Broadway too. It doesn't have the same exciting atmosphere, but it's cheaper than Akihabara, with lots of secondhand stores.
- **HOBBY OFF** - And the other "Off" stores like Book Off often have a small selection of anime figures (more so outside of Tokyo), as well as games, manga and CDs. This is where I've found the absolute cheapest figures - even as low as 390 yen!
- **OUTSIDE TOKYO** - DenDen Town in Osaka is a major destination. It's like Akihabara but with a more laidback feel. And there are merch stores like Animate and Mandarake in cities all around Japan.

GIANT GUNDAM

Life-size 19.7m tall Unicorn Gundam statue! Several times a day it transforms, and in the evening it lights up. There's also a Gundam Cafe and small trailer shop.
Outside Diver City Tokyo Plaza, Odaiba
There's also a Gundam Cafe near the station in Akihabara.

HOTEL TAVINOS

A manga-themed hotel in Hamamatsucho and Asakusa. The walls are covered with manga artwork, giant katakana and halftone patterns, even in your room! *hoteltavinos.com*

TOKOROZAWA SAKURA TOWN

An anime-themed compex outside central Tokyo in Saitama, opened in 2020, with a hotel where you can watch anime, shops, a library/museum and a modern take on a shrine. *Higashi-Tokorozawa Station, Saitama*

MANGA CAFES

At manga cafes (manga kissaten) you pay by the hour for a private booth with a library of manga (in Japanese!), internet, games and sometimes bottomless drinks packages. Popular chains are Manboo, Media Cafe Popeye and @Gran Bagus Cafe.

ONE PIECE

For some reason, Tokyo Tower is One Piece themed?! There's an indoor theme park (including films and a show) and theme restaurant. There's also a One Piece cafe and statues of the characters in the Fuji TV Building in Odaiba. *Tokyo Tower: Onarimon Station, Akabanebashi Station or Kamiyacho Station*

COSPLAY STUDIO

Take photos with themed backdrops!

- **Studio Crown** - Professional photoshoots, with optional costume and wig hire. *studio-crown.com/experience Akihabara*
- **Studio Booty** - Get a day or half day pass to use over 20 backdrops. No children. bootyjapan.jp (in Japanese) *Oshima Station*

CHEEPA'S CAFE

The owner of this cafe in Ginza used to work at a figure company and now displays their personal collection around the cafe, with mini exhibitions.

ANIME LOCATIONS

Anime settings are often based on real-life locations. The shrine from *Love Live* is Kanda Shrine, just a short walk from Akihabara. And the famous steps from *Your Name* are at Suga Shrine near Shinjuku.

SHIBUYA PARCO

The 6th floor has anime and gaming shops, including the first Nintendo store in Japan. The museum and art gallery house pop-up exhibitions, often featuring popular characters or anime. Check out Chaos Kitchen, the food floor in the basement!

POKÉMON CENTRE

Large Pokémon shop with all the merch you can think of! A must-visit for Pokémon fans. There's also a bakery with cute Pikachu cupcakes.
Sunshine City Mall, Ikebukuro

The largest is Pokémon Centre DX in Nihonbashi, with a Pokémon Cafe. It's surprisingly subtle-looking: light and airy, with themed food and exclusive merch. The cafe's reservation only - you can reserve online (use your browser to translate the page to English).
Takashimaya department store 5F, Nihonbashi Station or Tokyo Station

STUDIO GHIBLI

A must for fans of the films! It's nothing like Disneyland - much more quirky and whimsical, with a focus on the artwork. It's like exploring a magical old house! Rough sketches, unique exhibits, a Ghibli cafe and special films you can't watch anywhere else. While you're there, visit Inokashira Park next door, which has a lake with swan boats.

Numbers are limited so it's not too crowded. It sells out every day, so you'll need to book your tickets before you go to Japan, as early as you can. Follow the link from the official site for the agent in your country.

JR Chuo line from Shinjuku to Mitaka Station (15 mins). From there you can take a bus or walk alongside the waterworks (follow the Totoro signs!).

The tickets contain animation cells - they're all different!

STUDIO GHIBLI CLOCK

If you're passing through Shiodome, hop out and visit the large clock designed by Ghibli.
Near Shiodome Station

Gachapon

You'll need 100 yen coins to buy gacha. If you're short on coins, arcades / game centres have change machines.

Gachapon are capsule toys that you buy from mini vending machines. They're only 200 or 300 yen each. Each machine has a series of about 6 or 8 figures or variations - you don't know which you're going to get! Put your money in and turn the wheel until a capsule pops out!

Lots of gachapon are related to popular characters or anime, but there are also so many random series that are cute, funny or just bizarre! You can get little pouches, hats for your cat, keychains, mini figures and lots more. They make great souvenirs or presents - you might find yourself coming home with lots of them!! Watch my gachapon series on YouTube for a round-up of particularly strange ones I've found!

There are always new series coming out - they constantly change them so you never know what you'll find. Happy gachapon hunting!

WHERE TO FIND GACHAPON

Look out for gachapon machines in all the main city centre areas, especially in and outside arcades. There are lots in places that sell anime goods or character merch, like Akihabara, Ikebukuro, etc. Sometimes you'll come across whole banks of them!

COLLECTING A SERIES?

There are shops in Akihabara and Nakano Broadway with gachapon that have been opened, so you can pick the exact one you want.

GACHAPON GOLDMINES

There are several shops with nothing but gachapon machines!

- On the main street in Akihabara (same side as the station) with a pink sign, and another in the backstreets with a yellow sign - search on Google Maps for "Akihabara Gachapon Hall"
- Nakano Broadway (Nakano Station).
- The largest gachapon store in the world in Sunshine City, Ikebukuro (floor 3, beneath the aquarium).

Gachapon Challenge

Have your own Gachapon Challenge like in my video!

You have 20 minutes to find the cutest and strangest gachapon (or decide your own categories). It's not much time!

- Make sure both teams have enough 100 yen coins.
- Agree on a place to meet when the time's up.
- Hunt down the cutest and strangest gachapon you can find. You're only allowed to buy one for each category.
- Get back to the meeting place on time and compare what you found.
- Get a friend or family member to pick the winner (don't tell them whose is whose). Or post pics online and get your friends to vote!

Watch mine on cakeswithfaces.co.uk/gachaponchallenge

LOCATION:

PRIZE:

TEAM 1 VS TEAM 2

	TEAM 1	TEAM 2
CUTEST		
STRANGEST		

WINNERS

CUTEST:

STRANGEST:

Temples & Shrines

There are temples and shrines of various sizes all around Tokyo and the rest of Japan. Senso-ji in Asakusa is the main temple to visit in Tokyo (and the oldest, but you'd never know as it's so well-kept!), and there are lots of others too.

IS IT OK TO GO IN?

Everyone's welcome to come in and enjoy a moment of calm at temples and shrines. While the buildings are usually closed to the public, you're free to stroll around the outer grounds. Sometimes there's a small admission fee to part of the buildings or gardens.

ETIQUETTE

Remember it's a spiritual place, so be quiet and respectful - other people will be there to pray. Usually it's fine take pictures in the grounds but watch out for "no photos" signs, especially inside buildings.

WHAT'S THERE?

- Ema - Wooden boards to write your wishes on. Some places have special designs - like animal-shaped boards.
- Omikuji - Pay 100 yen and shake the box for a random stick with a number on. Open that drawer to receive your fortune. If it's bad, tie it with the others so it doesn't come home with you.
- Charms - Purchase good luck charms from kiosks. Some are dedicated to a certain theme, like relationships, work or studies.

GOSHUIN

A *goshuin* is a special seal from a shrine or temple, as proof of your pilgrimage there. You can collect them in a *goshuincho* book as souvenirs. Each consists of a rubber stamp and calligraphy, with the date you visited, and the design's unique to that place. There's a small fee, and you get to watch them do the calligraphy.

These stickers are senjafuda They're the names of pilgrims. It's a good omen if your name stays visible as the sticker wears away. (PS: You need special permission - it's not ok to sticker-graffiti shrines!)

TEMPLE OR SHRINE?

The terms shrine and temple aren't interchangable - they're for two different religions that coexist in Japan.

Shrines are for the Shinto religion:

- "Jinja", "taisha", "gu" or "jingu" in the name eg "Meiji Jingu".
- Tori gate at the entrance.
- Purification fountain at the entrance, with ladles for cleaning your mouth and hands.
- Ropes (shimenawa) around sacred places or things, to ward off evil.

Temples are Buddhist:

- "Dera", "in" or "ji" in the name eg "Senso Ji".
- Large incense burner - the smoke's said to have healing properties.
- Statues or images of the Buddha.
- Some have a pagoda.

KYOTO OF THE EAST

Kyoto's well known for its historic shrines and temples, but you don't have to go there to see them. There are lots all around Japan, and in Tokyo.

Kamakura is known as the Kyoto of the east. It's just 1 hour from Tokyo - an easy day trip if you want to see lots of historic temples and shrines. There's also my favourite bamboo garden at Hokokuji Temple. It's smaller than the one in Kyoto, but more peaceful and less crowded.

INARI SHRINES

Inari shrines are Shinto shrines dedicated to Inari, the god of agriculture and industry. They have the iconic red tori gates and fox statues. The foxes (kitsune) are messengers - they're also mischievous tricksters! Foxes are thought to enjoy tofu, which is why tofu sushi pockets are called inarizushi.

Onsen (Hot Springs)

Onsen are natural hot spring baths. Japan has lots of volcanic activity, which means there are numerous hot springs. The water's thought to be good for your skin, with healing properties. While personally I'm not a bath/spa person, for many people it's high on their to-do list, and I've heard lots of good things.

Onsen towns are in the countryside, situated around natural concentrations of hot springs. The towns are usually really pretty, with charming ryokan (hotels). Baths can be indoors or outdoors (called a *rotenburo*), sometimes surrounded by beautiful scenery.

RYOKAN

Traditional Japanese hotels (ryokan) often have hot spring baths, so you can stay overnight and relax. They give you yukata to wear while you stroll around the gardens and enjoy a fancy meal. Some onsen offer day passes if you just want to try the bath without staying overnight.

PRIVATE BATHS

If you don't want to be naked in front of other people, there are places where you can rent a smaller, private bath (an option if you have tattoos).

SENTO

A sento is a public bath-house. Whereas onsen have natural spring water (there are laws about it!), sento are manmade with hot tap water. There are also "super sento" offering a variety of themed baths.

IF YOU HAVE TATTOOS

Most onsen don't allow people with tattoos, because they're traditionally associated with the yakuza. However there are some that allow them - including all seven onsen in Kinosaki (2.5 hours from Tokyo by train). There are lists of them online; search for "tattoo friendly onsen".

ETIQUETTE

- Most onsen are communal and yes, you have to be naked. Swimwear would contaminate the water. There are separate areas for men and women.
- Wash before going in the water, in the shower area. Rinse off all the soap suds before going in.
- You can use a small towel to cover yourself when you're going in.
- Don't put your towel in the water - put it on your head!
- Tie your hair up so it doesn't go in the water.
- If the water's too hot, pour it over your body to get used to the temperature. Go in halfway first so you can adjust.
- Don't shower afterwards - that would wash off all the minerals (unless you have sensitive skin). Dry yourself lightly then go to the changing room.

ONSEN TOWNS NEAR TOKYO

- **Hakone** - Near Mount Fuji.
- **Ikaho** - Picturesque town; the main street is a 300m staircase.
- **Kinugawa** - Beautiful scenery, north of Tokyo near Nikko.
- **Kusatsu Onsen** - A longer journey but unique as the water's cooled outside in the centre of town.

DRINK MILK

It's traditional to have a refreshing drink of milk after bathing to cool down. You might see vending machines with little bottles of milk!

AQUARIUMS

There's no shortage of aquariums in Tokyo! There's Sunshine Aquarium in Ikebukuro, Sumida Aquarium at the SkyTree, and Shinagawa Aqua Park. In summer, look out for the Art Aquarium, an installation with atmospheric displays, lighting and projections (July - Sept).

INOKASHIRA PARK

Park with a large lake in Kichijoji right by the Studio Ghibli Museum. Beautiful cherry blossoms in spring, swan boats and a shrine. There's also a small, low-key zoo with a duck sanctuary, and you can play with guinea pigs.
Kichijoji Station

INSTITUTE FOR NATURE STUDY

More a nature reserve than a park, with trees, rivers and ponds and a natural feel. Visitor numbers are limited so it's never crowded.
Meguro Station

Togo Shrine, Harajuku (with turtle pond!)

SHINJUKU PARK

A pocket of greenery in the heart of the city with a traditional Japanese garden and large open spaces for picnics. There's a small entrance fee.
Shinjuku-Gyoenmae Station (you can walk from Shinjuku Station)

NATIONAL MUSEUM OF NATURE & SCIENCE

Natural history museum with exhibits about biodiversity, plants, animals dinosaurs, and a herb garden on the roof. *Ueno Park*

Shinjuku Park

MACHIDA SQUIRREL GARDEN

Feed and play with squirrels, rabbits and guinea pigs.
Slightly outside central Tokyo.
Go to Machida Station (half hour from Shinjuku on the Odakyu Odawara line), then take the no. 21 bus (20 mins)

DAY TRIPS

Really the best way to see nature is by taking a day trip out of the city. There are plenty of places within an hour or two by train, like Mount Takao and Nikko National Park.

TODOROKI GORGE

If you don't have time for a full countryside day trip, this ravine park's only 15 mins from Shibuya. An easy stroll by the river; see small shrines and hear birds singing. It's not huge but it's a short break from the skyscrapers and busy city.
From Todoroki Station take the south exit, turn right and take the first left. Past the supermarket with the pink sign, the start of the trail's on the right (take the steps down by the bridge).

ANIMAL CAFES

Play with cats, rabbits, reptiles, owls or hedgehogs while you have coffee and cake. An only-in-Japan experience. If you're looking for a cafe that puts animals first, at Cafe Lua in Machida (slightly outside Tokyo) the dogs and cats are rescue animals for adoption.

UENO ZOO

The main attraction is the pandas (that's why you see pandas around Ueno). Note: This is an old-fashioned zoo; some of the enclosures are concrete and small.

Inside Ueno Park (Ueno Station)

NOTE: ANIMAL WELFARE IN JAPAN
Sadly, standards of animal welfare aren't always high. Enclosures can be small, crowded and aren't always suitable. Before visiting a zoo or animal cafe, please check reviews and make sure they care for their animals responsibly before supporting them.

Modern Tokyo

ODAIBA

Ride the driverless Rinkai or Yurikamome line over the Rainbow Bridge to Odaiba, a futuristic area in Tokyo Bay with space-age-style architecture, like the Fuji TV Building above. Visit the giant Gundam at Diver City and meet robots at Miraikan, the science museum.
Yurikamome Line to Odaiba Kaihinkoen. Most places around Odaiba are walkable.

SKY CIRCUS

With the abundance of observation decks in Tokyo, Sunshine City put theirs into overdrive and made it a VR theme park. Experience a giant swing or be shot from a canon over the city! (Some attractions cost extra). *Inside Sunshine City mall in Ikebukuro*

PLANETARIA

Tokyo's newest planetarium. As well as regular planetarium shows (with earpieces for foreign languages), there are romantic shows with live music, luxurious round seats, virtual reality experiences (and galaxy doughnuts in the cafe!).
Yurakucho or Ginza Station

MIRAIKAN RECOMMENDED

Tokyo's science museum is ultra-modern and not just for kids! Watch demos of Asimo, Honda's robot that can run and kick a ball, see a model explaining how the internet works and go inside a model of the space station.
Telecom Center Station in Odaiba. Most locations on Odaiba are walkable if you're going to the seaside area and malls as well.

ARCADES

Try and win figures and plushies in UFO catchers, play video games, play dancing and rhythm games, take purikura photos with cute stickers. Anyone can go in and wander around - save up your 100 yen coins! (There are change machines).
Find them in major nightlife areas: Ikebukuro, Shinjuku, Shibuya, and lots in Akihabara.

CAPSULE HOTEL

Stay a night sleeping in a pod in a capsule hotel for the experience. There are lots; cheaper than regular hotels. The most futuristic one's called *9 Hours* (in Shinjuku & Narita Airport). At *The Millennials* in Shibuya, the high-tech pods have full-size reclining beds, controlled by touchscreen.

CONVEYOR BELT SUSHI (KAITENZUSHI)

Seems modern but it was actually invented in 1958. It's cheap (from 100 yen per plate), fun and easy if you don't speak Japanese! There are lots of restaurants to choose from all around Tokyo, including some where you order on a touchscreen (at many you can change the language to English, or they have pictures!).

SHIBUYA PARCO

The Parco department store in Shibuya was refurbished in 2020 with some unique new features. On the basement level, the restaurant floor Chaos Kitchen is themed like retro alleyways mixed with cyberpunk neon signs. Currently there's a cafe serving insect ice cream parfaits and a bar staffed by drag queens. Cyberspace Shibuya on floor 6 has anime and gaming shops, including an official Nintendo store, Pokemon, Capcom and Shonen Jump. Parco Museum Tokyo and Gallery X have pop-up exhibitions showcasing anime, characters and pop culture, such as Akira. There's also a chilled roof garden.

TEAMLAB BORDERLESS (DIGITAL ART MUSEUM) RECOMMENDED

Not a museum in a conventional sense, or an art gallery either. It's a completely unique, immersive experience with projections and music. It's also really fun! Book in advance on borderless.teamlab.art. Avoid weekends and allow at least 3-4 hours. *Aomi Station on the Yurikamome Line in Odaiba. The entrance is under the ferris wheel.*

TeamLab, the company that created the museum, also occasionally put on temporary exhibitions and installations. There's a similar company called Naked - one of their popular installations is called "Flowers by Naked". Check their websites to see what's on:

naked.co.jp/en
teamlab.art

JOYPOLIS

Indoor theme park with rides, VR experiences and games.
Inside Decks Tokyo Beach Mall in Odaiba (Odaiba Kaihinkoen Station).

TeamLab Borderless

Observation Decks

There's no better way of getting a sense of the immense scale of one of the largest cities in the world. A stunning view of skyscrapers as far as you can see in every direction. Your biggest decision is: day view or night view? Or go at sunset for a taste of both!

TOKYO SKYTREE

The tallest tower in the world. The priciest but also the highest, literally on a whole different level! Avoid weekends and holidays - it can get busy.
Tokyo SkyTree or Oshiage Station - or walk across the bridge from Asakusa.

TOKYO TOWER

Based on the Eiffel Tower, but painted in red and white. An older, more traditional tower - and for some reason I can never work out, it's *One Piece* themed. It's right next to Zojoji Temple - for the perfect contrast of historic and modern architecture!
Kamiyacho, Akabanebashi or Onamiron Station

SHIBUYA SKY

Tokyo's newest observation deck on the tallest building in Shibuya, right by the scramble crossing. There's an open air deck with glass walls and great photo opps.
Shibuya Station

From the Metropolitan Gov Building

TOKYO CITY VIEW, ROPPONGI HILLS

Large, stylish and modern, with indoor and outdoor decks. Centrally located, so you're right in the middle of the city - and there's a view of the Tokyo Tower. *Roppongi Station*

SKY CIRCUS

An observation deck with a difference: there are virtual reality games and experiences, plus a 360° view from the edge of central Tokyo. Ride a rollercoaster through the city or be shot from a giant canon.
In Sunshine City mall, Ikebukuro

ASAKUSA CULTURE & TOURISM CENTRE

FREE

Only 7 storeys tall, but you can get a unique view of Senso-Ji temple and the SkyTree. The building's really interesting, and there's a cafe so you can have a drink while you enjoy the view. It's also a tourist office so they can help you out with maps and advice.
Asakusa Station

METROPOLITAN GOVERNMENT BUILDING

FREE

It's free! And open till late. So you could see this view during the day and another at night. On weekdays you can get a cheap meal with a view of the city at the staff canteen (Building 1, 32nd floor). *Shinjuku Station*

View of the SkyTree from Asakusa

Tokyo Tower & Zojoji Temple

Everything's so tiny from the SkyTree!

Omoide Yokocho

Yanesen

Yanesen

Nezu Shrine

Yanesen

Shimokitazawa

Picturesque Tokyo

If you enjoy photography or Instagram, or if you just want to see some charming Japanese streets, head to these places! It's not too hard to find picturesque alleyways if you just walk away from the main, built-up areas into the backstreets.

YANESEN RECOMMENDED

Made of three areas: Yanaka, Nezu and Sendagi. Lots of small alleyways, charming houses and shrines. Nezu Shrine has a trail of red tori gates, and there's also a famous graveyard that's home to stray cats. Start at touristy Yanaka Ginza, grab some street food snacks, then explore the smaller streets away from the crowds and walk along winding Hebi Michi (Snake Road!).
Nippori Station (on the JR Yamanote line)

KOENJI

Thrift stores, small bars and cafes - perfect for Instagram shots of bikes leaned up against cute shops decorated with pot plants. Feels much more chilled than central Tokyo.
Koenji Station - 5-10 mins from Shinjuku on the JR Chuo Line

URA-HARA

The backstreets of Harajuku (cross the road at the end of Takeshita Street) and the alleyways around Cat Street are full of creatively-decorated shops, quirky boutiques and cafes.
An easy walk from Harajuku (Harajuku / Meiji-Jingumae Station)

DAIKANYAMA

Stylish, trendy area near Shibuya, known as the Brooklyn of Tokyo.
Walk from Shibuya or Ebisu Station

GOLDEN GAI

Alleyways with tiny bars - most have only 6-8 seats. You might have heard that foreigners aren't welcome, but that's only true for a couple of places. Most are very friendly - just pop your head in the door and they'll invite you in. Watch out for cover charges (entrance fees) if you're bar-hopping - they can add up. Also, because these bars are so small, it's a faux pas to hang around too long after you've finished - the culture is: drink up and move on (or order another drink!).
Walk from Shinjuku, Higashi Shinjuku or Shinjuku Sanchome Station

OMOIDE YOKOCHO

The food version of the Golden Gai (see above). Small izakaya (bars serving food) and yakitori bars in narrow alleyways.
Close to Shinjuku Station East exit

SHIMOKITAZAWA

Like Koenji but more built up. Lots of indie shops, thrift stores and cosy-looking bars. It's an alternative, creative area with lots of street art and interesting-looking shops. The north/west side of the station is the most indie, but both sides are worth a look.
Shimokitazawa Station is 5 mins from Shibuya on the Odakyu Line or 10 mins from Shinjuku on the Keio Inokashira Line.

Festivals (Matsuri)

There are festivals (matsuri) throughout the year in Japan. If there's one during your stay, I'd highly recommend going along. The best one I've been to is the annual festival in Kawagoe - the town was crammed full of people but it was an amazing experience and definitely worth it. See what's happening, soak up the atmosphere - and if nothing else, enjoy the street food stalls (there'll likely be lots of them!).

WHAT HAPPENS AT FESTIVALS?

It depends on the festival - there'll be food stalls, side shows and lots of people! They might be at a temple or shrine, or in a town centre. Usually it's free, and anyone's welcome to come along, join the crowds and see what's going on.

STREET FOOD

Often at festivals there'll be food stalls. It's not just burgers and chips - there's an amazing selection! Takoyaki, yakisoba, dango and all sorts of street food snacks you might not be familiar with, like fried spaghetti! Go with an empty stomach and make the most of it.

FESTIVALS IN TOKYO

There are lots of small matsuri all year round, at various locations around Japan. This is just a few of them, so check what's on during your visit! Search online for the place you're going, the month and "matsuri" eg "Tokyo matsuri February". There are also listings on Tokyo Cheapo and japanvisitor.com/japanese-festivals

JANUARY

- New Year and Coming of Age Day.

FEBRUARY

- Setsubun - Bean-throwing and demons for the start of spring.
- Nishiari Daruma Kuyo - Daruma burning.
- Plum blossoms (Ume Matsuri).

MARCH

- Jendaiji Daruma Ichi - Buy Daruma dolls to make your goals for the year (see p86).
- Cherry Blossoms (Sakura Matsuri).

APRIL

- Cherry Blossoms (Sakura Matsuri).

MAY

- Kanda Matsuri: 100 portable shrines.
- Asakusa Sanja Matsuri - Huge parade of portable shrines.

JUNE

- Sanno Matsuri - Floats and parades.

JULY

- Sensoji Hozuki Ichi - On this special day, 1 prayer is worth 46,000 prayers.
- Yasukuni Shrine Mitama Matsuri - 30,000 glowing lanterns.

AUGUST

- Tomioka Hachimangu Fukagawa Hachiman Matsuri - Shrine carrying and water fights!
- Koenji Awa-Odori - Dancing and street parties.
- Harajuku Super Yosakoi - Dancing and stages.

SEPTEMBER

- Akasaka Hikawa Matsuri - Parade, floats and stalls.

OCTOBER

- Kawagoe Matsuri - Floats and stalls.

NOVEMBER

- Asakusa Tori No Ichi - Giving thanks for the past year.

DECEMBER

- Gishisai Festival - For the 47 Ronin.

MATSURI DURING YOUR TRIP

FESTIVAL	WHERE	WHEN	NOTES

Rainy Days

It can rain any time of year in Japan, so take waterproof shoes and be prepared that you might get a rainy day or two. But it'll take more than rain to spoil your trip!

NAKANO BROADWAY

Nakano RECOMMENDED

Get lost exploring shops full of all sorts of bizarre action figures, toys and collectables. Great food options in the basement level and the Sun Mall.

ODAIBA

Unique shopping malls (Venus Fort's themed like ancient Rome), Toyota Megaweb, Sega Joypolis, Miraikan science museum, Trick Art Museum and Legoland Discovery Centre (families only).

There's lots to do indoors, but also worth visiting in good weather - you can't go swimming but the beach area's gorgeous when it's sunny.

UMBRELLAS

Hotels sometimes have umbrellas for guests to borrow. They also sell them at convenience stores for just a few hundred yen - the clear plastic umbrellas that you'll see lots of people using. I like them because they let lots of light through!

Shops have umbrella racks and plastic bags at the entrance for your umbrella so you don't drip water everywhere.

MUSEUMS & GALLERIES

There are so many museums in Tokyo, especially in Ueno Park. Or try a more obscure one like the Tokyo Metro Museum, the Yayoi Kusama gallery or the Meguro Parasitological Museum.

ARCADES

Go arcade-hopping in Akihabara. Take all your 100 yen coins and master a new game!

AQUARIUMS

There's no shortage of aquariums in Tokyo: Sunshine Aquarium in Ikebukuro, one at the SkyTree, Shinagawa Aqua Park (with creative music and lights) and Sea Life Park Odaiba.

TEMPLES & SHRINES

Some say Japan's more beautiful in the rain, making the colours more intense. Especially if you're somewhere like Kyoto, make the most of the popular sites while they're less crowded and more atmospheric.

Remember it might not rain all day. If there's a shower, take a break in a cafe or restaurant and it might be finished by the time you're done.

IKEBUKURO

Sunshine City's a huge shopping mall with several attractions: an aquarium, planetarium, observation deck/VR playground called Sky Circus and Namco Namja Town (and the Pokémon Centre!). There are also arcades in the area, and karaoke where you can hide from the rain for an hour or two.

RAINY DAY PLANS

Karaoke

Karaoke's so much fun - even if it's not usually your thing, I'd highly recommend giving it a try!

HOW IT WORKS

You get a private room just for you and your group - so you don't have to get up on stage in front of strangers! Even if you're bad singer, it's so much fun - just go for it.

First go to the desk and tell them how many people are in your party, and how many hours you'd like a booth for. They'll give you a little clipboard with the room number.

There's a touchscreen controller; change the language to English, then you'll be able to search and queue up songs. You can adjust the echo and volume of the mics. Some offer more facilities than others, but there'll be disco lights, and sometimes even costumes and tambourines!

They often phone you when your session's almost up, but keep an eye on the clock just in case - the time goes very quickly! You can ask to extend your time by taking the clipboard to the desk (or by phone if you can).

ARE THERE ENGLISH SONGS?

There's a huge choice of western music. Chart songs, classics and genres you might not expect, so even if you're not into mainstream music you'll still find a good choice of songs to sing.

ORDERING DRINKS

You can order drinks and food to be delivered to your booth. Order a round at reception when you arrive. After that, order on the phone and they'll bring it up to you. (Yes, that can be challenging sometimes!). You'll have to order a drink for each person every round.

HOW TO PAY

You pay at the end - take the clipboard back to reception. Remember to keep an eye on the clock; time can run away with you and you're paying by the hour. It's not a cheap night out, but it's a lot of fun! The price varies depending on the day and time - evenings and weekends are more expensive.

WHERE TO FIND IT

There are hundreds of karaoke bars in all the main city centre areas and nightlife districts. Some of the main chains are Big Echo, Karaoke Kan and Shidax. If you can read katakana, you'll spot the カラオケ signs EVERYWHERE.

Tokyo Day Trips

Day trips give you a flavour of Japan outside the city. Especially if you're staying in Tokyo for your whole time, they add contrast and might even be the highlight of your trip! These are all within a couple of hours of Tokyo - so you won't be spending the whole day on the train.

MOUNT FUJI & HAKONE

About 75 min from Shinjuku + bus

Visit the iconic Japanese mountain (it's actually an active volcano!). It's often obscured by cloud so you're not guaranteed a perfect view, but it's a popular day trip from Tokyo, or stopping point on the way to Kyoto/ Osaka.

There isn't just one definitive Mount Fuji trip; there are many options and it can be confusing! Consider whether you want to climb Fuji or see a view of it. The climbing season's from July to September, and there are great views from Lake Kawaguchiko in the five lakes area, as well as other things to do. There are buses to help you get around (search for "Fujiyuko Bus"; day passes are available).

Staying overnight in a ryokan (traditional Japanese hotel) in Hakone is another option, where you can experience bathing in an onsen (hot spring).

On my first trip to Japan I went on a day trip to Mount Fuji with Viator. I'm not a big fan of group coach trips but it's an easy, stress-free way to see Mount Fuji, and we reached the 5th station without any hiking!

TRAIN PASSES

- Hakone Free Pass (5,700 yen for 2 days) from Odakyu Railways covers the return trip from Shinjuku, local buses, trains, the Souzan Cablecar, Hakone Ropeway and boats on Lake Ashinoko. The Odakyu website's useful for planning your route (search for "Hakone Free Pass Odakyu").
- Fuji Hakone Pass (around 10,000 yen for 3 days) from Odakyu Railways also includes the Fuji Five Lakes Area.
- Flex Ticket for Hakone from JR Tokai Tours (7000 yen) includes the fastest bullet train to Odawara Station and a 2 day bus pass.
- JR Tokyo Wide Pass (around 10,000 yen for 3 days) includes Fuji and Kawaguchiko, as well as many other Tokyo day trips including Nikko.

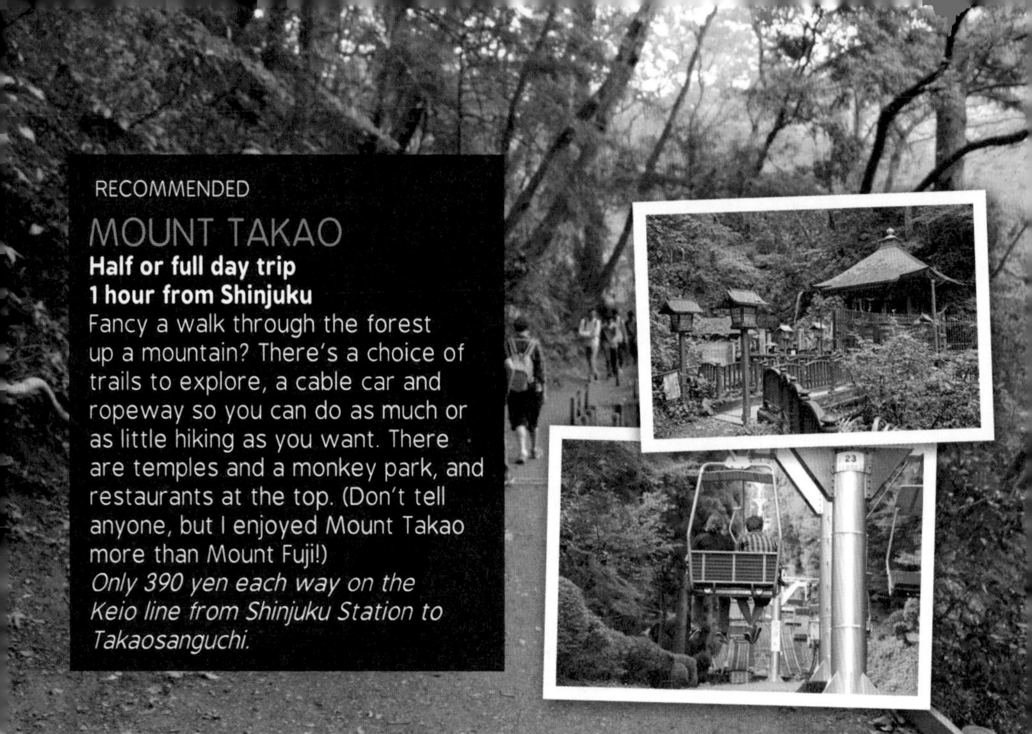

RECOMMENDED

MOUNT TAKAO

Half or full day trip
1 hour from Shinjuku

Fancy a walk through the forest up a mountain? There's a choice of trails to explore, a cable car and ropeway so you can do as much or as little hiking as you want. There are temples and a monkey park, and restaurants at the top. (Don't tell anyone, but I enjoyed Mount Takao more than Mount Fuji!)

Only 390 yen each way on the Keio line from Shinjuku Station to Takaosanguchi.

KAWAGOE

Half day trip
30-60 minutes from Ikebukuro

Head to the warehouse district (centred around the clock tower) for historic black warehouse buildings, restaurants and traditional street food, sweets and snacks.

Get the Kawagoe Discount Pass from Tobu Railways: 710 yen for your train there and back. Available from the Tobu helpdesk at Ikebukuro Station. Take the Tobu Tojo line from Ikebukuro to Hon-Kawagoe Station.

ENOSHIMA & KAMAKURA

1 hour from Shinjuku

Enjoy the seaside then walk across the bridge to explore Enoshima island with shrines, caves and an observation tower (the Sea Candle).

From there, move on to Kamakura, known for its temples and a great alternative if you can't make it to Kyoto. But the highlight for me is the bamboo garden at Hokokuji Temple - so peaceful and serene as you walk through the tall, rustling bamboo.

Get the Enoshima Kamakura Free Pass (1470 yen) from the Odakyu counter at Shinjuku Station to save money on the train.

YOKOHAMA

30 mins from Shibuya

Have a noodle-themed day out at the Cup Noodles Museum and the Ramen Musem (which isn't really a museum - it's just a lot of restaurants and an excuse to binge on ramen). There's also the Minato Mirai port area, Chinatown, traditional Japanese gardens, an aquarium and the Kirin beer factory.

Take the Tokyu Toyoku line from Shibuya (make sure you get a limited express or express train) for 280 yen each way - use your IC card.

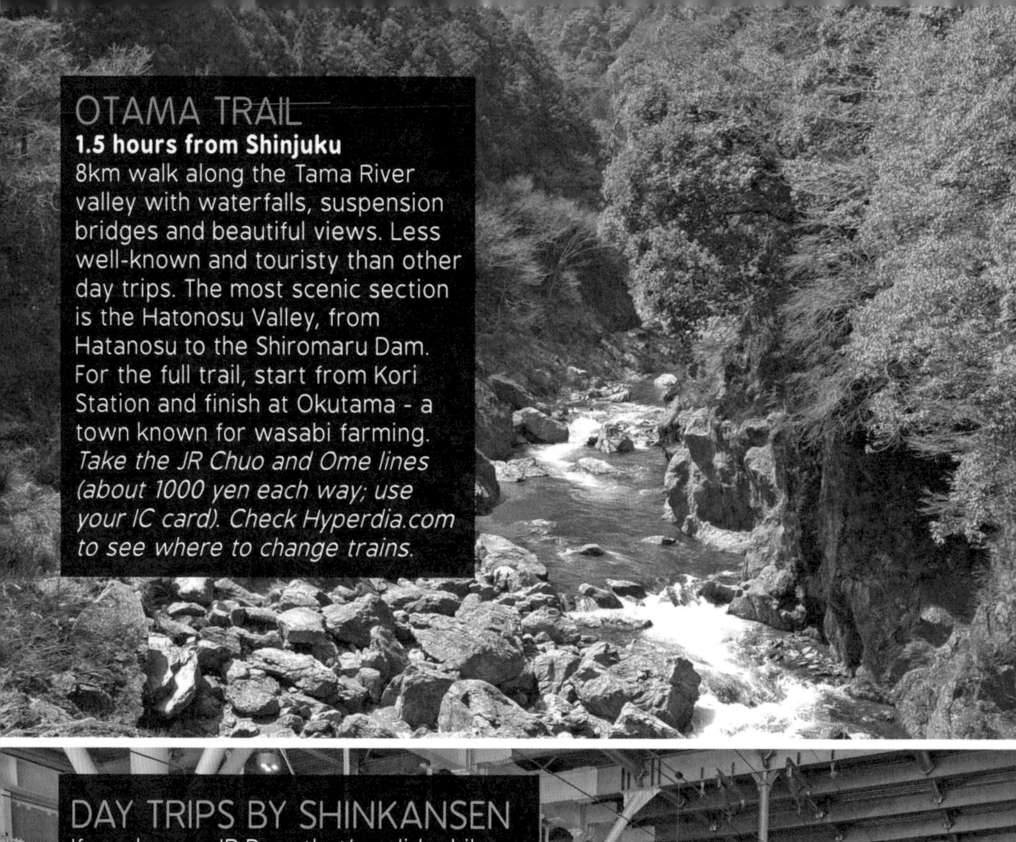

OTAMA TRAIL

1.5 hours from Shinjuku

8km walk along the Tama River valley with waterfalls, suspension bridges and beautiful views. Less well-known and touristy than other day trips. The most scenic section is the Hatonosu Valley, from Hatanosu to the Shiromaru Dam. For the full trail, start from Kori Station and finish at Okutama - a town known for wasabi farming. *Take the JR Chuo and Ome lines (about 1000 yen each way; use your IC card). Check Hyperdia.com to see where to change trains.*

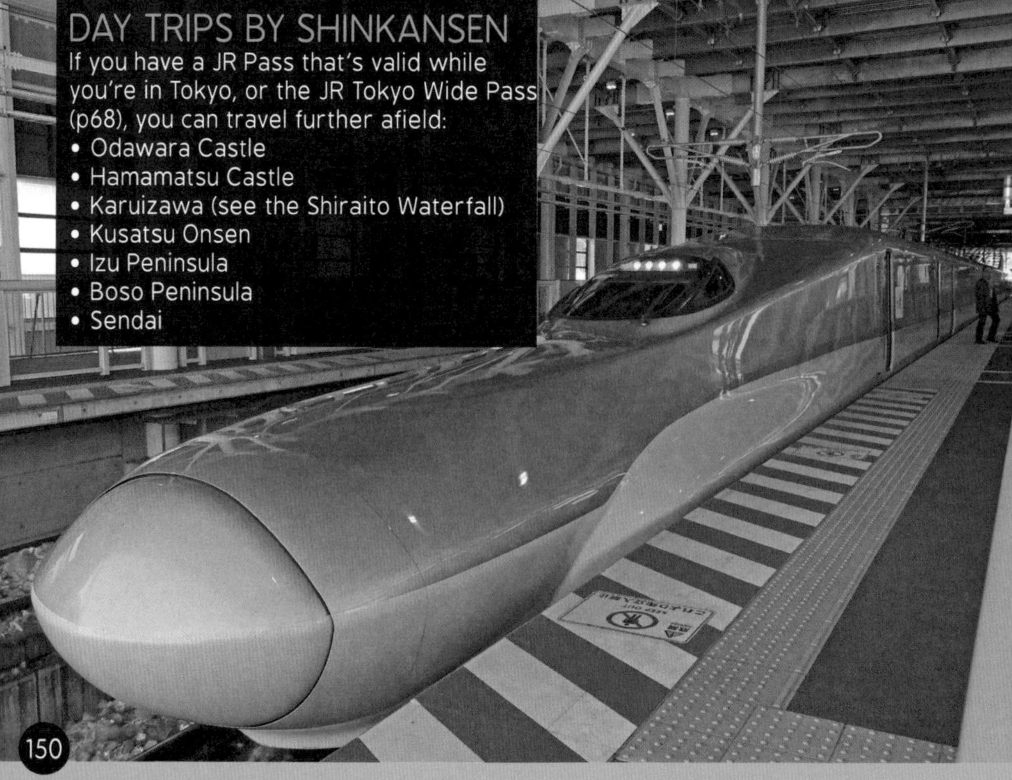

DAY TRIPS BY SHINKANSEN

If you have a JR Pass that's valid while you're in Tokyo, or the JR Tokyo Wide Pass (p68), you can travel further afield:

- Odawara Castle
- Hamamatsu Castle
- Karuizawa (see the Shiraito Waterfall)
- Kusatsu Onsen
- Izu Peninsula
- Boso Peninsula
- Sendai

SHIBAMATA

Half day trip
30 mins from Keisei Ueno Station

A retro town with temples, traditional snacks, sweets and souvenirs.
Walk through the backstreets to a quintessential Japanese floodplain with the only remaining traditional river crossing boat. A relaxing, easy half day trip to see an older, small town.
Take the Keisei line from Keisei Ueno Station. At Takasago, change to the Keisei Kanamachi line to Shibamata. 260 yen each way; use your IC card.

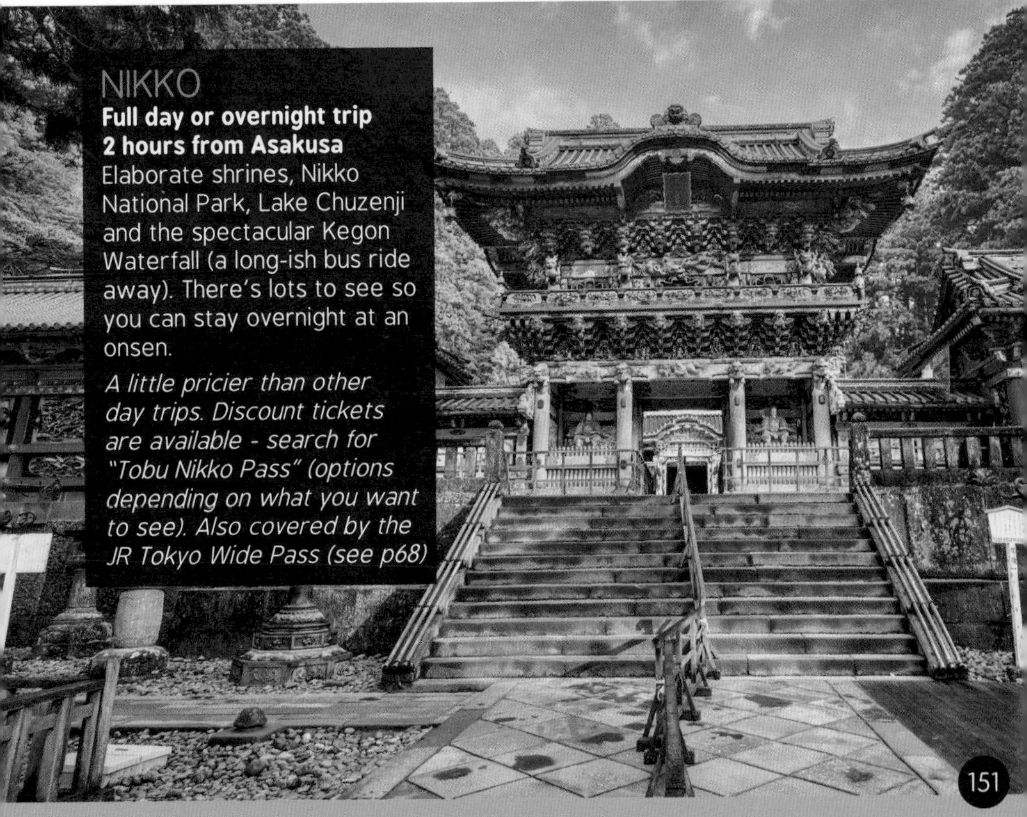

NIKKO

Full day or overnight trip
2 hours from Asakusa

Elaborate shrines, Nikko National Park, Lake Chuzenji and the spectacular Kegon Waterfall (a long-ish bus ride away). There's lots to see so you can stay overnight at an onsen.

A little pricier than other day trips. Discount tickets are available - search for "Tobu Nikko Pass" (options depending on what you want to see). Also covered by the JR Tokyo Wide Pass (see p68)

Tokyo Disney

Tokyo Disney is similar to other Disney parks around the world - however what makes it special is the theming. It's beautiful and you'll be amazed at the attention to detail. Look out for special merch and snacks, especially all the different flavours of popcorn (and super-cute souvenir popcorn buckets)! There are two parks, Disney hotels and Ikspiari, a mall with shops and restaurants.

TOKYO DISNEYLAND

Similar to the Magic Kingdom, with the castle and classic attractions you'll recognise, plus some that are exclusive to Tokyo Disney. The best is Pooh's Hunny Hunt, a trackless ride that's just so much fun, and Monsters Inc Ride & Go Seek, where you shine a torch to interact with characters and items along the way.

DISNEY SEA RECOMMENDED

Completely different to any other Disney park around the world. Amazingly detailed theming, centred around a volcano, with areas themed around Jules Verne, an American harbour, the Little Mermaid, a Mediterranean coast and more. The highlight's Journey to the Centre of the Earth, a ride inside the volcano.

DISNEYLAND OR DISNEY SEA?

If you've been to any of the other Disney resorts, I'd recommend Disney Sea because it's completely different and unique to Japan. However there are unique attractions at Disneyland too, so it's worth a visit if you're into Disney or you want the classic experience with the castle and famous rides like Space Moutain and Big Thunder Mountain.

AVOIDING CROWDS

The parks can get very crowded at times, with long wait times. Avoid weekends and holidays. Get there early and buy your tickets in advance so you're not queuing at the gates.

HOW TO GET TICKETS

- Online 3 months in advance, from tokyodisneyresort.jp
- From the Disney Store in Japan
- On the day, at the gate

TICKET TYPES

- Single day tickets (fixed day).
- Open tickets (no specified day). Park admission isn't guaranteed if it's busy.
- Starlight Passport evening tickets for entry after 3pm weekends/ holidays and 6pm weekdays.
- Multi-day tickets - You may have to specify which park you want to visit on each day.

HOW TO GET THERE

Take the JR Keiyo line from Tokyo Station to Maihama Station (about 15 mins - use your IC card). From there you'll need to get a ticket for the Disney monorail, a loop line that takes you to the parks.

DISNEY HOTELS

Tokyo Disneyland is easily accessible from the city by train as a day trip, so there's no need to stay there unless you want to. There are Disney hotels on-site which offer stunning theming (at a price!), as well as more affordable partner hotels. They're right by the parks; Hotel Miracosta is actually inside Disney Sea! I stayed there, with a stunning view of the park, parade and fireworks from the window. You can book through the Tokyo Disney website (which can be a little confusing to navigate at times).

Right: Tokyo Disneyland Hotel

TOKYO DAY TRIP IDEAS

DAY TRIP	
HOW TO GET THERE	
JOURNEY LENGTH	
THINGS TO SEE/DO	
NOTES	

DAY TRIP	
HOW TO GET THERE	
JOURNEY LENGTH	
THINGS TO SEE/DO	
NOTES	

Things to Do in the Rest of Japan

The rest of Japan is nothing like Tokyo! It's so varied and there's so much to explore. It's easy to travel around the country by bullet train - and with a JR Pass you can take as many trips as you like.

There's nowhere near enough room to include everything, so here's a selection of places that I think are interesting! For regions I haven't visited yet, I've included places from my wishlist.

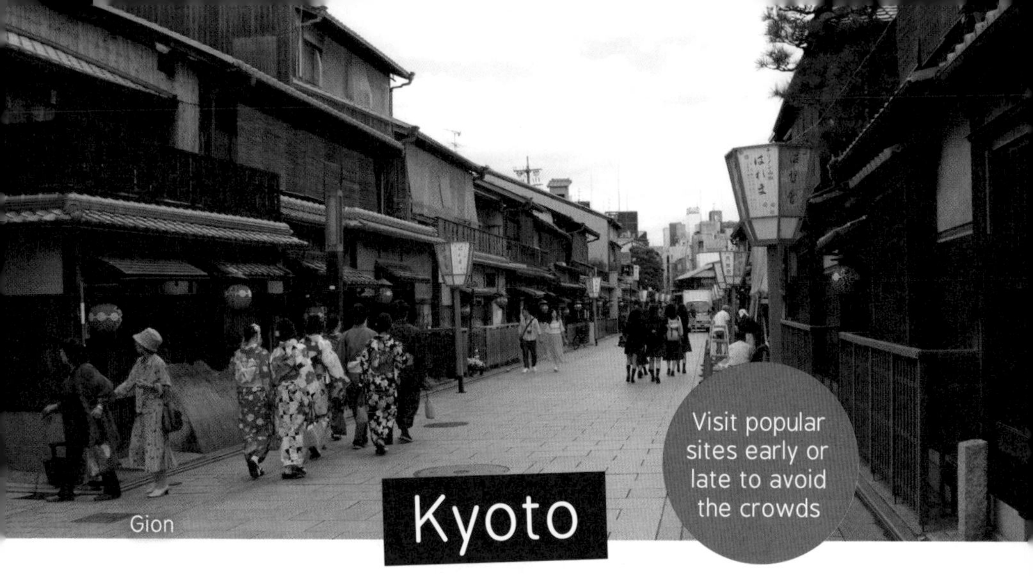
Gion

Kyoto

Visit popular sites early or late to avoid the crowds

The home of traditional Japan. If the Japan of your imagination is temples, gardens, shrines and historic streets, that's Kyoto! Kyoto and Osaka are very close (only 15 mins on the shinkansen, or 30 mins on regular trains), so you can easily visit both together. And there are lots of good day trips around the region.

FUSHIMI INARI SHRINE RECOMMENDED

Famous shrine with thousands of tori gates. I love all the red gates and fox statues. The highlight of my time in Kyoto - it really is stunning, and more of a hike than I expected! The trail of gates goes up a small mountain, with a view of the city at the top. The further you go up, the less crowded it gets, so persevere and you'll be able to get photos away from the crowds, especially if you go late in the day (or very early).

Take the train to Inari or Fushimi-Inari Station and follow the crowds.

KIYOMIZUDERA

Major temple with a pagoda and building built on a wooden platform. It's in the picturesque Higashiyama district - you can walk to Ninenzaka and Sannenzaka from here.

Walk from Kiyomizu-Gojo Station.

NINENZAKA & SANNENZAKA

Picturesque, sloping streets in Higashiyama near Kiyomizudera. This area's full of touristy souvenir shops, snacks, matcha ice cream and kimono rental places. I found the famous streets a bit too crowded with tourists - keep wandering and the backstreets nearby have more atmosphere.

Walk from Kiyomizu-Gojo or Gion-Shijo Station

KYOTO TOWER

Tallest tower in Kyoto, next to the station, for a view of the city. There's also a view from Kyoto Station next door - not as high but it's free, and station's an amazing building (with a floor of ramen restaurants!).

North side of Kyoto Station

KAMOGAWA RIVER

A wide river through the centre of Kyoto. Perfect for taking the scenic route or just sit and take a break.

ALTERNATIVES TO KYOTO

As tourism to Japan increases, Kyoto's become more crowded. If you want to see historic Japanese streets and temples, Kyoto has lots, but it's not the only place you can see them. There are small towns all around Japan where you can have a more atmospheric experience. Some are even known as "Little Kyoto":

- Kanazawa
- Takayama
- Hida Furakawa (a location from the film *Your Name*)
- Gujo Hachiman
- Kamakura

...and many more!

GION

RECOMMENDED

Kyoto's geisha district, and my favourite of the old, preserved areas. Will you spot a geisha? The area has a mysterious feel, with all the wooden shutters and private houses, alongside small canals. Stroll around and get lost! In the morning it was fairly quiet and it'd be very atmospheric in the evening. Shinbashi Dori is very beautiful, with willow trees, historic buildings and a stream.

Gion-Shijo Station

Shinbashi Dori

PHILOSOPHERS PATH

2km path alongside a canal in northern Higashiyama, where a philosopher used to walk to the university every day. Very beautiful in cherry blossom season. It runs between Ginkakuji (the silver temple) and Nanzanji temple.

1 mile walk from Keage Station or bus 5, 17 or 100 from Kyoto Station to Ginkakuji Temple

GINKAKUJI

The Silver Temple is much more understated than the Golden Temple. It's a zen temple with a moss garden and a sand garden. The gardens are very calm and peaceful, and there's a view of the city from behind the buildings.

At one end of the Philosopher's Path.

PONTOCHO

Kyoto's nightlife district - a narrow, charming alleyway with lanterns, small restaurants and bars. In the summer, restaurants by the river build wooden decks (kawadoko) for al fresco dining.

Gion-Shijo, Sanjo or Kawaramachi Station

Fushimi Inari Shrine Gion

Arashiyama

GOLDEN TEMPLE (KINKAKUJI)

One of the most famous temples of Kyoto. It's covered in gold and looks absolutely stunning, surrounded by a lake and a short trail around the gardens. I couldn't believe how perfect it looks. Kinkakuji's a little awkward to get to, and not that close to the other main areas of Kyoto.
Take the train to Enmachi Station, then it's a 1.7 mile walk or bus 205.

TRAM BETWEEN KINKAKUJI AND ARASHIYAMA

You can travel between Kinkakuji and Arashiyama on the Keifuku Electric Railway (aka Randen tram). IC cards are accepted. It goes from Arashiyama Station to Kitano Hakubaicho (change at Katabiranotsuji Station). To get to Kinkakuji it's a 1 mile walk or bus 102, 204 or 205.

ARASHIYAMA

You're still on the edge of town, but Arashiyama feels a bit more like the countryside. This is where you'll find the famous bamboo forest and monkey park. The centre is a wide, open river with the Moon Crossing Bridge. You can also go on a scenic railway, boat trips along the river and walking trails around the hills.
Saga-Arashiyama Station, 15 mins from Kyoto Station on the JR Sagano Line (aka JR Sanin Line)

NISHIKI MARKET

A long, covered market street with street food and snacks. Make sure you're hungry! Here's where to find all the local specialities, as well as Japanese knives and cookware.
Shijo, Karasuma or Kawaramachi Station

PRACTICAL INFO

WHERE TO STAY

- **Higashiyama and Gion** are close to the main tourist sites.
- **Kawaramachi** is downtown Kyoto, also close to the main sites.
- **Kyoto Station** area is convenient if you'll be doing lots of day trips. It's not the best-looking area of the city but it's practical.
- **Where not to stay:** Arashiyama and the areas near Kinkakuji and Fushimi Inari are a little out of the way.
- **Osaka** is very close to Kyoto (only 15 mins on the bullet train). If you want to stay somewhere livelier where everything's open later, get a hotel in Osaka and visit Kyoto on day trips.

HOW TO GET AROUND KYOTO

Walking - Not everywhere is walkable, but you can easily get between Higashiyama and Gion on foot. I walked there from Kyoto Station - not a short walk but do-able!

Train - There are also a couple of subway and train lines. You can use your Suica/Pasmo card or other IC card (the local one's called ICOCA) on trains, subways and buses.

Bus - A popular way of getting around but they can be crowded. Day passes are available from the Bus Information Centre at Kyoto Station.

Cycling - The city's flat, so renting bikes is also an option.

There are hundreds of temples & shrines; visit less famous ones for a more atmospheric experience.

Fushimi Inari Shrine

Osaka

Before I went to Osaka, everything I read about it only seemed to mention the food. The city's philosophy is *kuidaore* = eat till you go broke! While the food's excellent, there's actually a lot more to the city than that. It's also known for its friendly people who like to have a good time. Osaka's a huge, bustling city with lots going on. To me, it felt like Tokyo the Sequel - and it's a really fun sequel!

DOTONBORI

If you've seen a picture of Osaka, it's probably Dotonbori, the area around the canal. It really comes alive at night - and it's full on! Prepare yourself for a busy, crazy evening. Join the crowds, grab some takoyaki, take pictures of the giant crabs and statues on the buildings, watch a j-pop performance in the street - and make sure you're hungry - Osaka's known as the kitchen of Japan, and this is its centre.
Namba / Shinsaibashi Station

DON QUIJOTE FERRIS WHEEL

Unusual elliptical-shaped ferris wheel on top of Don Quijote, a large shop on Dotonbori that sells *everything*. The circular pods rotate as you go round, and there's a view of the city from the top. There's also a ferris wheel on top of Hep Five shopping mall - and one in the bay. *Namba / Shinsaibashi Station*

AMERICA MURA

Also known as Amemura, America Village is an alternative area with vintage shops, street art and music stores. It's like the Harajuku of Osaka - you'll find some of the same brands here, but it's more street than kawaii. Look out for the retro pinball arcade in Big Step shopping centre.
Head for Triangle Park (Sankaku / Mitsu Park), which is the centre of the area.

It's mandatory to take a cheesy photo with the Glico sign on Dotonbori.

RECOMMENDED

UMEDA SKY BUILDING

A really unusual building (above), made of two connected towers. There's an observatory at the top with one of the most stunning city views I've seen. The diagonal bridges you can see below the platform are the highest escalators in the world! Umeda is a skyscraper district that feels a lot like Tokyo.
Osaka / Umeda Station

FUN FACTS ABOUT OSAKA

The Kansai region has its own dialect. Instead of thanking you with "arigatou", people say "ookini".

Osaka was traditionally a city of merchants and business owners. That's why you'll see large, showy statues on the front of shops and restaurants. As a greeting, people say "Mokarimakka", which literally means "Are you making money?".

People stand on the right hand side of escalators, instead of the left like elsewhere in Japan. Osaka likes to be different!

Conveyor belt sushi was first invented in Osaka, in 1958. The aim was to serve more people without needing extra staff. There are now 11 stores in the chain, called *Mawaru Genroku Sushi.* If you want to visit the original, it's in Fuse in east Osaka, near the station.

SHINSEKAI

An older, retro district centred around Tsutenkaku Tower. When it was built, the north section was modelled on Paris and the south on Coney Island.
Shin-Imamiya Station, Dobutsuen-mae Station or Ebisucho Station

AQUARIUM KAIYUKAN

The world's largest aquarium with large and impressive displays, some spanning several floors. In the bay area there's also another ferris wheel (the largest in Osaka), shopping malls and you can even climb a mountain! Mount Tempozan is the smallest mountain in Japan, less than 5m tall.
Osakako Station in Osaka Bay

UNIVERSAL STUDIOS

Similar to the US theme park. There's the Wizarding World of Harry Potter, Jurassic Park, Snoopy, Hello Kitty, Sesame Street, Minions and lots more, as well as temporary anime-themed attractions.
Universal City Station in Osaka Bay

LOCAL SPECIALITIES

Osaka's known for its food. Japanese food's often thought to be healthy, but Osaka's specailities are deep-fried, smothered in mayo and delicious:

- **Takoyaki** - Balls of batter containing a small piece of octopus - but don't let that put you off!
- **Kushikatsu** - Meat/veg on sticks, deep-fried in breadcrumbs with dipping sauce.
- **Okonomiyaki** - Pancake batter with shredded cabbage, toppings and tasty, savoury sauce.

On Dotonbori there's a kiosk called "Gourmet Map"for restaurant recommendations: *gourmetmap.net*

ASAHI BEER FACTORY

Free guided tour of Asahi's first brewery - and yes, there's free beer in a tasting session at the end! Tours are in Japanese apart from certain days, but you can download an audio guide to your phone.
Slightly north of central Osaka at Suita Station

BOAT TRIP

Cruise past Osaka Castle on the Aqua Liner. There's also the Santa Maria Bay Cruise in Osaka Bay, and a short cruise along Dotonbori (Tombori River Cruise).

OSAKA CASTLE

Beautiful Japanese castle housing a museum, with an elegant Japanese garden.
Osakajokoen Station

MINOO PARK

Walk along a river to a 33m waterfall! An easy half day trip less than 30 mins from the city in a quasi-national park. Try the local speciality along the way: tempura maple leaves.

Take the Hankyu Takarazuka line from Hankyu Umeda Station to Ishibashi Station (15 mins). Transfer to Hankyu Minoo Line to Minoo Station (5 mins).

DENDEN TOWN

The Akihabara of Osaka, with anime merch, figures, cosplay shops, games shops, arcades and maid cafes. It feels more chilled than Akihabara, and there's more on street level. It's not wall-to-wall anime; the shops are dotted around the area east of Namba Parks shopping mall. (Walking distance from Dotonbori).

Namba Station

PRACTICAL INFO

WHERE TO STAY

The centre of Osaka is Dotonbori, so I'd recommend staying within walking distance of the canal (either north or south), in Namba or Shinsaibashi.

The shinkansen station (Shin-Osaka) is in the north of the city and not really close to the main centre.

HOW TO GET AROUND OSAKA

Subway - There are several subway lines. It's very similar to other metros. You can use your Suica or IC card from elsewhere in Japan.

Walking - The central area is walkable ie between Shinsaibashi / Amemura, Dotonbori and Namba / DenDen Town.

Cycling Osaka's fairly flat so cycling's very popular. Watch out for cyclists on the pavement when you're walking.

Day Trips from Osaka / Kyoto

Kyoto and Osaka are very close together, so you can easily stay in one and visit the other on day trips. They're completely different - Osaka's a buzzing, modern city and Kyoto's full of elegant history and tradition. If you have a JR Pass, you can travel between the two in only 15 minutes; otherwise it's still only half an hour on local trains. There are lots of places to visit around the Kansai region:

MIYAJIMA RECOMMENDED

30 mins from Hiroshima

One of the most beautiful places I've been in Japan. A beautiful "floating" tori gate in the water, wild deer and a mountain with cable cars. It's 30 min from Hiroshima, then a ferry across to the island (covered by your JR Pass). Or you can take a boat the whole way from Hiroshima. It's possible to visit Hiroshima in the morning and Miyajima in the afternoon. Alternatively, stay overnight in a ryokan on the island to see the beautiful sunset over the tori in the water.

NARA

1 hour from Osaka

A very popular and beloved day trip; Visit a park with large temples and deer that bow to you (in exchange for food!).

HIROSHIMA

1.5 hours from Osaka

Visit the Peace Park and Museum and see the A-bomb dome. Seeing the city today, it's hard to believe what happened there. While it's hard-hitting and not an easy visit, the museum is excellent. There's also a castle, and Miyajima's only 30 minutes away. Hiroshima also has its own style of okonomiyaki - try it at one of the many stalls in Okonomiyaki Mura.

KURAMA & KIBUNE

Less than 1 hour from Kyoto

Rural towns in the mountains north of Kyoto with hiking trails and shrines. In the summer, restaurants build platforms over the river (*kawadoko*) so you can sit outside and enjoy the cool air.

Miyajima - when the tide's out!

Kobe

Kurashiki

KOBE

30 mins from Osaka

If I went back to Kansai, Kobe would definitely be on my list! It's not just about Kobe beef; there's a lively harbour area, sake breweries, Chinatown, a fashion museum in a building that looks like it's from Star Trek and an earthquake museum. In Kitano-cho there are European-style houses where foreign traders from the port used to live.

Kobe's surrounded by mountains; you can even go skiing from November to March! There's a ropeway or cablecar up to the Kikuseidai Observation Platform on Mount Maya to see one of Japan's top 3 night views. It's called the ten million dollar view, referring to the cost of the electricity to power the thousands of lights twinkling in Osaka and Kobe.

There are several waterfalls near the shinkansen station that you can hike to, and get a view of the city. The closest is only 15 mins walk (Nunobiki Falls). There's also the Shin-Kobe Ropeway up to Nunobiki Herb Garden and a rose garden.

MOUNT KOYA

Less than 2 hours from Osaka

Also called Koyasan, a mountain with mysterious woodland hikes and over 100 Buddhist temples and monasteries, some of which you can stay at (*shokubo*).

KURASHIKI

70 mins from Osaka

Quiet, picturesque town with historic buildings around a canal, relaxing boat trips and traditional street food. It's famous for producing denim - you can even get blue denim ice cream and burgers in blue buns!

HIMEJI

30 mins from Osaka

Home to Himeji Castle, a World Heritage Site, considered the most beautiful castle in Japan, with extensive grounds.

JR KANSAI WIDE AREA PASS

A useful train pass for exploring the Kansai region (if you're not getting a JR Pass for the whole of Japan, or if you need extra days). It's about 10,000 yen for 5 days (slightly cheaper if you buy it before travelling - I use japan-rail-pass.co.uk). Take unlimited trips on the bullet train and JR trains in the area, plus a few non-JR lines. Visit Kobe, Himeji, Kinosaki Onsen and Kurashiki, and even go as far as Tottori and its sand dunes, Takamatsu on Shikoku and Amanohashidate to see the sandbar (one of Japan's top 3 scenic views).

KANSAI THRU PASS

This pass covers a smaller area and is only for non-JR trains. Bullet trains aren't included. Currently it's 4,300 yen (2 days) or 5,300 yen (3 days). The days don't have to be consecutive. It's worth it if you're going further afield than Osaka / Kyoto / Kobe.

Momochi Seaside Park

Kyushu

Kyushu is the southernmost of Japan's main islands. It's subtropical, with lots of volcanic activity and onsen (hot springs). The shinkansen line makes it easy to get around the island. I stayed in Fukuoka as a base; Kumamoto would also be a good, central place to stay.

FUKUOKA

The largest city on Kyushu. A modern city by the sea with a laidback feel.

- **Tenjin** - The main downtown shopping area.
- **Daimyo** - Trendy area with cafes and independent shops.
- **Canal City** - Large shopping mall with interesting architecture like a slot canyon. Nightly water and light shows - currently *One Piece* themed.
- **Momochi Seaside Park** - Sandy beach with Fukuoka Tower, a pretty wedding pavilion and boat trips across the bay.

Canal City mall

- **Uminonakamichi Seaside Park** - Peninsula with family attractions including Marine World, a petting zoo, flower parks and bike hire.
- **Shika Island** - Wild island at the end of Uminonakamichi with walking trails and hidden shrines in the woods.
- **Ohori Park** - City park centred around a large lake.
- **Maizuru Park** - Home to Fukuoka's castle ruins. A good place for cherry blossoms (along with Uminonakamichi).
- **Nokonoshima** - Island in Fukuoka Bay with a flower park, trails and noko noko ball, a version of croquet.
- **Yatai** - Food stalls that set up mini restaurants in the evening, mainly on Nakasu, the nightlife district.

BEPPU HELLS RECOMMENDED

A Day in Hell! The seven hells are a varied collection of unusual natural hot springs: dramatic steam vents, a pond of blood-red water, a natural geyser spouting boiling water and bubbling mud pools. Really unusual natural phenomena, and my favourite day trip in Kyushu. Get individual or combined tickets from the entrance of any hell. Head to Yukemuri Observatory to see steam rising up from springs around the city. *From Fukuoka take the shinkansen to Kokura, then the Sonic Limited Express to Beppu (2 hours total). From Beppu Station, take a bus to Kannawa terminal (also a tourist info centre). Five hells are in that area, and there's a bus from the terminal to the other two.*

There are onsen baths in Beppu, but not these - they're 100°C!

DAZAIFU & YANAGAWA

Popular day trip from Fukuoka.

Dazaifu is a historic town with a major temple, beautiful gardens and a museum.

Yanagawa is the Venice of Japan; relax in a punting boat drifting along tranquil, picturesque waterways that used to be the castle moats.

Ticket packages are available from Nishitetsu railways. Both are within an hour of Fukuoka so you can visit either or both as an easy day trip.

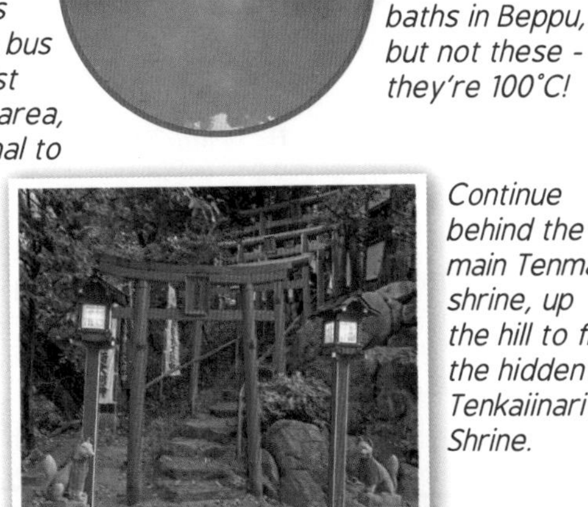

Continue behind the main Tenmangu shrine, up the hill to find the hidden Tenkaiinari Shrine.

Dazaifu

Beautiful Yanagawa

Yakushima

YAKUSHIMA

If you want to go somewhere really remote, Yakushima is a subtropical island south of Kyushu. Explore ancient, mossy forests - Princess Mononoke-style, it's really somewhere else!
Take a boat from Kagoshima or an internal flight from Fukuoka or Osaka.

ARU ARU CITY

The Akihabara of Kyushu: a shopping mall with anime and gaming stores.
Take the shinkansen to Kokura Station (15 mins from Fukuoka).

GUNKANJIMA

An abandoned island off the coast of Nagasaki. It used to be a coal mine, and had the highest population density in the world. It closed in 1974; now you can take a sightseeing cruise to visit parts of the island and see the deteriorating buildings.
Several companies run cruises from Nagasaki.

VISIT KOREA

It's not cheap, but you can take a ferry from Fukuoka to Busan in Korea. There are 3 hour and overnight options.

YUFUIN

Pretty onsen town near Beppu. From the town you can take a walk past rice fields and farmhouses to Lake Kinriko, which is famous for atmospheric morning mist. Nearby Yufuin Floral Village is themed like the English countryside. It's extremely cute and very Studio Ghibli.
80 mins by train from Beppu

SAKURAJIMA & KAGOSHIMA

Travel to the south of Kyushu and take a ferry from Kagoshima to explore Sakurajima, an active volcano! There's a minor eruption most days, but it's usually quite safe - people live there! You can see smoke coming from the volcano and black ash collected by the side of the road. A famous site is a tori gate buried in the ground by lava. There are walking trails, observation decks and it'd be a great place to hire bikes - then relax in the free foot baths. There's also a dinosaur park. Elsewhere in Kagoshima, you can take a steam sand bath, buried in geothermal black sand. It's said to be good for the circulation and more healing than an onsen bath.
1.5 hours from Fukuoka by shinkansen

 Sakurajima - an active volcano

FRUIT BUS STOPS

In Konagai (Nagasaki prefecture) there are super-cute fruit-shaped bus stops! Where else can you can wait for the bus in a giant melon or strawberry?!
PS: There's not much else to do in town so while they're adorable, it might not be worth the trip unless you're nearby!

NAGASAKI

Visit the peace park commemorating the atomic bomb. Take a boat tour round Gunkanjima, an abandoned island, see one of Japan's top 3 night views from Mount Inasa and visit Huis Ten Bosch, a Dutch theme park.
2 hours from Fukuoka by train

UNZEN HELLS

Steaming hot springs in an onsen town and national park near a volcano, Mount Unzen. There's also a Disaster Museum about volcanic eruptions.
Take a bus from Nagasaki. Or from Kumamoto, take a ferry to Shimabara then a bus to Unzen Onsen.

MOUNT ASO

Active volcano with one of the world's largest caldera. Check conditions as it's not always safe to go near the crater.
2 hour bus ride from Kumamoto. Easier to access by car.

KUMAMOTO

Home of popular bear mascot Kumamon! Visit the castle, gardens and historic houses, and support the city's recovery from the 2016 earthquake.
Only 45 mins from Fukuoka by shinkansen

TAKACHIHO GORGE

Beautiful gorge with a tall waterfall. Walk along the trails and take a rowing boat along the river. *3 hour bus from Kumamoto (only 2 buses per day). Easier by car, or stay in the area.*

SHIMABARA

Known as the "City of Swimming Carp", with carp swimming in the water in drainage canals along the streets. It's a castle town with historic, preserved streets.
Nagasaki prefecture. Connected to Kumamoto via the Kyusho Ferry (60 mins) and Kumamoto Ferry (30 mins).

Takachiho Gorge

Okinawa

The Hawaii of Japan! The tropical / sub-tropical islands are far south of the mainland. It looks like paradise, with perfect beaches, snorkelling and diving. Experience a different type of Japanese culture where spam is a sushi topping, US military bases give a western influence and there's one of the longest life expectancies in the world. I haven't been yet, but these places are on my list:

Way south of here!

MIYAKO-JIMA

One of the prettiest islands, with the loveliest beaches (best from April to November). It's about 300km southwest of Okinawa's main island. It has the clearest blue water in Okinawa, perfect for diving and snorkelling among coral reefs, with tropical fish and sea turtles, as well as surfing and stand up paddling.

Fly from Tokyo, Osaka, Nagoya or the other islands of Okinawa.

SWIMMING IN THE SEA

The water's warm enough for swimming between May and October on the main island, and April to November further south in the Yaeyama Islands. Only swim in the sea in designated areas (there are signs in English). Outside these areas there can be strong currents and venomous jellyfish.

AMERICAN VILLAGE

US-themed entertainment complex with shops, restaurants and a ferris wheel, in an area of US military bases.

Mihama, Honto (main island)

American Village

CHIRAUMI AQUARIUM

Said to be Japan's best aquarium. There are huge tanks, including one with whale sharks. Tickets are discounted after 4pm.
Northern Honto (main island)

VALLEY OF GANGALA

Looks as exotic as it sounds! Dine under the stalactites in a limestone cave with a cafe, then take a tour through a mysterious forest with vines and huge banyan trees with long roots.
Southern Honto (main Island)

OKINAWA WORLD

Theme park with a traditional Okinawan village, snake exhibition and spectacular 5km long cave with stalactites.
Southern Honto (main island)

CLIMATE

Okinawa's southern tropical / sub-tropical climate is warmer than the rest of Japan. The winter's mild but you'll need a jacket, and it can be windy. Like the rest of Japan, summer's humid. Most people prefer spring and autumn. It's a popular destination for Golden Week (end of April/start of May) and Silver Week (September), so they're busy times. Rainy season's earlier than the rest of Japan, in May/June. Okinawa's more affected by typhoons than the other islands, between May and October. August and September are the peak months.

Valley of Gangala

REGIONAL SPECIALITIES

- Purple sweet potato (beni-imo)
- Goya champuru - Stir fry made with goya, a local vegetable that's extremely bitter. An acquired taste!
- Taco rice - Taco fillings served on rice; a Japanese/American fusion.
- Umibudo - "Sea grapes": seaweed capsules of salty liquid.

PINEAPPLE PARK

Theme park about pineapples. See where they're grown, try various products and ride through the fields in a pineapple-shaped Jeep.
Northern Honto (main Island)

Lion/dragon statues on rooftops (shisa) ward off evil spirits.

ISHIGAKI ISLAND

The main island of the Yaeyama Islands, which are the furthest inhabited islands to the south and west. It's a beautiful island with beaches and clear water where you can swim with manta rays. Some of the beaches have star-shaped grains of sand. There's snorkelling, diving, kayaking and glass-bottomed boat trips to see the underwater world in the reef below, including manta rays. Or say hello to the multicoloured monster statues at the sculpture garden at Yonekoyaki Craft Centre, opposite Yonehara Beach. You can also take ferries to smaller nearby islands.

IRIOMOTE ISLAND

A wild island close to Ishigaki (you can take a ferry there). It's a trip to the jungle! It's a protected national park but locals offer guided tours. Go hiking and kayaking, cruise along the river through mangrove forests and even go swimming in a waterfall.
50 minute ferry from Ishigaki Island

GETTING AROUND OKINAWA

To get to Okinawa from the mainland, check budget airlines, and tourist packages for internal flights (JAL Japan Explorer & ANA Experience Japan fares). It may be cheaper to fly from Osaka.

To get between the islands, there are some ferries but most involve internal flights, so visiting more than one can be pricey.

TAKETOMI ISLAND

An easy day trip from Ishigaki Island. Taketomi is small so you can easily cycle around it. See traditional houses, or take a tour in a cart pulled by water buffalo. Go swimming on Kondoi Beach and see the star-shaped sand at Kaiji Beach.
15 minute ferry from Ishigaki Island

 Mangrove swamp on Iriomote Island

Trains and buses are less frequent in remote areas, so plan carefully around the schedule.

Shikoku

Shikoku is the main island that's least visited by tourists, which I think makes it all the more intriguing! There are some pretty remote areas, definitely off the beaten track. It's known for the 88 Temple Pilgrimage, a 1,200km trail that takes 30-60 days. Shikoku means "four provinces", named after the four prefectures on the island.

IYA VALLEY

I first heard about Iya Valley in Alex Kerr's book *Lost Japan*. It's impossible to read the book without wanting to go there! It's a remote valley crossed by vine rope bridges. The bridges (Kazurabashi) actually look quite terrifying, with large gaps, but the scenery's stunning. Nearby, you can go on a cruise along Oboke Gorge. There's also a famous statue of a boy peeing into the valley 200m below, which used to be a local rite of passage.

Awa-Ikeda or Oboke Station. From there you can take a bus (only a few per day).

Naoshima

TATSUKUSHI MARINE PARK

Rugged, rocky coast near the southern point of Shikoku. Take a glass-bottomed boat into the bay to see coral reefs and tropical fish. At Ashizuri Underwater Observation Tower you can go below the surface to see the underwater wildlife swimming by.
Kochi prefecture

NARUTO WHIRLPOOLS

Natural whirlpools twice a day off the coast of Tokushima, between Shikoku and Osaka. You can see them from a sightseeing boat, a walkway underneath Onaruto Bridge called Uzu no Michi, or viewpoints in Naruto Park. Check the schedules as there's more to see on some days than others, depending on the tides.
Naruto Station, Tokushima

LOCAL SPECIALITIES

- Sanuki udon (Kagawa) - Shikoku's udon noodles are thicker and chewier than elsewhere in Japan.
- Tokushima ramen - Rich pork bone broth, with a rice on the side.
- Iya soba noodles
- Katsuo no Tataki - Bonito fish grilled on the outside but raw inside.
- Citrus fruits and yuzu

ART ISLANDS

Several islands including Naoshima, Inujima and Teshima are known for galleries, sculptures and public artworks. The most famous is Naoshima, home to Yayoi Kusama's spotty pumpkin (left).
Take a ferry from Uno (Okayama) or Takamatsu (Kagawa).

SHODOSHIMA

An island between Shikoku and the mainland, connected by ferry. There are olive groves, a soy sauce factory museum and Kankakei Gorge, one of Japan's top three valleys. At the Olive Park you can visit the bakery from Kiki's Delivery Service and even take photos on a broom! At Angel Road there's a sandbar you can cross to a tiny island when the tide's out. Tonosho's known as "maze town" for the twisting, picturesque alleyways.
Take a ferry from Takamatsu, or several places on Honshu including Himeji and Okayama.

KOTOHIRA-GU

Also known as Kompirasan. A major shrine dedicated to sailors and seafaring. Getting to the entrance involves climbing almost 800 steps, with shops and snacks along the way, and there's a great view at the top from the main hall. Most people only make it that far but there's an inner shrine if you can face even more steps.
Kotohira Station, Kagawa

DOGO ONSEN

One of several onsen said to be the inspiration for the bathhouse in Ghibli's *Spirited Away*. It's 3000 years old; one of the oldest bathhouses in Japan. You can still bathe there and have snacks in the tatami mat lounge. Look for heron motifs; legend has it that an injured heron was healed by the waters.
Dogo Onsen Station, Matsuyama

SHIMANAMI KAIDO

A 70km route connecting Shikoku with the main island, Honshu. It's a popular cycling track across tall suspension bridges, six islands and the Seto Inland Sea. There are stunning views of the islands and small towns along the way. (The bridges are quite high if you're afraid of heights!).

The track runs between Onomichi and Imabari. Intermediate level cyclists can complete it in a day, or there are guesthouses and campgrounds along the way if you want to spread it over several days. Or just cycle a section and take a bus or ferry on the way back!

Onomichi, the town at the Honshu end of the trail, has lots of historic temples and several pagodas. There's a 2.5km temple walk to see 25 of them, and a ropeway with a view over the islands of the Seto Inland Sea.

The closest stations to the start/end of the route are Onomichi and Imabari.

MORE THINGS TO DO IN SHIKOKU:

- findshikoku.com
- setouchifinder.com
- shikokurailwaytrip.com

BIKE HIRE

You can hire bikes (including electric-assisted bikes!) at the start and end of the track. There are drop-off terminals along the way if you're not doing the whole route. Details are on shimanami-cycle.or.jp/rental/english

Note that there's another bike hire place (Giant rentals), which has higher-end bikes but is more expensive, with only two rental stations, at the start and end.

LUGGAGE

Yamato Transport Co (the delivery company with the cute cat logo) offer a same-day delivery service to send your luggage to your next hotel.

ROUTE GUIDE

Excellent information is available from one of the guesthouses along the way: cyclonoie.com/shimanamikaido-e.php

Chubu

Chubu is the central region of Japan, between Kanto (the region around Tokyo) and Kansai. While lots of tourists zoom through this area on the way between Tokyo and Kyoto, this middle section of Japan is often forgotten as a destination. But there are lots of interesting and less well-known places, as well as the Japanese alps and winter sports resorts.

KANAZAWA

An excellent alternative to Kyoto - a place to see historic Japan without the crowds. Experience preserved streets and elegant gardens, wandering through geisha districts and historic samurai areas. It's known for gold leaf - you can even eat it on ice cream.
2.5 to 3 hours from Tokyo on the shinkansen and 2 hours from Kyoto on the excitingly-named JR Thunderbird limited express train.

SHIRAKAWAGO

A world heritage site of traditional villages with triangular thatched roof houses (called *gassho-style* farmhouses) and rice fields. Relax and experience country life by staying overnight in a *minshuku* (guesthouse). There are several villages: the largest is Ogimachi; Suganuma and Ainokura are smaller and less developed.
1.5 hours by bus from Toyama or 75 mins by bus from Kanazawa.

Traditional meets modern at the stunning entrance to Kanawa Station.

Kurobe Gorge

KUROBE GORGE

A day trip from Kanazawa. Take a scenic railway that criss-crosses the gorge over 20 bridges, giving you stunning views with the snowy mountains of the Japanese alps in the distance. You can get off at stations along the way to explore. The railway runs from mid April to the end of November. *kurotetu.co.jp/en/*
Take the shinkansen to Kurobe-Unazakionsen Station. Cross the road to Shin-Kurobe Station and take a local train to Unazaki Onsen Station for the start of the Kurobe Gorge Railway.

GUJO HACHIMAN

A charming town known as the water city, with beautiful waterways and canals. There's a castle, lots of shrines and temples, and just outside the town you can visit limestone caves. It's also where they make plastic food models for restaurant window displays! You can try making your own in a workshop, or buy them as souvenirs.
Fairly remote: 80 mins from Takayama or Nagoya by bus, or 2.5 hours from Nagoya by train.

HOKURIKU ARCH PASS *hokuriku-arch-pass.com*
Explore many of these places with a regional train pass from Japan Railways. Follow an alternate version of the Golden Route from Osaka/Kyoto to Tokyo, via the Japanese alps, through Kanazawa, Toyama and Nagano. The pass covers the entire route, stopping wherever you like over 7 days. Note that it doesn't include the direct shinkansen route between Tokyo and Osaka.

Naraijuku on the Nakasendo Trail

NAKASENDO TRAIL

An ancient road between Tokyo and Kyoto, which is now a hiking route through the Kiso Valley. Along the way it passes through historic post towns with old wooden houses, rice fields and woodland. The most popular stretch is between Magome and Tsumago.
A day trip from Nagoya or Matsumoto, or stay in a guesthouse along the way.

GHIBLI THEME PARK

Opening late 2022. While Studio Ghibli in Tokyo is more of a whimsical museum of drawings, at the new park you can visit magical locations from Ghibli films, including the forest from My Neighbour Totoro, Mononoke Village and Kiki's house in Valley of the Witches.
Nagakute city in Aichi prefecture (on the outskirts of Nagoya).

MAGLEV MUSEUM

A must-visit museum for train nerds, all about the shinkansen! See retired bullet trains, simulators and dioramas of mini trains.
25 mins from Nagoya at the end of the Aonami Line.

TATEYAMA-KUROBE ALPINE ROUTE

Walk through a corridor of snow with walls up to 20m high! The complete route goes through the mountains via several buses, cablecars and a ropeway. It's open from mid April to late November, and you can walk along the snow corridor until late June.
The route runs between Toyama (on the shinkansen line) and Ogizawa (accessible by train from Matsumoto or by bus from Nagano).

MATSUMOTO

A castle town near the mountains, known as the gateway to the Japanese alps. The castle's called the crow castle because it's painted black to make it look more intimidating! It's artist Yayoi Kusama's home town; the art gallery has a permanent exhibition. Nearby there's Daioh Wasabi Farm for wasabi flavoured treats and picturesque boat trips. You can also hire bikes and cycle through rice fields at Azumino.
2 hours 40 from Tokyo on the train.

KAMIKOCHI

A mountain resort with hiking trails through a beautiful national park. Open from mid April until mid November.
A day trip from Matsumoto / Takayama.

Kamikochi

Tohoku

Tohoku is the area north (or east) of Tokyo, between the capital and Hokkaido. I've stopped over in Sendai and visited Matsushima on the way to Hokkaido, to break up the trip, and it was great to see more of the country on the way. It was interesting to see it start to become snowy as we travelled north on the bullet train. You could easily spend more time just travelling around Tohoku, and there are so many unique places beyond those mentioned here.

MATSUSHIMA RECOMMENDED

One of Japan's top three scenic views. Unique coastal town with over 260 tiny islands dotted around the bay. Must-do: cross the 250m red bridge and explore Fukuura Island for walking trails and amazing views of the bay. You can also go on a boat trip and explore temples (Entsuin Temple is so picturesque). It's known for oysters and seafood. *Only 1.75 hours from Tokyo by shinkansen, then 25 mins train from Sendai to Matsushima.*

Matsushima bay - one of Japan's top three scenic views

MOUNT ZAO

A mountain resort where you can go hiking in summer and skiing in winter. Mount Zao is an active volcano; the geothermal activity is why there are hot springs and onsen. Take a ropeway and hike up to see the otherworldly Okama Crater lake. In February when it's snowy, there's a unique phenomenon where snow collects on the trees to form snow monsters! Yamagata's known for high quality beef, so look out for grilled beef and hotpot dishes as a local speciality. *Yamagata prefecture.*

ZAO FOX VILLAGE

Foxes are thought to be messengers of the gods (that's why there are fox statues at inari shrines). Here you can see 6 different breeds, including snow foxes. You can feed them and even have photos with younger foxes. *Take a shuttle bus from Sendai or Shiroishi-Zao Station, Miyagi prefecture. Buses are infrequent; details on zao-fox-village.com/en Taxis are about 4000 yen each way.*

HIRAIZUMI

This used to be a major city in the 1100s, so it's home to historic temples and gardens, including Chusonji Temple, a world heritage site. There's a hall covered completely in gold called Konjikido. The most unusual temple is Takkoku no Iwaya, which is built into a cliff with red wooden scaffolding.
Hiraizumi Station (only 8 mins from Ichinoseki Station on the shinkansen line), Iwate prefecture.

YAMADERA

A mysterious hike through a forest up around 1000 steps, past small and larger temples. There are stunning views of the valley and mountains. It's particularly beautiful in the autumn. Risshakuji is a mountain-top temple, sometimes called a temple in the sky. The observation deck has stunning views (below).
Yamadera Station (1 hour from Sendai), Yamagata prefecture.

Yamadera

Ginzan Onsen

GEIBIKEI GORGE

Take a relaxing boat trip along a beautiful gorge - especially gorge-ous with the autumn colours in late October/November. Be careful not to get it mixed up with Genbikei Gorge, which isn't too far away.
Geibikei Station, Iwate prefecture.

GENBIKEI GORGE

Less popular than Geibikei Gorge but also scenic. You can get "flying dango" from a shop on the opposite side of the river. There's a ropeway across the gorge; put your money in a basket, hit a gong and send it across, and your dango will be sent back to you when the basket returns.
Genbikei Gorge is a 20 min bus ride from Ichinoseki Station.

WINTER SPORTS

It gets snowy in Tohoku! The ski season's from Nov/Dec until April or May. The resorts are less well known than Hokkaido and Nagano, so it's less crowded. You can even relax in an onsen after a day on the slopes.

GINZAN ONSEN

Beautiful hot springs town in the mountains. Extremely picturesque, especially in the snow. There's a short trail to a waterfall and you can go underground into an old silver mine ("gin" in the town's name means "silver" in Japanese).
Yamagata prefecture

SANRIKU COAST

300 km of rocky coastline and an area of natural beauty, which was hit by the 2011 tsunami. Spend your holiday yen helping the area recover.

- Iwate Tsunami Memorial Museum
- Ryusendo Cave with stalactites, bats and underground lakes.
- Kesennuma City Memorial Museum - Used to be a high school.
- Kitayamazaki Observatory - Views of the cliffs (sightseeing cruises from Shimanokoshi Station).
- Jodogashima - Lovely pebbled beach with craggy rocks and walking trails. Go on a boat to see the Blue Cave with beautiful blue water, only accessible by sea.
- Fish markets for fresh seafood.

Aomori, Iwate, Miyagi prefecture

Hokkaido

Explore Japan's winter wonderland: winter sports, snow festivals and beautiful landscapes. The summer's not as hot and humid as the rest of Japan, and it also escapes the rainy season. And if you've missed the cherry blossoms in Tokyo, they bloom slightly later up north. It starts to get snowy in November, and the snow lasts until April.

SAPPORO

The largest city on Hokkaido, known for the Sapporo Snow Festival in February. The streets are built on a grid system, and it has less of a Japanese feel.

- Sapporo TV Tower
- Odori Park
- Susukino (nightlife distruct)
- Fish market - Enjoy a fresh seafood breakfast. Nijo market is the most central; Sapporo Central Wholesale Market is less touristy.
- Sapporo Beer Museum
- Tanuki Koji - Covered shopping street
- Pole Town - Underground shopping street to escape the cold
- Mount Moiwa - A city view
- Moerunuma Park
- Shiroi Koibito Park - Chocolate biscuit factory

OTARU

Quaint town by the sea, only 30 minutes from Sapporo. Known for the warehouse district by the canal (above), with the biggest icicles I've ever seen! As it's by the coast, it's known for sushi, picturesque architecture and glassware. Visit in February for the enchanting Snow Light Path Festival (overlaps with the Sapporo Snow Festival).
JR Hakodate line to Otaru Station

LAKE TOYA

The Shikotsu-Toya National Park is made up of Lake Toya and Lake Shikotsu, two caldera lakes. Nearby on the Kompiriyama and Nishiyama Crater Walking Trails you can see newly-formed craters from an eruption in 2000, damaged buildings and a destroyed road.
Toya Station is 2 hours from Sapporo by train

SKIING

The ski season in Japan starts in December and runs through until April, depending on the area. The snow's deepest from January to March.

- Rusutsu - Largest ski resort in Hokkaido.
- Niseko - Gets the most snowfall of any ski resort in the world.
- Furano - Smaller, but with amazing views.
- Teine - Closest to Sapporo, formerly home to the Winter Olympics.

There are also ski resorts in Tohoku on Japan's main island, and several in Hakuba in the Japanese alps.

SOUNKYO VALLEY

Beautiful national park with forests and a gorge with high cliffs. It looks amazing in autumn with the colours.
From Kamikawa Station (JR Sekihoku Line) or Asahikawa Station, take the Dohoku Bus to Sounkyo (35 mins from Kamikawa or 110 mins from Asahikawa)

LOCAL SPECIALITIES

- Fresh seafood from the cold waters around Hokkaido. Try *kaisendon* (seafood rice bowls) at fish markets.
- Melon - At fruit stalls in the markets.
- Hokkaido milk - You'll see lots of soft serve ice cream - but you might not fancy it in the cold!
- Sapporo ramen - Rich miso ramen with butter to warm you up.

HAKODATE RECOMMENDED

Coastal town at the end of the shinkansen line. See one of Japan's top three night views and stroll through Motomachi, with picturesque European style architecture and churches. A good stopover on your way to Sapporo.
Shin-Hakodate Station's currently at the end of the shinkansen line.

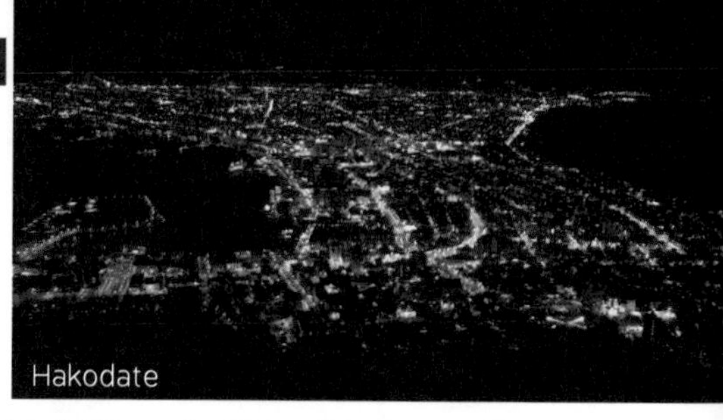
Hakodate

NOBORIBETSU

Aka Hell Valley! The hells are hot springs, and this is an onsen town. Explore walking trails with steam vents, hot spring pools and a warm river with natural footbaths.

1 hour 20 mins from Sapporo by train, then 15 mins bus to the onsen town.

JEWELLERY ICE

A natural phenomenon where large chunks of ice wash up on the shore. They shine different colours like jewels as the sun rises. Occurs from mid January to late February.
Otsu beach, Tokachi Toyokoro

BIEI / FURANO

Rural towns in central Hokkaido with beautiful countryside. Known for flower fields in summer and skiing in winter. The famous blue pond is nearby.
2 hours from Sapporo on the "Furano Lavender Express" train.

DRIFT ICE

Go on a cruise on the frozen open sea through drift ice, which can only be seen in a few places in the world. Occurs from mid January to mid April (the best time is late February).
Tours are operated by Aurora Drift Ice Sightseeing Tours and Garinko Ice Breaker Cruise.

Sapporo Snow Festival

Huge festival in Sapporo at the start of February, with giant snow and ice sculptures. At night they're lit up and brought to life with projections and music (including mini concerts with Snow Miku!). There are three sites:

- **Odori Park** - Main site with giant snow sculptures and food stalls.
- **Susukino** - Smaller ice sculptures, just a short walk from Odori Park.
- **Tsudome** - Snow slides and activities for children. A bus ride away from the city centre.

The festival's free, including the snow slides. There's only a fee for some of the activities at Tsudome.

FOOD STALLS

There are lots of stalls with all kinds of food and snacks to warm you up. This is *oshiruko*: sweet red bean soup with mochi, a traditional winter treat. The version from vending machines is delicious too!

TIPS TO ENJOY THE FESTIVAL

- Avoid the weekend if you can - it's a lot busier
- Book your hotel early - everywhere will be fully booked. Expect prices to be higher than their usual rates.
- If you're travelling there across Hokkaido on the train, reserve your seats as it'll be busy.
- Don't miss the night-time shows - they're the best part.
- Yes, it's extremely cold - even down to -20°C! But it's worth it. Wear layers and take breaks indoors to warm up.
- Buy heat packs (*kairo*) from the convenience store to put in your pockets and warm up your hands.
- Get hot drinks from the vending machines - they'll keep your hands warm too.
- Be careful of slippery patches on the ground - mostly it's fine but don't rush, especially crossing the road.
- Remember phone/camera batteries don't last as long in the cold.

Other Snow Festivals

While Sapporo's the largest and most famous, it's not the only snow festival in Japan. There are lots in Hokkaido and Tohoku that are smaller but less commercial, offering a different kind of experience. This is just a selection; there are many more!

SOUNKYO ICE WATERFALL FESTIVAL

Late Jan - March, Hokkaido

Snow sculptures, ice bars, fireworks and 100m of tunnels full of icicles in an onsen town. Everything's lit up with colourful lights at night - it looks amazing! You can even try climbing a frozen waterfall.

YOKOTE KAMAKURA SNOW FESTIVAL

February, Akita

Enjoy mochi and warm, sweet sake in cosy igloos made of snow, surrounded by glowing snow lanterns.

ZAO SNOW MONSTER FESTIVAL

End of Jan/start of Feb, Yamagata

Snow turns the trees at this ski resort into "snow monsters"! They're illuminated at night and you can go on snowmobile tours. During the festival weekend, lights dance between them as skiers zoom down the mountain with torches.

ICICLES OF MISOTSUCHI

January - February, Saitama

Magnificent large icicles, lit up with coloured lights. The closest event to Tokyo.

OUCHIJUKU SNOW FESTIVAL

February, Fukushima

Ouchijuku is a village with historic thatched buildings. It looks even more picturesque in the snow. The festival's more traditional than others, with fireworks, snow lanterns, period costumes and taiko drumming.

OTARU SNOW LIGHT PATH FESTIVAL

Early Feb, Hokkaido RECOMMENDED

This smaller festival overlaps with the end of the Sapporo Snow Festival in early February, so if you get your timing right you can visit both. Volunteers fill the town with lamps made of snow and ice, making really charming displays with a homegrown feel. It's magical, enchanting and creative, with a lot of heart. Only 30 mins from Sapporo by local train.

Your Plans

There are so many places to discover in Japan! With the increase in tourism, the most popular destinations are becoming increasingly crowded, so I'd encourage you to research and explore less-visited places. It's impossible to include them all in this book, so use this space for notes about places to visit. Plan your itinerary based on what interests you. Use the websites from the start of this section, read blogs and watch videos to find unique places in the area you're visiting.

PLACE	
HOW TO GET THERE (Train line, journey time)	
THINGS TO SEE/DO	
NOTES	

PLACE	
HOW TO GET THERE (Train line, journey time)	
THINGS TO SEE/DO	
NOTES	

PLACE

HOW TO GET THERE
(Train line, journey time)

THINGS TO SEE/DO

NOTES

PLACE

HOW TO GET THERE
(Train line, journey time)

THINGS TO SEE/DO

NOTES

PLACE	
HOW TO GET THERE (Train line, journey time)	
THINGS TO SEE/DO	
NOTES	

PLACE	
HOW TO GET THERE (Train line, journey time)	
THINGS TO SEE/DO	
NOTES	

PLACE

HOW TO GET THERE
(Train line, journey time)

THINGS TO SEE/DO

NOTES

PLACE

HOW TO GET THERE
(Train line, journey time)

THINGS TO SEE/DO

NOTES

Language

Do I Need to Know Japanese?

Before I first went to Japan I was really worried that everything would be in Japanese and I wouldn't even be able to understand anything. The good news is, it's really not like that at all! There's lots of English, and Japan's more foreigner-friendly than you might think. As English speakers, we're so lucky that we can travel all the way around the world and there are still signs in English.

TRAINS

All the signs you need are in English as well as Japanese, as well as displays inside the train and spoken announcements. You can change the language on ticket machines at stations.

If you're making train reservations with your JR Pass or purchasing a tourist ticket package, there's usually someone who speaks English at the counter. Customer service is excellent in Japan and they're really helpful.

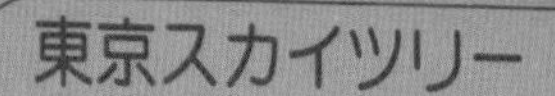

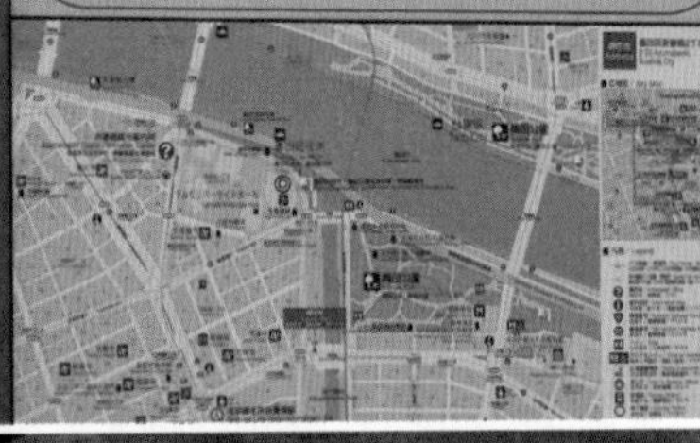

Most signs you need are in English as well as Japanese

RESTAURANTS

Most restaurants have an English menu, especially in cities and touristy places. Some smaller restaurants might not. You might need to ask for it, but often the staff will recognise that you're a foreigner.

Picture menus are common, which make it easy because you know exactly what you're getting, and you can point to order.

At restaurants where you order on a touchscreen, like some sushi bars, you can often change the language, and pictures are common.

Picture menus are common - so you can see what you're getting!

RESTAURANTS WITH TICKET MACHINES

Some restaurants have ticket machines to place your order. It's so they can operate with fewer staff. Sometimes they have English on the buttons and sometimes they don't.

If there's no English, try matching up the prices with the menu to find the items you want. Sometimes there's a staff member nearby who can help.

A useful phrase is: *"Chigaimashita"* = I made a mistake!

HOW TO USE TICKET MACHINES AT RESTAURANTS:

- Put in your money (you'll need cash; very occasionally they take IC cards).
- Press the button(s) for the items you want. A ticket will be printed for each item.
- Give the tickets to the staff inside the restaurant when you go in. Your food will be prepared and brought to your table as usual.

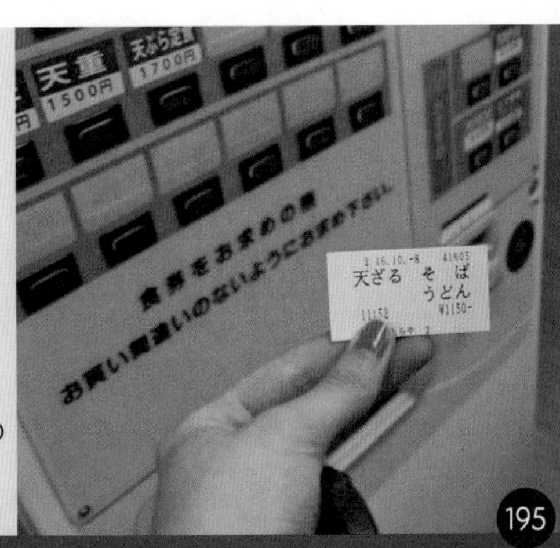

Not all packaging has English - but you can often see what things are!

CONVENIENCE STORES

Some labels and packets have English on them, but not all of them. Lists of ingredients and instructions on the packaging will be in Japanese. For most items you can work out what they are, but a few surprises are all part of the fun! If you have allergies or a special diet, I'd recommend using Google Translate and researching brands/products to look out for.

Onigiri (rice balls) were typically a challenge but all the major convenience stores now have English on their labels, making it much easier to know what the fillings are!

VENDING MACHINES

Drinks in vending machines don't always have English. Sometimes you can work them out from the packaging or get a rough idea. But as for the exact type of coffee in a can, that's still largely vending machine roulette!

BUYING THINGS IN SHOPS

The price will be shown on the till (or on a calculator in some cases) so there's not much need to say anything when you're making a purchase. You can gesture to your credit card to ask if they're accepted and the assistant will know what you mean.

Displays at the station alternate between Japanese and English.

DO YOU NEED TO LEARN HIRAGANA/ KATAKANA?

There's no need to learn to read Japanese unless you want to. All the signs you'll need are in English, and so are instructions/signs at touristy places.

Knowing hiragana and katakana will help you work out labels and packaging (eg convenience store snacks and ice cream flavours) but you can usually have a fairly good guess - it's rarely a complete mystery!

I'm constantly distracted trying to read signs in Japanese. However, nine times out of ten there are too many kanji for me to understand, or there's an English translation anyway. So by all means learn for fun if you want to, but it's not essential.

DO PEOPLE SPEAK ENGLISH?

Some do, some don't. English is taught in schools so people often understand it to a certain extent, but don't always feel confident speaking it.

At places where it's common to deal with foreigners, like hotel check-in desks and ticket counters, there's a good chance there'll be someone who speaks English.

Often when I speak Japanese to someone in a shop or restaurant, they'll reply in English.

LEARN JUST A FEW WORDS

It's amazing how much you can communicate with pointing and gestures. However, if you can learn a few words like 'please' and 'thank you' it certainly helps. Your efforts will definitely be appreciated, even if you make a mess of them!

Station signs are good for practicing your hiragana and kanji!

Essential Words

If you only learn 5 phrases, these will make life a lot easier:

hai
yes

iie
no

arigatou
thank you

kore o onegaishimasu
this please
Useful in shops and for ordering in restaurants - point at what you want.

sumimasen
sorry / excuse me
Use as an apology and also to get someone's attention

SIGN LANGUAGE

It's amazing how much you can communicate with the international language of gestures!

- Point with your whole hand or several fingers - it's more polite than one finger.
- When you enter a restaurant, hold your fingers up to show how many people are in your group.
- Crossing your arms like a big X in front of you means no (like the cute mascot on the sign below!). If you see someone do this gesture, it's not rude or aggressive - it's just like shaking your head.

Useful Phrases

GENERAL

arigatou gozaimasu
thank you very much

domo arigatou gozaimasu
(even more) thank you very much

daijoubu desu ka?
is it alright? / may I?

chigaimashita
I made a mistake / did something wrong

wakarimasen
I don't understand

nihongo ga wakarimasen
I don't understand Japanese

eigo ga wakarimasuka?
do you understand English

__________ wa doko desu ka?
where is _________?

toire wa doko desu ka?
where are the toilets?

IN SHOPS

Kurejitto kado wa tsukaemasuka?
Are credit cards accepted?

IN RESTAURANTS

eigo no menu ga arimasu ka?
Or just: eigo no menu?
is there an english menu

__________ hitotsu
one (portion) of __________

__________ futatsu
two (portions) of __________

beeru ippon
one bottle of beer

gochisosama deshita
(thank you for the delicious meal)

o kanjou onegaishimasu
can I have the bill please

oishii
delicious

AT THE HOTEL

Heya o yoyaku o shimashita
I reserved a room
(for checking into your hotel)

O nimotsu o azukatte itadakemasen ka?
Can I leave my luggage here please?
(before check in / after check-out)

PRONUNCIATION

Japanese pronunciation's based on breaking words down into single syllables (from hiragana/katakana), without any specific emphasis. Trying to explain this on paper is difficult so watch my video to hear how these are pronounced: cakeswithfaces.co.uk/pronunciation

Emergency Phrases

If it comes to the worst, here are some emergency phrases you can point to:

財布をなくしました saifu o naku shimashita	I lost my wallet
チケットをなくしました chicketto o naku shimashita	I lost my ticket
携帯電話 をなくしました keitaidenwa o naku shimashita	I lost my phone
具合が悪いです guai ga warui desu	I don't feel well
風邪をひきました kaze o hikimashita	I caught a cold
熱があるんです netsu ga arun desu	I have a fever
頭が痛い atama ga itai	I have a headache
おなかが痛い onaka ga itai	I have a stomach ache
脚 ashi / 足 ashi / 腕 ude が痛い ga itai	My leg / My foot / My arm hurts

(Ashi means both foot and leg. Point to show which you mean.)

__________アレルギーがあります __________ arerugii ga arimasu	I'm allergic to ________

Station Announcements

Announcements at the station are in English as well as Japanese, so you don't need to learn these. But I think its fun to be able to understand what they're saying, especially if you're learning Japanese. Trains are the main way to get around, so you'll be hearing these a lot while you're waiting on the platform.

Mamonaku ichiban sen ni, Tokyo yuki ga mairimasu.

Soon on platform 1, the Tokyo-bound train will arrive.

Abunai desu kara kiiroi sen made osagari kudasai.

(It's dangerous so) stand behind the yellow line.

Hakusen no uchigawa ni sagatte omachi kudasai.

Please wait behind the white line.

ON THE TRAIN

Doa ga shimarimasu.

The doors are closing.

Shimaru doa ni gochuui kudasai.

Be careful of the closing doors.

Tsugi wa, ______

Next is ______ (for the next station)

Mamonaku, _____

Soon, _________ (for the next station)

Deguchi wa hidarigawa desu.

Exit will be on the left (ie doors on the left side will open).

Deguchi wa migigawa desu

Exit will be on the right (ie doors on the right side will open).

Words & Phrases

How to Learn Japanese

There's really no need to learn Japanese unless you want to. You can absolutely get by with just a few words. But if you're interested in learning Japanese anyway, now's a great time! Preparing for a trip is a perfect source of motivation.

Often when you speak Japanese to someone in Japan, they'll either reply in English or come back with a stream of fast Japanese that's too complex to understand. But it does make certain situations easier, and people definitely appreciate your efforts! Plus, it's fun to be able to speak the language, even if it's just a few words at complete beginner level.

READING JAPANESE

There are three "alphabets" in Japanese:

- **Hiragana** - Phonetic and relatively easy to learn.
- **Katakana** - Again, phonetic and relatively easy to learn. It's used for foreign, borrowed words.
- **Kanji** - Pictogram-style characters. There are literally thousands of them - even most Japanese people don't know them all.

Katakana is used for foreign terms, so if you learn it first, you'll be able to recognise words once you start to sound them out. You'll then be able to pick out words in Japan, on signs and packaging, etc. You'll spot karaoke signs everywhere, and you'll be able to tell the difference between plain and custard cream melon pan in convenience stores.

If you learn hiragana too and know some Japanese words, you'll be able to pick out a few more words - although on most occasions I find it's in English too anyway!

Kanji are notoriously difficult, so don't worry about them until you've mastered hiragana and katakana.

I found audio courses useful to get used to recognising how words sound.

There are so many resources for learning Japanese. Everyone learns in different ways, so work out whether you get on better with books, flashcards, videos or audio. There are also lots of YouTube videos, podcasts and free apps; Memrise and Anki are both very popular. Try them and find out what works for you! These are just a few that I've tried and how I got on with them:

PIMSLEUR (AUDIO COURSE)
My number one favourite method of learning Japanese! An audio course based on remembering phrases after various intervals of time, so they go from your short term to long term memory. It's not cheap so try the free lesson first. There are monthly subscriptions, and it's available through Audible.

DR MOKU'S HIRAGANA / KATAKANA (APP) Flashcard-based app for learning to read Japanese characters. It uses mnemonics - silly pictures that look like the characters to help you remember them. The app includes tests to make sure you remember what you've learnt. The easiest way to learn hiragana/katakana!

INSTANT JAPANESE (BOOK & CD)
Part of the yellow *Teach Yourself* series, with exercises, vocab lists and bite-size grammar. The blurb promises you'll speak Japanese after 6 weeks! That might be a bit optimistic but you'll definitely learn something! I like the conversation scripts in English on one page with Japanese on the opposite page, so you can compare and work out what's what.

ROSETTA STONE (SOFTWARE)
Connect a microphone for speaking practice, and there are multiple choice exercises. A very well-known platform - but personally I wouldn't recommend it; it's expensive and gets quite repetitive.

JAPANESEPOD101 (AUDIO COURSE / PODCAST)
As well as the subscription there are lots of free lessons. The format's based on conversations, which are repeated slowly and discussed, explaining new vocabulary and grammar. Personally I much prefer Pimsleur because it tests you more - but there's lots of free content here.

WHITE RABBIT FLASHCARDS
Flashcards for learning kanji, the most complex of the three writing systems. There are free flashcard apps like Anki, but I prefer having a break from looking at screens sometimes! I like using physical cards so you can build decks of kanji you need to practice, add in new ones, sort and shuffle them.

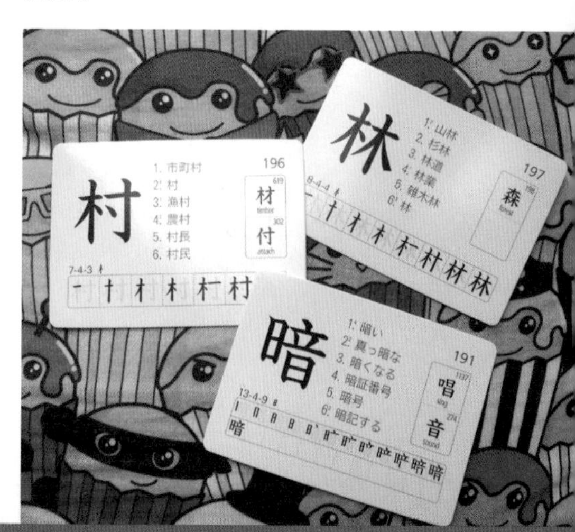

Money

Money in Japan

The currency in Japan is **Japanese Yen**. Get ready for some large numbers - prices are in the hundreds, thousands and tens of thousands.

CONVERTING CURRENCY

xe.com is a really useful website for converting currency. There's also a free app for your phone.

1 YEN COINS

You'll end up with hundreds of them! They're worth very little, and vending machines and arcades don't take them. Try and pay with them when you can, to avoid drowning in change!

HOW TO WORK OUT PRICES

An easy way of quickly working out prices is to remember how much 1,000 yen is in your currency.

From there you can easily work out 100 yen and 10,000 yen without too much mental arithmetic. Then you can double or multiply for a rough idea of prices.

100 yen =	
500 yen =	
1,000 yen =	
2,000 yen =	
5,000 yen =	
10,000 yen =	

CONSUMPTION TAX

There's a tax of 10% on purchases in shops in Japan, and 8% on food and drinks. If there are two prices on labels and signs, one will show the price with tax included.

TAX-FREE SHOPPING

Some shops are tax free for foreigners. You'll see the signs dotted around.

Show your passport when you pay, and you won't have to pay the consumption tax, which is 10%. There's usually a minimum spend.

DO'S AND DON'TS

Japan's a safe country so it's ok to carry cash with you. Pickpocketing doesn't tend to be a problem - but use your common sense just to be on the safe side!

No tipping - It's just not part of the culture. The total on the bill is the price you pay.

No haggling - This would come across as rude.

You might notice a tray on the counter in shops. When you pay, put your cash or card in the tray rather than handing it directly to the assistant.

How Much Money You'll Need

Tokyo has a reputation for being expensive. In reality, while the flights and hotels cost a lot, once you're in Japan it's more affordable than you might think, especially for food at restaurants.

Watch my "How Expensive is Tokyo" video on YouTube to see how much I spent in 3 days.

FOOD

- Onigiri rice ball 100 yen
- Ice cream cone 250-400 yen
- Bowl of ramen 700 yen
- Conveyor belt sushi 800 yen (per person, depending how much you eat!)
- Coco Curry 800 yen
- Dinner in a restaurant 1000-1500 yen each (or more, depending on how fancy the place is!)

DRINKS

- Bottle of soft drink 100-160 yen
- Coffee in a cafe 280 yen
- Alcohol cans/small bottles from the convenience store 100-200 yen
- Drinks in bars 500 yen+ Plus a cover charge of ~1000 yen per person (like an entry fee)

TRANSPORT

- Trains/metro in Tokyo 170-310 yen per trip
- Metro: 1 day pass 900 yen
- Day trip to Mount Takao (1 hour away) 780 yen
- Day trip to Kamakura (tourist ticket package) 1,470 yen

ADMISSION FEES

You'll probably spend most of the time wandering around exploring, so there might not be admission fees every day.

- Museum 600 yen
- Tokyo Tower 900 yen
- SkyTree 2,060 yen
- Aquarium 2,200 yen
- Temples 300-600 yen (many are free)
- Tokyo Disney 7,400 yen (1 day)

YOUR BUDGET

	PER DAY
Food (breakfast, lunch, dinner, snacks)	
Drinks	
Transport	
Evening: Drinks / going out	
Admission fees	
Spending money	
Total per day =	
x _____ days =	
+ Day trips / one-offs	
TOTAL	

Cash or Cards?

While it may seem like an ultra-modern place, Japan is largely a cash-based society (and they still use fax machines!). Credit/debit card usage is becoming more widespread, but there are still quite a few places that don't take them.

This means you'll need both your credit/debit card AND more cash than you'd normally take on a trip abroad.

WHERE TAKES CARDS?

In reality, lots of shops and restaurants do accept cards, but smaller places don't. You can't assume you can always use your card everywhere.

WHAT YOU'LL NEED CASH FOR

- Smaller shops and restaurants
- Restaurants where you order on a vending machine
- Street food, snack kiosks, ice creams
- Vending machines
- Train ticket machines (including topping up your Suica/Pasmo card)
- Entrance fees at certain places eg temples and shrines
- Games arcades

WHAT I TAKE

- **Cash**
  More than I'd usually take on a trip.
- **Credit card**
  (Commission-free for foreign currencies). For everyday spending where it's accepted.
- **Debit card**
  (Commission-free for ATMs). As a back-up, just in case I run out of cash and need to withdraw some more.

CARRYING CASH

Japan's a safe country with low crime levels, so you don't need to worry about carrying cash with you. Pickpocketing isn't a generally a problem.

However, use your common sense as you would anywhere - just because theft is rare, doesn't mean it never happens.

Where to get Yen

Lots of places have a bureau de change: supermarkets, department stores, travel agents and specialist travel money companies. Rates vary, so shop around to get the best deal.

1

Watch the yen rate on xe.com
It varies over time, so try and buy when it's a good rate.

2

Compare rates from different providers
A really useful comparison site is:
travelmoney.moneysavingexpert.com

Some providers will deliver to your house, and some are over the counter at a shop.

3

Pick a reliable provider that you've heard of
Or check reviews, especially if you're exchanging a large amount of money.

CAN'T I JUST WITHDRAW CASH WHEN I'M THERE?

Withdrawing cash from an ATM when you're in Japan can give you a better rate.

However, personally I prefer to get it sorted beforehand. It saves time when you're there, and can you imagine if your card didn't work and you were stuck without cash?!

CASH MACHINES

Your card should work in these ATMs:

- Post Office
- 7-Eleven convenience stores
- Some Family Mart and Lawsons convenience stores (but not all)
- Aeon Bank (at Aeon malls)

CLOSEST ATM TO YOUR HOTEL:

Credit/Debit Cards

Japan uses chip and pin, but you may be asked to provide a signature instead. Sometimes neither is required - the easiest approach is to put your card in the tray on the counter and see what the assistant asks for. Contactless payments are increasing in popularity but they haven't yet been adopted everywhere.

Not everywhere takes cards, so make sure you have plenty of cash too.

USE YOUR CARD FOR THE BEST RATE

Travel money providers always take a cut and give you a rate lower than what's on xe.com.

When you use a commission-free card in Japan you get the actual exchange rate, so you get the most yen for your money.

IS YOUR CARD COMMISSION-FREE?

It's important to make sure your card is commission-free for foreign purchases, so you don't get charged for every transaction. It should tell you on your bank's website. If you don't have one, it's worth getting one for your trip.

A card that's commission-free for cash withdrawals might not be commission-free for purchases. I take one card for ATMs and one for purchases.

CHECKLIST

- [ ] **Get cash**
- [ ] **Notify your bank that you're going to Japan**
  So they don't think your card's been stolen and cancel it!
  You can usually do this via online banking.
- [ ] **Check which of your cards are commission-free abroad**

  For purchases: ______________________

  For ATM cash withdrawals: ______________________

Food

Japanese food is amazing and you've got to try your favs. Here are my recommendations; you'd be missing out if you went to Japan and didn't have:

1 OKONOMIYAKI

My favourite Japanese meal! You hardly ever find it at western Japanese restaurants and I don't know why! It's fun to make your own with a grill at your table. My fav toppings are cheese and mochi rice cake.

2 CONVEYOR BELT SUSHI

Obviously you've got to have sushi. Conveyor belt sushi is lower quality than restaurant sushi - but compared to the UK, it's better than most restaurants at home. And it's unbelievably cheap. And fun. Feast away and stack up those plates!

3 STRAWBERRY SHORTCAKE

This is actually Japanese birthday and Christmas cake! Sweet whipped cream, light sponge and strawberries. As well as looking perfect (just like in an anime!), it's absolutely delicious. Japanese gateaux are particularly light and fluffy - it's too easy to devour all that whipped cream. Look out for Cozy Corner for a delicious selection of cakes. They even put a frozen ice pack in the box to keep it fresh.

4 RAMEN

As one of Japan's most beloved dishes, I'm sure ramen's already on your list - and there are so many different types to try! One of my favs that you don't often find outside Japan is curry ramen, or curry udon.

5 TAIYAKI

Fish-shaped waffles with fillings - traditionally red bean paste (which is sweet but has a definite bean flavour), or custard, chocolate cream or matcha cream. Find them freshly made at stalls and kiosks.

6 MELON PAN

Not melon flavoured, but like a melon with soft bread on the inside with a firm, cookie-like shell. The flavour isn't anything amazing but there's just something satisfying about them. Find them in convenience stores or bakeries. Pretty much anything from a Japanese bakery is amazingly soft, fluffy and magical - I wish I could try everything!

7 MOCHI / DANGO

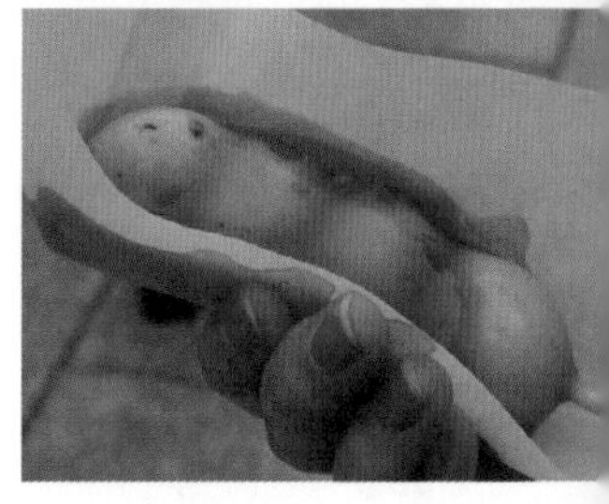

All the mochi I've had in Japan has been so much fresher and softer than mochi overseas - even pre-packaged mochi in convenience stores. It's soft, chewy rice cake. It's not really sweet and doesn't even have that much flavour - it's more about the texture and mouth-feel. Dango are very similar but on a stick (technically mochi's made from rice and dango's made from rice flour).

8 COCO CURRY

You've got to try Coco Curry! Satisfying katsu curry in large portions, that you can customise with toppings. You choose the spice level - and it's not for the faint-hearted! I apologise in advance because once you've been, you'll miss it so much once you're back home.

9 ONIGIRI

Rice balls (with or without seaweed wrapping) with various fillings. Find them in convenience stores - they're the equivalent of sandwiches, only about 100 yen. Perfect for breakfast or lunch. There are all sorts of fillings; I like wakame seaweed, pickled plum and even the plain onigiri are somehow satsfying.

10 SOFT SERVE ICE CREAM

This might not seem like a Japanese speciality but it's definitely a treat! In touristy places you'll find matcha green tea flavour, Hokkaido milk... but sometimes you'll come across a kiosk with hundreds of different flavours. My favourite is black sesame - and there are lots of novelty flavours, like garlic or squid ink!

How to Order in Restaurants

Most restaurants have food models outside, so you can easily see what type of food they serve. It's also very common to have a picture menu. In the main areas, most restaurants have an English menu - sometimes you have to ask for it - but smaller places in the backstreets might not have one.

1. **When you go in** hold up your fingers to show how many people are in your party. You'll be shown to your seat.

2. **To ask for the English menu:**

   Eigo no menu ga arimasu ka?
   Or just: *Eigo no menu?*

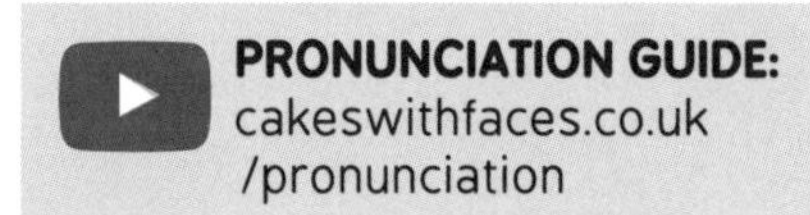

3. **To place your order** point at what you want and say:

   Kore o onegaishimasu (this please)

   It's polite to point with your whole hand rather than one finger.

   Or to ask for their recommendation, say: *Ososume wa?*

   Dishes are brought to your table as they're ready, which might not be all together at the same time.

4. **The bill** will usually be on your table. They'll update it if you order additional items.

   If you need to ask for the bill, say: *O kanjou onegaishimasu*
   Or just *O kanjou*

   Usually you get up to pay at the till, but just follow what everyone else is doing! Not everywhere accepts credit cards, so make sure you have cash just in case.

   There's no tipping in Japan (even though the service is usually so good you'll want to tip). The stories are true about waiters running after customers to return their money when they left a tip!

Restaurant Etiquette

- **Don't hang around, especially in small restaurants - leave once you've finished eating.** Especially in the city, lots of restaurants are very small and can only make enough money by having a high customer throughput. Often you'll see queues outside, so it's polite to give up your space once you've finished eating to let the next group in.
- No tipping - it's not part of the culture.
- It's ok to call the waiter over (politely) if you need something. Just raise your hand and say "sumimasen" (excuse me).
- Don't stand your chopsticks up in your rice - it's associated with funerals.
- If you're passing food to someone else, don't pass it from chopstick to chopstick - that's also a funeral custom.

- If you're taking food from a shared dish, use the other end of your chopsticks.
- There might be a basket for your bag, so you don't have to put it on the floor, to keep it clean.
- Usually you go up to the till to pay at the end.

As a foreigner, no one will expect you to know all the nuances of the local etiquette. The important thing is to be polite, respectful and follow what other people are doing.

VENDING MACHINE ORDERING

At some restaurants, usually ramen or noodle places, you order at a vending machine!

It's a way of making the restaurant easier to run, so the staff don't have to take orders or handle cash.

Insert your cash and press the buttons of the items you want. Hand the tickets to the staff and they'll prepare your meal.

Types of Japanese Food

Make the most of being in Japan and try as much authentic, local cooking as you can. Here are various types of Japanese food - tick the ones you want to try, and make a must-eat list!

☐ SUSHI

In contrast to sushi restaurants abroad, in Japan sushi is often quite simple, focussing on quality, well-prepared ingredients rather than lots of flavours.

CURRY RICE ☐

Japanese curry is brown and gravy-like. Often served with pork katsu (katsu curry). My fav is Coco Curry - you can choose your spice level and toppings. A filling, satisfying meal!

☐ PORK KATSU

Pork cutlet in breadcrumbs. Japanese panko breadcrumbs are large and crunchy. It's basically the meat from a katsu curry, but served with rice, tonkatsu sauce (fruity, tangy and delicious, like brown sauce) and shredded white cabbage as a salad.

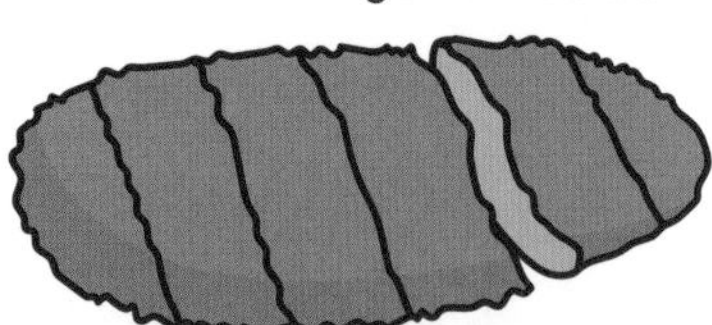

☐ GYUDON

Beef rice bowl. Very cheap at Yoshinoya, a Japanese fast food chain. "Gyu" means beef and "don" or "donburi" means food on a bowl of rice. You can also get seafood donburi.

☐ YAKISOBA

Noodles stir-fried in a tasty, tangy-sweet sauce, with cabbage, pork or shrimp and topped with fried egg and katsuoboshi (dried fish flakes). A popular street food at festivals. You'll also find it at some izakaya or teppanyaki grill restaurants, or sometimes where you can get okonomiyaki. The green topping is seaweed flakes, and it's also served with red pickled ginger (beni shoga).

☐ TEMPURA

Seafood and vegetables deep fried in light, crispy batter. It takes a lot of skill to cook properly, at the correct temperature and timing. If it's cooked correctly, it's very light and not greasy like you might expect, bringing out the flavour of the ingredients.

☐ SOBA NOODLES

Buckwheat noodles in soup or served cold with dipping sauce (zaru soba). They have a more distinctive flavour than regular noodles and are very healthy! Traditionally you drink the water the noodles were cooked in (soba yu) as a final course - it's thought to be nutritious.

UMAMI

Umami is a type of flavour in Japanese cuisine, just like sweet, sour or spicy. It means tasty and savoury, and is used to describe satisfying or meaty-type foods.

Foods rich in umami include miso, soy sauce, dashi (stock). In western cuisine: gravy and the tasty Italian cheese/tomato combination.

☐ RAMEN

Another well-known favourite. The best is at tiny ramen bars where you sit at the counter. There's not just one type of ramen - there are many (see the ramen page for more!).

☐ UDON

Thick white noodles served in hot soup. You can also get them cold with dipping sauce (zaru udon) - surprisingly refreshing!

☐ GYOZA

Dumplings with a filling made of pork, garlic and vegetables, served with a dipping sauce. Find them at izakaya and as a side dish. How many can you eat??

☐ SHABU SHABU

Thin slices of meat and veg that you cook at your table by swirling them in a hot broth. Then at the end you can drink the soup! Some restaurants offer all-you-can-eat sets (tabehodai).

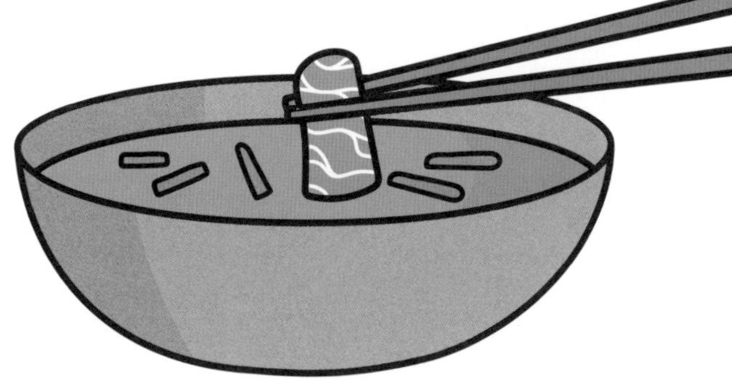

☐ OMURICE

Chicken and tomato fried rice wrapped in an omelette and topped with ketchup. It's comfort food, popular with children. It's said to be a western-influenced dish (yoshoku).

TRY JAPANESE HOME COOKING

With *Nagomi Visit* you can see what it's like having a meal at someone's house. Your host will meet you at the station and cook dinner for you - a chance to find out all about what it's like living in Japan. Details on nagomivisit.com

☐ YAKINIKU

Grill your own bite-sized pieces of meat at your table - usually beef, pork and chicken. It's similar to a Korean barbecue. Some restaurants offer all-you-can-eat (tabehodai) and some also have all-you-can-drink plans (nomihodai)!

☐ YAKITORI / KUSHIYAKI

Grilled food (mainly meat) on sticks. Strictly speaking, yakitori is chicken, and kushiyaki includes other meats and vegetables too, but the terms are used interchangeably.

Typical bar food at izakaya (Japanese pubs), which are just as much about eating as they are about drinking!

☐ KUSHIAGE/ KUSHIKATSU

Deep-fried meat and vegetables in breadcrumbs, on sticks and served with tasty dipping sauce. Very popular in Osaka.

NON-JAPANESE FOOD

There are plenty of restaurants with other types of food eg pizza, pasta, curry, burgers, etc. So don't worry if you're travelling with picky eaters or if you're craving something familiar. But if you've travelled all the way around the world to Japan, it's a waste not to make the most of the local cuisine.

DO ONE THING & DO IT WELL

Japanese restaurants abroad serve sushi, ramen, katsu curry, tempura and a bit of everything. However in Japan, they tend to focus on just one style of food eg just sushi, or ramen. There isn't always a large selection on the menu - they focus on one type of cuisine, perfect the art and make it the best they possibly can!

☐ OKONOMIYAKI

Often called a Japanese pancake/pizza, but apart from being flat and round, it's not really much like either! It's made of shredded cabbage in batter with toppings, tasty brown sauce, mayo and seaweed flakes. It's one of my favourite Japanese dishes because it's quite hard to find abroad. The sauce is really tasty! Hiroshima-style okonomiyaki is layered, with the pancake at the bottom, also containing yakisoba noodles.

Mix your own okonomiyaki and cook it on a grill at your table.

MONJAYAKI is made of similar ingredients but stays semi-liquid - you eat it off the grill with a mini spatula.

If you want to try making your own, okonomiyaki and takoyaki sauce is sweet and tangy - similar to a mixture of ketchup, brown sauce, soy sauce and Worcester sauce.

☐ TAKOYAKI

Fried balls of batter with a small piece of octopus inside. Topped with okonomiyaki sauce, mayo, seaweed flakes and bonito (fish flakes).
A popular street food snack, especially in Osaka - find it at kiosks and food stalls.

☐ KAISEKI

Fancy (and expensive) traditional multi-course meal with lots of tiny dishes served on different plates. Definitely fine dining - not your typical midweek meal! If you stay at an onsen with dinner included, it'll probably be kaiseki. However, you don't need to go to an expensive restaurant to have a great meal in Japan; the standard is excellent across the board for all types of food.

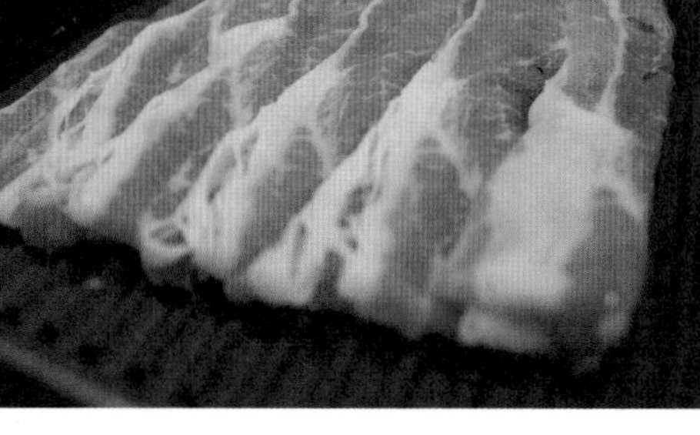

☐ KOBE BEEF

High grade, melt-in-your-mouth beef. Famously very expensive. There are various grades available, with A5 being the highest. Wagyu is a wider term that refers to beef from Japanese cattle breeds. On the whole, Japan isn't a place where you're likely to get ripped off, but if you want to try it, do your research to make sure it's genuine.

☐ ODEN

A winter food! Fish cakes, boiled eggs, tofu and vegetables in steaming hot broth to warm you up. In the winter you'll find it in convenience stores by the counter, where you can choose whichever pieces you want, like a kind of hot pick and mix. It's also served at some izakaya (bars), food stalls and mobile food stands (yattai).

☐ MISO SOUP

Tasty thin soup made with miso (fermented soy bean paste - watch how it forms clouds in the soup bowl!). It's topped with spring onion and small pieces of tofu. Full of umami - that savoury, tasty, satisfying flavour. Like other fermented foods, it's also very healthy (although high in salt). It's a common side dish in set meals, and part of a traditional Japanese breakfast.

Fast Food

If you go all the way to Japan and just eat McDonalds, pizza and foods you can get at home, you'll be missing out on some amazing Japanese food. But if it's late and nowhere else is open, or if you're craving a burger, fast food's always an option.

WESTERN CHAINS

There'll be chains you recognise (are there any countries without McDonalds?). Alongside your favourites, there might be a few less familiar menu items, like teriyaki burgers. Look out for novelty limited time specialities, like black burger buns or fries with chocolate sauce!

- McDonalds
- Burger King
- KFC
- Pizza Hut
- Dominos
- Subway

"Giga Meat", "Quattro Happy" and potato-mayo pizza at Domino's.

NOT JUST BURGERS & CHIPS

Fast food in Japan isn't always burgers, chips, pizza and deep-fried food! It's great that there are places where you can get a quick, cheap meal at all hours that's a little healthier (ok, maybe not that healthy...) but at least there's more variety.

- Yoshinoya - Beef bowls (gyudon) - beef on rice.
- Sukiya - Beef bowls.
- Coco Curry - My favourite! Cheap, satisfying and delicious katsu curry.
- Tenya - Tempura with rice or udon noodles.

JAPANESE FAST FOOD CHAINS

If you're craving a burger, why not try the Japanese chains?

- Mos Burger - My favourite! Most of the burgers can be made as soy burgers.
- Freshness Burger - Known for fresh, natural ingredients.
- Lotteria - Burgers and fries.
- First Kitchen - Burgers but also pasta, pizza and fried chicken.

Sushi Restaurants

You might be surprised how cheap sushi is in Japan! Compared to the UK, it's about a third the price. Of course, you can splash out on high-end, expensive restaurants, but in my experience even the cheapest sushi is a better standard than what's served in restaurants at home. In particular, the cuts of fish are higher quality and the rice is prepared really well.

CONVEYOR BELT SUSHI (KAITENZUSHI)

An essential Japanese experience! It's lots of fun, and also cheap. It may seem futuristic, but kaitenzushi was actually invented in 1958, as a way to serve more people without needing extra staff.

The sushi's usually not the highest quality, but I've found it's at least an equal standard to chains in the UK - and there's a greater variety.

Take what you fancy off the belt, then pay at the end when they count your plates. You can usually order from a menu as well.

At some places there's a touchscreen for placing your order (there's often an English language option, and pictures). Once it's ready, your order zooms along to your place - it's sometimes called bullet train sushi!

When you're done, press the button for the bill and they'll bring it over so you can pay at the till.

There are several sushi places that have become popular with foreigners, like *Genki Sushi* in Shibuya. There's always a crowd of tourists queuing outside. While they're great, they're not the only places with touchscreens and conveyor belts. There are lots of other fun, cheap sushi places with similar set-ups that are less well-known but just as accessible if you don't speak Japanese, like *Kura Sushi, Hamazushi, Sushiro* and *Sushi Go Round* - or search on Google Maps for "kaiten sushi".

STAND-UP SUSHI BARS

Fast and cheap sushi. You literally stand up at the counter, like at a bar, with no chairs. It's the quickest eat-and-go experience, for those sushi emergencies when you need nigiri, instantly!

FANCY RESTAURANTS

While there's lots of cheap sushi, there's also expensive sushi served at high-end restaurants. There's virtually no upper price limit if you want to splash out. But really, unless you're a sushi connoisseur and used to high-end, expensive places, it's not necessary to pay a lot to enjoy good sushi unless you want to!

Fresh nigiri at Tsukiji

SHOPS

Convenience stores and supermarkets have sushi bento boxes and pre-packaged rolls for picnic lunches. It's very cheap and much better quality than supermarket sushi you might have tried at home.

FISH MARKETS

If you're jet-lagged and wake up early, take a stroll through the quiet streets and head to a fish market for the freshest sushi you've ever tasted.

Tsukiji Fish Market in Tokyo's now moved to Toyosu in Odaiba. At the new market, you can watch the tuna auction at 5:30am through an upper window (no booking required). If you apply online, 10 minute slots for a closer window are assigned by lottery. It's free, but it's quite sterile compared to the old market. If you just want a fresh sushi breakfast, the original outer market with all its restaurants is still there in Tsukiji.

Many other towns and cities have fish markets too, especially if they're near the coast. Most of them have bars or food courts where you can eat. They often sell fruit and vegetables as well, if there's anyone in your group who doesn't like fish.

Types of Sushi

The name sushi doesn't necessarily mean raw fish - it simply refers to the method of preparing the rice. Sushi in Japan is fairly simple, usually with just one filling or topping, and without extra sauces or garnishes. It's all about the pure taste of quality ingredients and making simple dishes the best they can be.

MAKI ROLLS

Rolls with a single filling, wrapped in nori (seaweed sheet).

FUTOMAKI

Larger rolls with several fillings

NIGIRI

The most common type of sushi at restaurants in Japan. An oval-shape rice ball with a topping (no seaweed).

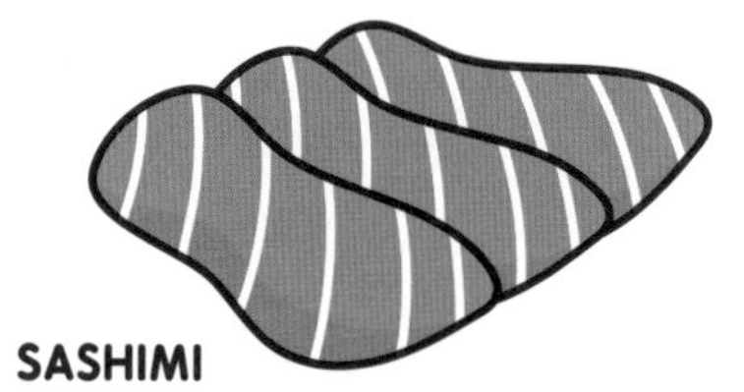

SASHIMI

Just the fish, without rice

CHIRASHI SUSHI

A bowl of rice with the fillings scattered on top. "Kaisendon" is very similar - a rice bowl with seafood on top. The difference is that the rice in chirashi sushi is seasoned. A "don" is any kind of dish that's a rice bowl with toppings (eg donburi).

TEMAKI

Hand roll - looks like an ice cream cone! When people make sushi at home, it's often hand rolls because they're the easiest to prepare.

GUNKAN

Similar to a maki roll but taller and oval-shaped. The name means battleship roll, because of its shape.

DON'T LIKE FISH?

Sushi places often have one or two options - enough for a meal, but don't expect a huge choice:

- Tamago nigiri (egg)
  *may be made with fish stock
- Kappamaki (cucumber roll)
- Inari sushi (sweet tofu pocket filled with rice)
- Oshinko maki (pickled radish roll)
- Kampyo roll (pickled gourd)
- Natto roll (fermented soy beans - famously an acquired taste!)
- Avocado isn't that common in Japan - it's not a traditional sushi ingredient. It was introduced in the west as a non-fish alternative to fatty tuna.

Ramen

One of the most loved Japanese dishes: huge bowls of noodles in soup - warm and satisfying. In Japan there are all different types of ramen. Restaurants often specialise in a particular variety, perfecting the recipe and turning it into an art.

TONKOTSU	Rich, creamy soup made from pork stock. Originally from Fukuoka.
SHIO	Light broth flavoured with salt - the closest to traditional Chinese-style noodle soups.
SHOYU	Flavoured with soy sauce.
MISO	The soup's flavoured with miso paste, like miso soup - savoury and full of umami!
CURRY	Curry soup, like a thinner version of katsu curry sauce. You can also get it with udon noodles.
TSUKEMEN	Dipping noodles. The noodles are served separately with a thicker sauce to dip them in.

RAMEN MUSEUM

Try different types of ramen from all around Japan at the Ramen Museum in Yokohama (about half an hour from Tokyo by train).

There are half portions (which are still pretty big) so you can try several varieties.

It has retro Japanese theming and an Okinawan bar in the middle. Look out for Orion, a beer from the islands of Okinawa!

ORDERING AT A VENDING MACHINE

At some ramen restaurants you order at a vending machine!

Put in your money, press the buttons for the items you want, and it'll give you a ticket for each item. Hand them to the staff when you go in and they'll cook your ramen for you.

If you press the wrong button, say "chigaimashita" = I made a mistake!

Convenience Stores

Convenience stores are EVERYWHERE. Especially in Tokyo, you're never more than a few minutes away from one (or three!). And the big surprise is: the food is actually good quality. There are healthy options (and lots of unhealthy options!). *And* it's cheap, making them perfect for grabbing a quick lunch, breakfast, snacks and drinks. They're usually open late, often 24 hours in Tokyo. The main chains are 7-Eleven, Family Mart and Lawsons.

ONIGIRI

Rice balls with different fillings (eg tuna mayo, cod roe, seaweed, pickled plum). A cheap snack or lunch - the Japanese equivalent of sandwiches - only about 100 yen! They're ingeniously packaged so the seaweed doesn't go soggy before you eat it. There are also cheap sushi boxes, whole sushi rolls and bento lunchboxes.

FRIED CHICKEN

Fall in love with convenience store kara age (fried chicken). Only about 100 yen a piece, you'll find it with the hot food on the counter.

FRUIT SANDWICHES

The softest, fluffiest bread (no crusts!), with light, whipped cream and fruit. The fruit's seasonal, so look out for different types. Egg mayo sandwiches are 100% delicious too.

STEAMED BUNS

On the counter, beside the cabinet for fried chicken there'll be a steam cabinet for steamed buns:

- Nikuman (meat buns)
- Pizzaman (cheese and tomato)
- Ankoman (sweet red bean paste)
- Curry or curry and cheese

Pizzaman

DRINKS AND ALCOHOL

Convenience stores are slightly cheaper than vending machines for drinks. There's a huge choice. They also sell alcohol, for your hotel room at the end of the day. There's fresh coffee, and one of the fridge cabinets is usually hot, with bottles of tea and coffee.

BAKERY ITEMS

One of my favourite sections! All kinds of treats, including melon pan, dorayaki, chocolate mochi bread and doughnuts, as well as some savoury options (including rolls filled with yakisoba... yep, carbfest!). If you get a chance to go to an actual bakery, they'll be fresh and even better.

SALAD & FRUIT

If you're in need of something healthy, there are salads, fresh fruit, pots of prepared fruit and packs of edamame.

CHOCOLATE, BISCUITS & CRISPS

More about these on the next page!

HOT FOOD

If you buy a ready meal or noodle dish that needs heating, the staff can heat it up for you in a microwave behind the counter. Sometimes there's a small counter for you to eat at.

ODEN

A winter dish of fish cakes, vegetables and boiled eggs in hot broth. You might see them in a kind of rectangular cauldron at the counter. Pick and mix items to take away.

ICE CREAM

Don't forget to check out the freezer - these are treats you can't bring home!

- Gari gari-kun - Ice lolly with unusual, seasonal flavours
- Packaged soft serve style ice cream cones (I don't know how they keep them so perfect-looking!)
- Coolish - soft serve ice cream in a packet
- Ice cream mochi

Ice cream mochi

Snacks & Treats

Convenience stores (konbini in Japanese) are full of treasures. Really, there are so many - see what there is and try as many as you can! Here are a few of my favourites:

KINOKO NO YAMA

My konbini snack of choice: little mushrooms made of biscuit and chocolate - the name means "mountain mushrooms". There's also Takenoko no Sato ("bamboo shoot village"). Look out for special edition flavours!

JAGARIKO

Potato crisp sticks in a tub. Very crispy. My fav is salad flavour - tastes nothing like salad but somehow satisfying nonetheless.

DARS CHOCOLATE

The ultimate convenience - chocolate already broken into squares for you. Like most Japanese sweets, it's not that sweet, which makes it less sickly than some white chocolate. There's also milk, dark and mint chocolate flavour.

FLAVOURED KITKATS

Japan's taken Kitkats to a whole new level, with hundreds of different flavours. The name sounds like "kitto katsu" meaning "you'll surely win", so they became popular good luck presents, especially for exams. They even have a space for writing a message on the back. Flavours are seasonal and regional, but you can usually collect several different varieties if you're on the look-out. There's a video on my channel about Kitkat hunting and where to look.

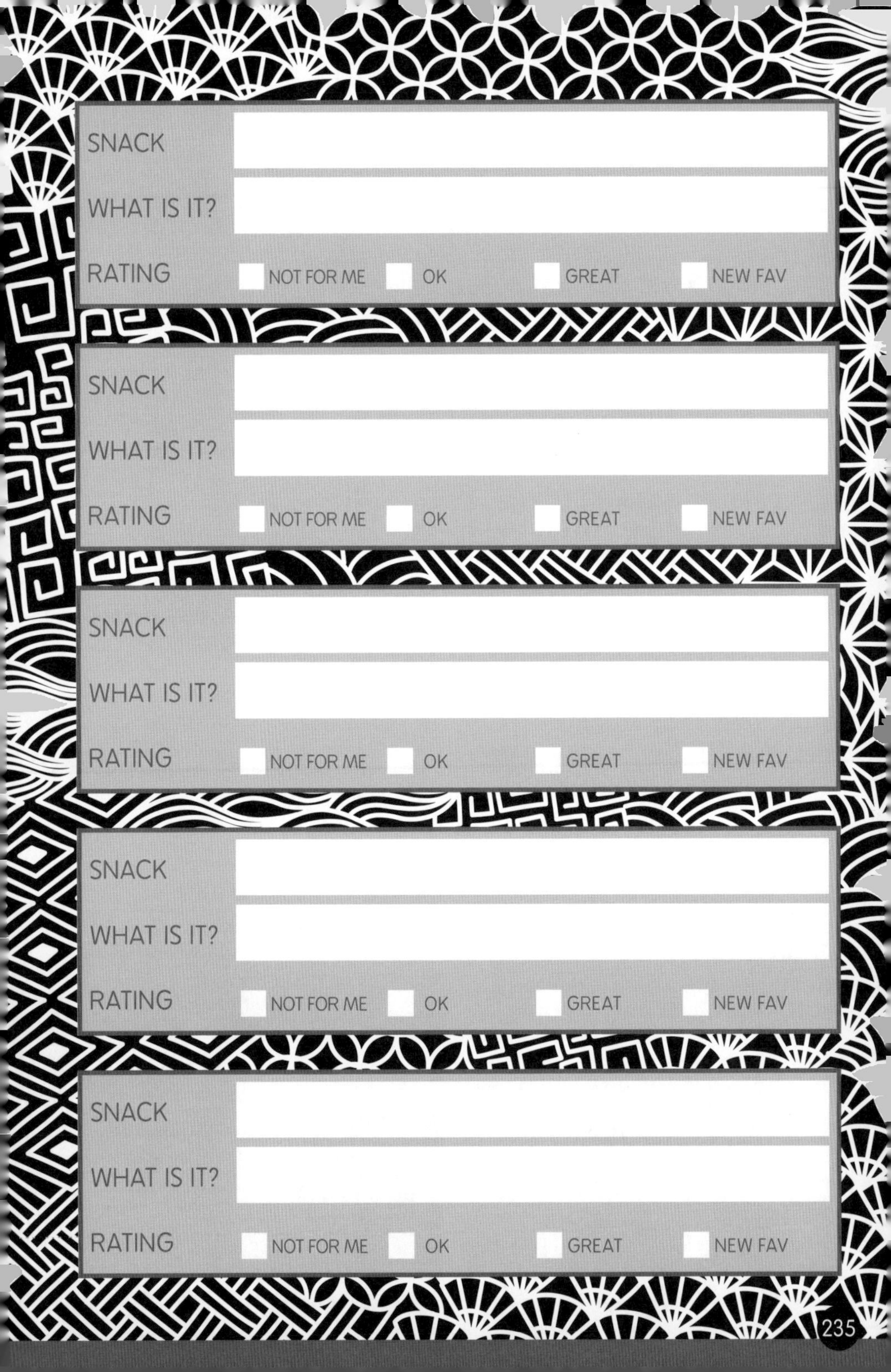
SNACK
WHAT IS IT?
RATING NOT FOR ME OK GREAT NEW FAV

SNACK
WHAT IS IT?
RATING NOT FOR ME OK GREAT NEW FAV

SNACK
WHAT IS IT?
RATING NOT FOR ME OK GREAT NEW FAV

SNACK
WHAT IS IT?
RATING NOT FOR ME OK GREAT NEW FAV

SNACK
WHAT IS IT?
RATING NOT FOR ME OK GREAT NEW FAV

Traditional Snacks

A taste of traditional Japan. You'll find these at kiosks, food stalls (especially at festivals), sometimes convenience stores and at traditional sweets cafes. Lots of places around Japan have their own regional versions as local specialities.

MOCHI

Soft, chewy rice cake made by pounding rice to a pulp. It doesn't have much flavour or sweetness - it's all about the chewy texture. Part of appreciating Japanese food is the "mouth-feel". Mochi in Japan, even from the convenience store, is so much fresher and softer than dry, pre-packaged mochi abroad.

Lots of sweets and snacks are variations of mochi. You can even get mochi cheese as a bar snack - the melty cheese goes really well with the chewy texture.

RED BEAN PASTE (ANKO)

A common ingredient in traditional sweets and snacks. Sometimes it's smooth, and sometimes there are whole or crushed beans. It's sweet but has a definite bean flavour - give it a try!

DAIFUKU

Mochi with a sweet filling, usually red bean paste. Strawberry daifuku have a whole strawberry inside!

Strawberry daifuku

Bean daifuku

TAIYAKI
Fish-shaped snack made of batter similar to a waffle, with a sweet filling. The most traditional is anko (red bean paste) and you can also get custard, matcha, strawberry cream and chocolate. All of them are delicious! Croissant taiyaki have flaky puff pastry instead of waffle.

WAGASHI
There are all kinds of mysterious, traditional sweets made of various types of jelly and mochi. It's traditional to pair them with green tea; the sweetness complements the bitterness of the matcha.

SENBEI
Rice crackers - a very traditional Japanese snack. There are various varieties, the classic flavour being soy sauce - tasty and full of savoury umami flavour.

MANJU
Small buns with a sweet filling, usually red bean paste. Essentially similar to taiyaki but not fish-shaped! There are lots of different types and variations.

DORAYAKI
A sandwich of two small, thick pancakes. The traditional filling is red bean paste (anko), but you can also get custard, chocolate cream, strawberry, maple syrup and matcha (green tea), and sometimes even ice cream. You can get them from kiosks and the bakery section in convenience stores.

DANGO
Very similar to mochi, but on a stick! The difference is that mochi's made from rice, and dango's made from rice flour. Dango come in different flavours - the famous pink, white and green one is for cherry blossom season. Another common flavour is sweet soy sauce, which is grilled then dipped in syrupy (not very sweet) soy sauce.

WHERE TO FIND STREET FOOD

- At festivals/matsuri
- Asakusa, around Senso-Ji temple
- Yanaka Ginza
- Togoshi Ginza (Tokyo's longest shopping street)
- Ameya Yokocho, Ueno

JAPANESE BAKERIES
If you get a chance to go to a Japanese bakery, don't miss out! Perfect for breakfast, lunch, picnics or snacks. There are so many treats, and things I'd never even dreamt of, like mochi-edamame-bread. While bread isn't traditionally Japanese, they've perfected the art of heavenly, extra fluffy dough. Pre-packed melon pan, etc at convenience stores are good, but the freshly baked versions are on another level. My fav bakeries:

- Little Bakery at 3-Chome, Shinjuku
- Bon Monsieur Bon, Nakano
- Fresh Bakery Kobeya, Shimbashi / Shiodome (underground in the station passageways)

MELON PAN

Sweet bread with a cookie-type coating. It's not melon flavoured; it's named after a melon because of the firm shell and soft inside. While they don't have a particularly delicious flavour, there's just something satisfying about them! I also enjoy the filled versions, like maple syrup, custard and cream, or pumpkin cream (right)!

MATCHA SOFT SERVE

Light soft-serve ice cream with a bitter note of green tea. Japan's mastered soft serve ice cream flavours for sure. Look out for specialities like black sesame, yuzu (a citrus like a less-sharp lemon) and bizarre, novelty flavours like squid ink, wasabi and garlic!

KORROKE

Deep-fried croquettes covered in breadcrumbs, with fillings like mashed potato and minced meat ("menchi katsu"), crab or pumpkin.

KAKIGORI

Shaved ice with syrup - perfectly refreshing and just what you need on a hot, humid day.

CURRY PAN

Curry bread (like the French word "pain"). Like a savoury doughnut, with a curry filling! It's deep-fried with crispy panko breadcrumbs on the outside. Japanese food's healthy, right?! Everyone I know who's tried them has loved them!

Drinks

When you're walking around all day you need plenty of drinks to stay hydrated, especially when it's hot. I always forget to drink enough! The good news is there are lots of places to get drinks when you're out and about. They're not expensive or difficult to find.

One of the fun things about travelling is trying new things that you can't get at home. There are so many different drinks - brands you recognise (sometimes with different varieties!), as well as exciting new types and flavours.

HOT DRINKS

You can also get hot drinks in cans and bottles from convenience stores and vending machines, like hot tea, coffee, cocoa and even soup! Perfect to put in your pocket and keep your hands warm!

MELON SODA
I love melon soda because it tastes so artificial! There are several brands, each with varying degrees of chemicalness. Fanta Melon's the best, and also melon cream soda (even if it sounds horrible!)

FANTA GRAPE
The finest of the drinks! Sweet and delicious. Look out for other flavours of Fanta, like peach, lemon, and seasonal limited editions.

CC LEMON
Fizzy lemon drink with vitamin C. Lemon's a popular flavour in Japan - not too sharp and so refreshing. Perfect for when it's hot.

POCARI SWEAT
Classic sports drink. Made to replenish your electrolytes.

CALPIS
Milky, yoghurt flavour soda.

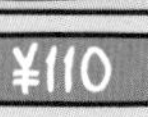

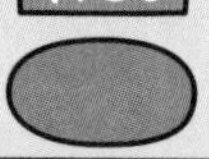

SURPRISE!
Take the opportunity to try unusual drinks that might surprise you: juice with jelly bits in, and unusual milkshakes, like pudding or pancake flavour!

SUPER-CUTE DRINKS
Look out for adorable juice drinks like Natchan - you'll want to keep the bottle!

RAMUNE
Classic marble soda. Push the glass ball down to open it up (gently so it doesn't fizz up!). You won't find it in vending machines - look on food stalls and kiosks. Lots of different flavours; to me they all have an artificial, bubblegum flavour.

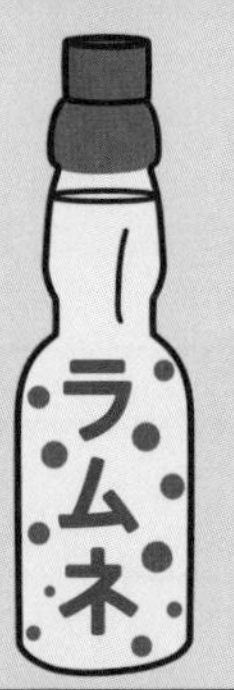

GREEN TEA
There are lots of different varieties. Usually they don't have English on the label so pick a random one!

SOUP
You can get hot soup from vending machines! There's sweetcorn soup, sweet red bean soup and potato soup!

ROYAL MILK TEA
If you're craving a cup of tea, you can get a bottle of Royal Milk Tea from the vending machine. It's often very milky and sweet.

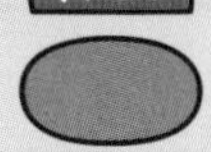

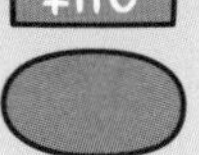

COFFEE IN A CAN
There are lots of different types! Black coffee, milky coffee, extra sweet... both hot and cold. Hot drinks have red price labels. There's even one called Rainbow Mountain Blend!

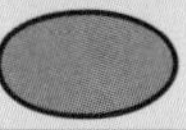

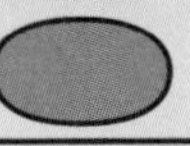

Vending Machines

There are lots of stories about "crazy" Japanese vending machines, but in reality, most of them sell drinks. You might spot some unusual ones though!

THEY'RE EVERYWHERE

You'll find vending machines literally EVERYWHERE - on the street, station platforms, in parks, even up mountains! It's not uncommon to see several banks of them just metres away from each other. So you'll never be stuck for where to get a drink.

CASH OR IC CARD

You'll need cash for vending machines. Sometimes you can pay using your IC card (your train pass).

VENDING MACHINE SHOP

In Shimbashi there's a small shop with nothing but vending machines. There are several different kinds of hot food, drinks and beers. (Unfortunately you need a Japanese ID to buy alcohol from the machines).

Search for 2-5-14 Higashi-Shinbashi on Google Maps. It's a small shop with a red neon sign in Japanese that says "benda sutando" (vendor stand).

Drinks from vending machines are 100-160 yen each.

Alcohol

Here are some common drinks you might come across:

- **Japanese beers** (eg Asahi, Kirin, Sapporo).
- **Sake** - Which can be served warm or cold.
- **Chuhai** (shochu highball) - Shochu mixed with fruit flavoured soda.
- **Highball** - Whisky and soda.
- **Ginger highball** - Whisky and ginger ale.
- **Lemon sour** - Shochu, lemon juice and soda.
- **Umeshu** - Plum wine.

Look out for Strong Zero in convenience stores - a blend of shochu and fruit soda for only about 100 Yen. But watch out, when they call it strong, they mean it: it's 9% alcohol.

Wine isn't always on the menu, but you'll see it in some places.

CONVENIENCE STORES

Alcohol's cheap at convenience stores, so if you want to save money, pick up a few drinks to take back to your hotel room.

When you're at the till, a message (in Japanese) will appear on the screen, saying "are you aged 20 or older?". You'll need to tap the touchscreen to say yes.

Bars

IZAKAYA

An izakaya is a Japanese pub. It's very much about sharing food as well as drinking. They'll serve a whole range of small plates, including edamame, fried chicken and yakitori (grilled skewers of meat and vegetables).

GOLDEN GAI

A unique, only-in-Japan experience! The Golden Gai (above) is an area of tiny bars in Shinjuku. And when I say tiny, I mean tiny. Most of them are a single row of 6-8 stools along a bar - and that's it! There are so many of them packed in tiny alleyways - it's a really unique place to explore.

You might have heard that foreigners aren't welcome in the Golden Gai. There are one or two bars that say "No gaijin" (no foreigners). It can be because they're only for regulars, or they don't speak English. Most are absolutely fine. Just poke your head through the door and if there's space, they'll welcome you in.

The legal drinking age is 20.

I've never been asked for ID in Japan, but as a foreigner you have to carry your passport with you at all times, so you'll always have ID if you need it.

TORIKIZOKU

Small izakaya are best for the authentic, friendly, local experience. However if you want somewhere that's easy for foreigners and ok to hang out the whole evening, Torikizoku's a fun chain to visit.

Everything's 298 yen, including the drinks. It's loud and relaxed. There's a whole range of yakitori (meat on sticks), snacks and small plates like edamame, and chips if that's what you fancy.

If you search on Google Maps, there are branches all over Tokyo, and a few in other cities.

LAST TRAIN HOME

Although Tokyo's very much awake late into the night, the metro doesn't run 24 hours a day. The last trains are usually around midnight or 1am.

COVER CHARGE

Something to be aware of is the **cover charge**. It's like an entry fee per person, and is added to your first drinks order. Sometimes it includes a drink, or a small plate of snacks. It's often advertised on a sign outside. Usually it's around 500 yen, so it can add up if visit lots of different bars. Not everywhere has one; if you search online you can find bars without cover charges.

ETIQUETTE

Especially at smaller places, either keep ordering or leave once you've finished your drinks, to let other people come in. It's a faux pas to nurse a pint all evening!

DRINKING ON THE STREET

Drinking in public is allowed in Japan. Most people don't really hang out drinking on the streets, but it's perfectly legal to grab a drink from the convenience store for the park or an evening stroll around the city.

Theme Cafes

Novelty, themed restaurants, cafes and bars are a unique and fun experience.

The food's themed too and very photogenic - sometimes too cute to eat! There are some really unique, creative dishes, especially the desserts, drinks and ice cream sundaes.

Theme cafes are quite pricey and the food isn't always as good as at regular restaurants. But really it's all about the experience, and immersing yourself in the world of your favourite characters.

Caterpillar, Cheshire Cat & Mad Hatter roll cake at an Alice in Wonderland cafe

LIMITED TIME POP-UPS

Look out for temporary pop-up cafes - they often coincide with anime or game launches. Sometimes there's special, limited edition merchandise.

These venues host pop-ups:

- Tower Records in Shibuya
- The Guest cafe
- Sweets Paradise
- Animate Cafe
- Harajuku Box Cafe & Space

Look on dangonews.com for listings of what's on.

MAKE A RESERVATION

At popular cafes, especially pop-ups, you might need to book. I learnt that the hard way when I missed out on the Hamtaro Cafe in Harajuku (sob!).

Check the website; sometimes you can reserve online or in person earlier in your trip.

- **Alice in Wonderland:** Several branches, in Ginza, two in Shinjuku, Ikebukuro, Shibuya. Each has different decor/theme.
- **Vampire Cafe:** Ginza
- **Christon Cafe:** Medieval/Christian themed, Shinjuku
- **The Lock-Up:** Genuinely terrifying prison/horror restaurant in Shinjuku.
- **Ninja Akasaka**, Akasuka. Ninjas do magic tricks at your table.
- **Eorzea:** Final Fantasy theme, Akihabara
- **Gundam Cafe:** Akihabara & Odaiba (by the giant Gundam!)
- **Pompompurin Cafe:** Kawaii overload in Harajuku and Yokohama.
- **Cinnamoroll Cafe**, Shinjuku: 100% adorable.
- **Sanrio Cafe**, Ikebukuro - with Hello Kitty and friends.
- **Pokémon Cafe:** Subtly-themed cafe in Nihonbashi. There's also a themed bakery at the Pokémon centre in Ikebukuro.
- **Cafe Mugiwara:** One Piece cafe at Tokyo Tower (with a One Piece indoor theme park).
- **Kaiju Sakaba:** Dine with monsters from Ultraman in Shimbashi.
- **Zauo Fishing Restaurant**, Shinjuku. Sit in a giant boat and catch your own dinner!
- **Luida's Bar:** Dragon Quest bar in Roppongi.
- **Artnia:** Egg-shaped Square Enix cafe in Shinjuku.
- **2D Cafe**, Shin-Okubo: Step into a cartoon line drawing, where everything's flat and monochrome.
- **Science Bar Incubator**, Shinjuku: Wear a lab coat and drink cocktails from test tubes and lab beakers.
- **Moomin House Cafe** at the SkyTree or Tokyo Dome City. If you're lonely, a plushie Moomin can sit with you.
- **Peanuts Cafe**, Meguro: With Snoopy and Charlie Brown.
- **Kirby Cafe** for Nintendo fans at the SkyTree mall.

Animal Cafes

In the city where people have small homes or apartments, pets aren't always allowed. So instead you can go out to play with cute animals while you have tea.

WHAT CAFES ARE THERE?

- Cats - the cutest is Temari no Ouchi in Kichijoji - it looks like it's straight out of Studio Ghibli (you can walk there from the Ghibli Museum).
- Rabbits
- Owls
- Dogs
- Hedgehogs
- Hamsters
- Birds
- Reptiles and snakes

You pay for the time you spend there, plus your snacks and drinks. As you'd expect, they're pricier than regular cafes. But you're not there for the food, you're there for the cute animals!

Some places might need a reservation if they're popular.

NOTE ON ANIMAL WELFARE

Sadly animal welfare in Japan isn't always the top priority. Not all animal cafes are necessarily bad, but please check reviews before visiting, and make sure the animals are treated with the love and care they deserve.

CAT & DOG CAFE LUA, MACHIDA

The animals at this cafe are rescue cats and dogs that are up for adoption. It's slightly outside central Tokyo, but it's definitely a place that puts animals first.

Maid Cafes

moe moe kyuun!

Escape the real world for an hour and enter the land of kawaii, where the waitresses are dressed as cute maids. They are lots in Akihabara, the otaku district, where you'll see maids on the street handing out flyers.

WHAT HAPPENS AT A MAID CAFE?

- Super-cute food - think curry with rice shaped like a teddy bear.
- If you order omurice, the maids draw cute doodles on it with ketchup.
- Clap along and chant the magic words to make the food more delicious: "Moe Moe Kyuuun!"
- Practice your Japanese chatting with the maids.
- Have your photo with a maid. Ask for a "chekki" and they'll doodle on a small polaroid for you. Taking your own photos isn't allowed.
- Live j-pop-style performances - some maids are mini idols.
- Play games with the maids.
- At the Heaven's Gate branch of Maiddreamin you can dress up in a maid outfit!

You pay by the hour, so keep an eye on the time. It's quite pricey! Extra experiences eg games and photos are paid for - you order them from the menu. Most maid cafes are completely innocent and it's all for fun.

Recommended for beginners:

- Maiddreamin' (there are many branches around Akihabara and one in Shibuya)
- @Home
- Akiba Zettai also looks very cute!

Food Bucket List

List your must-eats, so you don't miss any of them when you're in Japan! They could be foods or experiences eg ramen at a backstreet ramen bar, or a picnic under the cherry blossoms.

Restaurants to Visit

This book's not about prescribing a list of restaurants for you to visit. The best, most magical experiences are at places you discover yourself or stumble across by chance. The standard's excellent pretty much everywhere in Japan - you can't go too far wrong - so there's no need to stick to recommended places to have a good time. Be spontaneous, venture out and have your own, unique experiences! Try that little sushi place or that cute cafe you find, or see why that noodle bar has such a long a queue outside. But you might also come across places in videos or in your research that you want to try, so here's a space to note them down.

RESTAURANT	
AREA/STATION	
TYPE OF FOOD	
NOTES eg Opening times, what looks good)	

RESTAURANT	
AREA/STATION	
TYPE OF FOOD	
NOTES eg Opening times, what looks good)	

RESTAURANT	
AREA/STATION	
TYPE OF FOOD	
NOTES eg Opening times, what looks good)	

RESTAURANT

AREA/STATION

TYPE OF FOOD

NOTES
eg Opening times, what looks good)

RESTAURANT

AREA/STATION

TYPE OF FOOD

NOTES
eg Opening times, what looks good)

RESTAURANT

AREA/STATION

TYPE OF FOOD

NOTES
eg Opening times, what looks good)

RESTAURANT

AREA/STATION

TYPE OF FOOD

NOTES
eg Opening times, what looks good)

RESTAURANT

AREA/STATION

TYPE OF FOOD

NOTES
eg Opening times, what looks good)

RESTAURANT

AREA/STATION

TYPE OF FOOD

NOTES
eg Opening times, what looks good)

Special Diets

I love Japan, but as a vegetarian I don't always love it when I'm hungry! There've been times when I've been walking the streets for hours trying to find somewhere to eat, then resorted to pizza when what I really wanted was local, authentic Japanese food. Special diets can be difficult in Japan, but it's not impossible with a little preparation.

DO YOUR RESEARCH

While I'm all for spontaneity, it's so much easier if you're armed with a back-up list of restaurants in case you can't find anywhere. I've had a much less stressful experience when I've done a bit of research before travelling. There are restaurants for special diets, but you won't necessarily come across them on the street; you need to look them up.

ADAPTING THE MENU

Try asking if they can modify a dish from the menu eg yakisoba without the fish/meat, or okonomiyaki with different ingredients. Ask before you sit down, to avoid awkwardness. Not everywhere will be willing to do this, so be very polite to avoid offending anyone. It helps if you know a little Japanese. Politely ask something like: *Yasai yaki soba wa daijoubu desu ka?* (Would vegetable fried noodles be ok?).

EXPLAIN WHAT YOU CAN EAT

Terms like "vegan", "vegetarian" and "lactose-intolerant" aren't always widely understood. Instead, tell the waiter what you can't eat.

Dishes with broth (eg ramen) almost always contain fish or meat stock.

IF YOU DON'T SPEAK JAPANESE

Here's a link to free, printable cards explaining common special diets and allergies in English and Japanese, so you can show them to the waiter if you want to be 100% sure: *justhungry.com/japan-dining-out-cards*

SELF-CATERING

If you have a severe allergy or a restrictive diet, self-catering is an easier option, so you have complete control over what you're eating. You can try local Japanese ingredients, and it's a great option if you enjoy cooking.

PHRASES

Pronunciation guide video: cakeswithfaces.co.uk/pronunciation

Kore ni wa, ______ ga haite imasu ka? Is there ______ in this?

Bejiterien desu. Niku to sakana ga taberaremasen. Nanika ga arimasu ka?
I'm vegetarian. I can't eat meat/fish. Is there something?
(Not the most eloquent but it's worked for me!)

_________ ga taberaremasen — I can't eat _______

arerugii ga arimasu — I have an allergy - or just say "arerugii"

FOODS TO WATCH OUT FOR

VEGETARIAN

- Dashi (fish stock)
- Dishes with soup/ broth
- Ramen
- Fish flakes as a topping (katsuoboshi/ bonito)
- Japanese curry sauce

My restaurant list: cakeswithfaces.co.uk/ vegetarian

VEGAN

In addition to the list for vegetarians:

- Ramen noodles (udon and soba noodles are usually vegan)
- Okonomiyaki
- Bakery items
- Fried / boiled egg as a topping

NO FISH

- Dishes with soup/ broth contain fish stock eg noodles in soup
- Fish flakes as a topping (katsuoboshi/bonito)

There are plenty of meat options, not everything is fish!

NO MEAT

- Tonkotsu ramen / pork-based ramen
- Japanese curry sauce

Meat isn't traditionally part of the Japanese diet, so there are plenty of fish/seafood options.

GLUTEN-FREE

- Soy sauce (often used as an ingredient)
- Sushi rice (the seasoning contains barley malt)
- Miso (eg miso soup)

Look up gluten-free cafes.

LACTOSE INTOLERANT

- Chocolate
- Baked goods
- Desserts

Soy milk's available in convenience stores (search for images so you know what to look for).

NUT ALLERGY

- Snacks on the plane
- Desserts
- Baked goods
- Convenience store snacks

HALAL

- Soy sauce and mirin (both major cooking ingredients)
- Sake (also often used in cooking)
- Sushi rice seasoning may contain rice wine
- Dishes with broth/ soup
- Dipping sauce

There are Halal restaurants; look them up and make a list.

FOODS TO AVOID

Make your own list:

Food Favs

FIRST MEAL IN JAPAN

BEST EXPERIENCE

FAV DRINKS

BIGGEST SURPRISE

FOOD HIGHLIGHTS

DISHES TO COOK AT HOME

Survival Guide

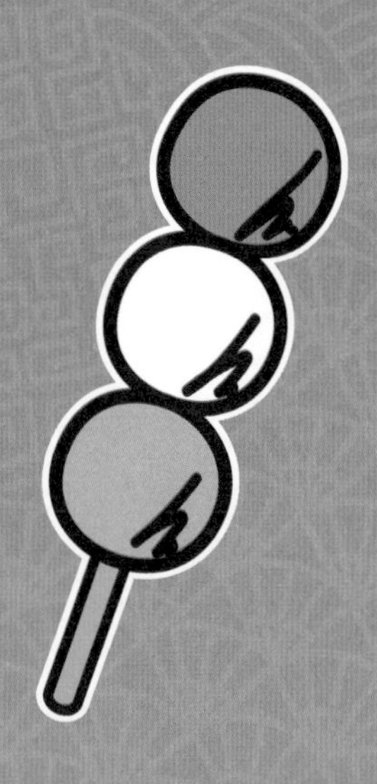

Etiquette Tips

MOST IMPORTANTLY: BE POLITE AND RESPECTFUL
Because Japan's population density is high, the culture's built around manners, being considerate and not being a nuisance to other people. People tend to be friendly but not necessarily outgoing - they're reserved, but happy to help. The most important thing is to be polite and mindful of other people.

DON'T EAT ON THE STREET
People don't tend to eat while walking along, apart from places where there are food stalls, like at a festival. There's also no eating on trains unless it's a long distance or bullet train.

QUEUING
Queues and lines are very much a thing in Japan: for restaurants, trains, tickets. Respect the queue and don't push in!

MEIWAKU
The concept of being a nuisance or causing inconvenience to others. Japan's social etiquette's all about everyone getting along without bothering each other.

WHEN YOU'RE ON THE TRAIN
Don't talk too loudly, and keep your phone on silent (in Japan it's called "manner mode"). It's ok to play on your phone, just make sure the sound's off. Don't put your bag on the seat next to you. Try and be considerate of other people, especially if you're wearing a backpack. Don't eat on the train unless it's a bullet train.

BAGS
When you're in a cafe or restaurant, people don't tend to put their bags on the floor because it's considered dirty (even though most places are immaculately clean). You might also notice people don't sit on the ground outside without a mat or sheet. Sometimes there are baskets beside your table in restaurants to put your bag in. No one will be offended if you put your bag on the floor - but sometimes waiters have picked mine up, thinking I've dropped it.

CHOPSTICKS
Don't stick your chopsticks into your food, and if you're passing food to someone else, don't hand it from one pair of chopsticks to another - both of these are associated with funerals. If you're taking food from a shared plate, use the other ends of your chopsticks - it's more hygienic.

POINTING
Pointing one finger can be considered rude. It's more polite to use your whole hand with the palm upwards.

TEMPLES AND SHRINES
Be respectful - they're places of worship. Avoid making too much noise or being rowdy, and remember that other people might be praying or paying their respects.

AS A GENERAL RULE

Try and follow what other people are doing, but don't worry too much about getting tiny things wrong. It'll probably be obvious you're a foreigner, so no one will expect you to know all the unwritten rules and minutiae of society.

The most important thing is to be polite, considerate and respectful of others.

NO HAGGLING OR TIPPING
There's no haggling - it would come across as quite rude. There's also no tipping (even if the service is so good that you want to!) - it's just not done.

BLOWING YOUR NOSE
If you have a cold, don't blow your nose in public. It might seem strange, but sniffing is thought to be more polite. One reason people wear masks in public is because they have a cold, or want to avoid getting ill (or because they didn't want to put make-up on!).

TAKING YOUR SHOES OFF
Look out for situations where you might need to take your shoes off. It's a custom related to cleanliness. This includes visiting someone's home, changing rooms in shops, going inside temples and shrines and some traditional restaurants with tatami mats.

Things You Should Know

CARRY YOUR PASSPORT
It's a legal requirement to have your passport with you at all times. If you're worried about losing it, keep a copy in your room or take a photo of it.

TIME DIFFERENCE
Japan's time zone is GMT +9 hours.

PLUG ADAPTERS & ELECTRICITY
Japanese plugs have two straight, flat pins; they look the same as US plugs. You'll need a travel adapter.

The voltage in Japan is 100V, lower than the USA and Europe. Most devices work with an adapter, including phone and camera battery chargers - they just take a little longer to charge. Some devices, including those that involve heating (eg hairdryers) or movement (eg shavers) might not work properly. Check the voltage range on the label. Hairdryers are usually provided in hotels so you don't need to take your own.

INSECTS
If you look up what deadly and terrifying insects there are in Japan, you'll never sleep again (for the sake of your sanity, don't search for Japanese hornets...!). However, despite the horror stories, I've never seen any, apart from some spiders on a countryside hike (and they were on their webs, away from the path). Apparently there are cockroaches in Tokyo, but I've never seen any. All the hotels I've been to have been scrupulously clean, with no bugs at all, and I've never seen any on the subway either.

SMOKING
The minimum age for smoking is 20. You can buy cigarettes at convenience stores, which are everywhere. Vending machines require a Japanese ID card to prove your age.

Smoking's not allowed on trains, in stations and on the streets of most city centres. A smoking ban was introduced in 2020 in many restaurants, cafes and bars. Some are exempt, so look for signs indicating whether smoking's allowed or if there's a smoking room or area. When you book your hotel, you'll need to book a room where smoking's allowed.

ALCOHOL
The minimum age for drinking is 20. You'll need to carry your passport with you anyway, so you can use it as ID. Drinking in public is allowed, but people don't tend to hang around drinking on the streets unless it's a festival.

MEDICINE
Some over-the-counter medicines aren't allowed in Japan, including Vicks inhalers and medicines containing pseudoephedrine and codeine. If you're not sure, check before you go. You can bring up to 2 months' supply of prescription medication. See p262 for medical emergencies.

BINS
There aren't many bins around the streets! It's linked to how people don't walk around eating. On the whole, Japan's very clean and you're expected to take your rubbish with you. There've been so many times I've carried wrappers and packaging around with me all day because there were no bins!

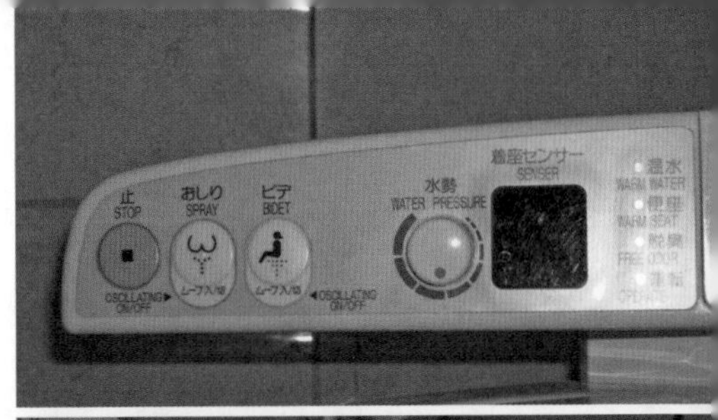

WHERE TO FIND TOILETS

- Stations
- Shopping malls
- Department stores
- Most tourist attractions
- Public toilets in parks, etc
- Convenience stores

SQUAT TOILETS

Most facilities are western (often with extra buttons for bidet and sound effects to protect your modesty!). You might come across squat toilets. Sometimes there are both types, with a sign on the door to indicate which is which. There's paper and they flush just like western toilets. They're actually not all that common - but don't be surprised if you come across one!

Natural Disasters

Japan's a seismically active country - that's why there are so many geothermal hot springs, onsen and volcanoes (like Mount Fuji!). But it does also mean there's the possibility of natural disasters like earthquakes.

EARTHQUAKES

Japan's well prepared for earthquakes, and buildings are built to withstand them. Most earthquakes are minor and nothing to worry about. I've been in the subway during a fairly strong earthquake and no one else even batted an eyelid. Don't let them put you off travelling to Japan - they'll happen or they won't. If an earthquake does occur, keep calm and follow what everyone else is doing.

TYPHOONS

An average of three typhoons hit Japan's main islands each year - more commonly in the south. Okinawa has around seven or eight.

Typhoons are usually between May and October - the peak months are August and September.

Strong typhoons may result in transport being shut down. It'll be windy with torrential rain. Their path can usually be tracked and predicted, and they lose momentum over land. If you're on the edge of a typhoon it might just be more rainy than usual.

Spotted at a town on the coast

Medical Emergencies

GOING TO A PHARMACY

It's easiest to take basic painkillers with you, but if you need over-the-counter medicine there are pharmacies and drugstores. They can also offer advice for simple ailments.

At the pharmacy they won't necessarily speak English, so you might need to use Google Translate, a phrasebook or miming.

IF YOU NEED A DOCTOR

Contact your travel insurance medical emergency helpline and follow their instructions. Call them before making any appointments, to make sure you'll be covered.

Your hotel or a tourist information centre may be able to help you make any calls to doctors, etc in Japanese.

The emergency number for an ambulance is 119.

Image: Wikimedia Commons, Osamu Iwasaki CC-BY-SA-2.0

CHECK YOUR MEDICATION

Some over-the-counter medicines are illegal in Japan, including Vicks inhalers, Sudafed and some medicines containing codeine. Check the regulations or ask your doctor before taking them with you.

HELP FROM THE TOURIST OFFICE

The Japan National Tourism Organisation (JNTO) have a useful guide for what to do if you're unwell in Japan.

On their website there's a list of institutions that care for foreigners. There's also a pdf "Guide for using medical institutions" with phrases you can point to, to describe your symptoms. To find it, search for "JNTO emergency".

Crime & Safety

Japan's a very safe country, with low crime levels. People tend to be honest and respectful of other people, so crimes like petty theft and pickpocketing aren't a problem. You don't need to worry about carrying money with you, but remember to use your common sense like you would anywhere.

The stories of people leaving their wallets on cafe tables to save their place when they go to the bathroom are true. People are respectful of other's property. I've even seen people running in the street to return items that strangers have dropped.

EMERGENCY NUMBERS

Police emergencies: 110

Fire & ambulance: 119

Coastguard: 118

BREAKING THE LAW

Be aware that penalties for breaking the law are strict in Japan, and you won't necessarily get special treatment for being a foreigner.

KOBAN (POLICE BOXES)

You can find the police at *koban*, small police boxes around the city like the one on the left. They can help with directions if you get lost!

ARE THERE ANY BAD AREAS?

Kabukicho in Shinjuku is sometimes called the bad area of Tokyo. It's the red light district, and traditionally a yakuza hangout.

However, it's not dangerous to simply walk around the streets. You might get approached by touts who want you to go to their bars, but just ignore them and you'll be fine. All the reports I've heard of tourists getting into trouble have involved them going into bars, where their drinks were spiked or they were overcharged for drinks. There's no need to be scared of going to Kabukicho or walking around the streets. In fact it's one of my favourite places to stay; a really lively area with lots of bright lights - and even a statue of Godzilla!

Roppongi can be a bit sketchy at night-time, also with lots of touts (again, it's best to just ignore them). It's probably only an area you'd want to go in the evening if you're going out clubbing.

Arriving in Japan

You might need to pick up a few things before you leave the airport. I always make a checklist, because I don't trust myself to remember when I'm tired after a long flight!

THINGS TO PICK UP

	WHERE FROM
☐ POCKET WIFI	
☐ JAPAN RAIL PASS	
☐ IC CARD	
☐	
☐	

HOW TO GET FROM THE AIRPORT

FINDING YOUR HOTEL

There are two airports for Tokyo (Haneda and Narita), so check which one you'll be arriving at. Recommended routes from the airport are on p60.

The last thing you want when you're tired after a long flight is to be walking around, dragging your suitcases in search of your hotel, so check the directions and make a note here. If you're staying near a major station, check which exit you'll need. There can be multiple exits that come out at different places.

It's a good idea to look up your hotel on Google Street View so you know what you're looking for!

HOTEL	
STATION	
WHICH EXIT?	
DIRECTIONS	
CHECK-IN TIME	

TRAVELLING WITH LUGGAGE

I usually carry my suitcase with me on the train. Take your time; some station transfers involve a fair amount of walking. Not all exits have escalators/lifts but there's usually an accessible route somewhere if you look for signs.

Once you get into the city, the trains won't have luggage racks. Just try and keep out of other peoples' way as much as you can!

If you're on the Tokyo Metro at rush hour, be prepared! At busy times it can be very crowded on the train. Keep calm, leave yourself plenty of time and prepare to have zero personal space for 15 minutes or so!

LUGGAGE DELIVERY

If you'd prefer not to carry your suitcase, there are delivery services. Your luggage will arrive next day (2 days if it's long distance).

The cost depends on the destination and size of your suitcase; expect about 1000-2000 yen per item. Look for counters at the airport, and for the way back ask at your hotel.

Checking in to your Hotel

CHECKING IN

Most hotels have lots of foreign guests, so don't worry if you don't speak Japanese. Usually even if I speak Japanese, the staff reply in English anyway!

If you want to practice your Japanese:

Heya o yoyaku o shimashita	*I reserved a room*

Don't worry if they ask to see your passport and take a photocopy - that's normal if you don't live in Japan.

DROPPING OFF YOUR LUGGAGE

If you'll be arriving earlier than check-in time, most hotels will hold your luggage for you, so you can go out start exploring straight away!

O-nimotsu o azukatte itadakemasenka?	*Can I leave my luggage here please?*

Jet Lag

Personally, I don't notice jet lag too much when I arrive in Japan. I'm too excited to go out and do things! It's when I come home and back to my everyday routine that I feel tired. But everyone experiences it differently.

It's easier if your flight arrives in the afternoon or later in the day. You can check in, have a long-awaited shower, grab some dinner then get to sleep.

However, if your flight arrives in the morning, try not to waste the day. Take it easy and plan something that's not too hectic, because you might not be feeling 100% after the flight. If it's too early to check in to your hotel, there are showers at the airport to freshen up. Drop off your bags at the hotel, refuel with breakfast/lunch, and take it easy for the first day.

TIPS FOR COPING WITH JET LAG

- Adapt to Japanese time as soon as you can.
- Get as much sleep as possible on the plane (noise-cancelling headphones really help!).
- Have a short nap when you check in if you need to - but not too long.
- It's tempting to go straight to the places you're most excited about, but plan something relaxed and low-key for the day you arrive.
- Try and stay up at least until the evening.
- If you wake up early and can't get back to sleep, make the most of it and take a walk around the quiet streets, or visit the fish market.

Shopping

Buying Things in Shops

DO I NEED TO KNOW JAPANESE?
Don't worry if you don't speak Japanese. When you're at the till buying something, everyone knows the procedure so you don't need to say much - but a quick "arigatou" (thank you) will always be appreciated.

If you need to ask for something, point with your whole hand and say:

Kore o onegaishimasu
This please

PRICES
The price will be displayed on the till. At smaller shops they'll hold up a calculator to show you the price.

The little tray on the counter is to put your money or card in, instead of handing it directly to the assistant.

CASH VS CARDS
Japan's traditionally a cash-based society. While cards are now accepted fairly widely, not all shops take them so it's best to have cash with you as well, as a back-up. There's more info in the Money section, including where to get yen and conversion tables to help you work out prices.

CONSUMPTION TAX
There's a tax of 10% on purchases in shops in Japan. All shops and restaurants are now required to show the price with sales tax included – so you'll know exactly how much the bill will be, with no surprises at the till!

TAX FREE SHOPPING
Look out for signs to see which shops are tax-free for foreigners. There's a minimum spend of 5,000 yen.

When you pay, you'll need to show your passport (which must be carried with you at all times anyway) and you won't have to pay tax.

Love this cute logo for Yamato Transport delivery company!

TAKING YOUR PURCHASES HOME

I usually pack my purchases in my suitcase and carry them back with me. This is fine for most things, as long as they're not restricted items.

Remember there are limits on how much you can bring back for certain items like alcohol and cigarettes, without paying tax and duty at customs when you get home.

SHIPPING ITEMS HOME

It's cheaper to carry your purchases with you if you can. If that's not possible, you can ship items home at the post office. You can find them on Google Maps. They usually sell boxes too.

There's also the option of paying for an extra suitcase at the airport - or check if your airline allows more than one checked bag per person by default.

PACKING TIPS

If you're planning on buying a lot, pack as lightly as you can!

- Some airlines allow two suitcases per person. Fit a medium suitcase inside a larger suitcase, then pack your clothes in that. Then you have an extra suitcase for the way back if you need it. If you don't have extra suitcases, take an empty holdall or backpack.
- Some airlines allow a handbag or personal item in addition to your main hand luggage. Check what's allowed on the airline's website.
- Take a mini suitcase as hand luggage.
- Pack as lightly as you can, and (unless it's a summer trip!) wear your clothes more than once.
- Wear your bulkiest clothes and shoes on the plane.
- Throw away boxes or packaging to fit more in, and use your clothes to wrap breakable items.

Shopping Districts

In Tokyo there are several areas with concentrations of specialist shops, where you can indulge your obsession:

CLOTHES

- Shibuya - Popular shopping area with the iconic Shibuya 109 mall.
- Harajuku - Home of alternative and cute fashion.
- Shinjuku & Ikebukuro - Both have plenty of shops and restaurants.

DESIGNER LABEL FASHION

- Ginza has lots of designer stores along the main street.
- Omotesando (near Harajuku) is also a high-end area.

THRIFT STORES

- Koenji - A chilled area slightly outside central Tokyo.
- Shimokitazawa - Could this be the new Harajuku? Lots of trendy boutiques and thrift stores.

FABRIC

Browse cute and colourful fabric prints in Nippori (on the Yamanote line). One of the main shops is called Tomato!

CAMERAS

It's not wall-to-wall cameras but there are several shops dotted around the west side of Shinjuku Station with new, used and vintage cameras. One of them's called Lemon!

SWEETS & JAPANESE KITKATS

- Okashi no Machioka - A sweets shop with many branches. Great for presents for friends back home.
- Don Quijote - A crowded shop that sells all sorts of things including costumes, novelty gadgets and sweets. Pretty cheap for Kitkats.
- Haneda/Narita airport - Stock up on Kitkats last minute before you go home. The duty free shops have a variety of flavours in multipack boxes.
- Gift Shop the Akiba (in Radio Kaikan near Akihabara Station) and Gift Shop the Daiba in Odaiba - Good for finding extra Kitkat flavours and a great selection of interesting sweets.

ANIME MERCH & GAMES

- Akihabara - Otaku central, the main place to go for anime, manga and games. Also called "Electric Town" because of the electronics stores.
- Book Off - Used DVDs, games, books and music at great prices. You never know what you'll find! Sister stores Hobby Off, Hard Off, etc are also definitely worth a look. ("Off" refers to taking money "off" the price.)
- Nakano Broadway by Nakano Station is a treasure trove of figures, collectables and retro toys. It's slightly cheaper then Akihabara.

KPOP MERCH & KOREAN COSMETICS

- Shin Okubo near Shinjuku is Korea Town. There are also lots of Korean restaurants.
- Etude House (a cosmetics brand) has a super-cute store in Harajuku.

BOOKS

In Jimbocho there are 150+ stores with new, used and antique books, and cosy cafes to stop at.

SPORTS GOODS

Kanda-Ogawamachi has sports clothes and equipment, including skiing, snowboarding, skateboarding, golfing and cycling.

STATIONERY

- Itoya (Ginza) is a well-established stationery store with multiple floors. There's even a postbox so you can buy, write and send postcards.
- Sekaido (Shinjuku) - 5 floors of art supplies and stationery!
- Loft (Shibuya) is great for cute, colourful stationery. Like Tokyu Hands, it also sells homeware, gadgets and all sorts of bits and pieces (great for gifts).
- Daiso and other 100 yen shops have cheap, cute stationery.
- Bunbougu Cafe is a stationery cafe in Omotesando! As well as selling cute stationery, there's a selection for everyone to use. If you become a member, you get a key to secret drawers under the tables with even more goodies.

CUTE CHARACTER MERCH

- Character Street in Tokyo Station has lots of brand stores, like Sanrio and Sumikko Gurashi. It's tricky to find; follow signs to First Avenue.
- Kiddyland has all sorts of western and Japanese character goods. The largest branch is in Harajuku.
- Village Vanguard has books, CDs and anime, manga and character merch.
- Yamashiroya, a toy shop in Ueno, also has kawaii character goods.

DEPARTMENT STORES

Department stores are often attached to major stations, and they're elsewhere too. Typically there's a food marketplace on the basement level, fashion concessions and a restaurant floor at the top. If you get there as the store opens, staff bow and greet the first customers. Stores include Isetan, Marui (the sign says 0101), Parco and Seibu. Mitsukoshi is the oldest; the Nihombashi store is very grand inside.

Left: Wako, a luxury department store in Ginza.

MUSICAL INSTRUMENTS

- Ochanomizu has lots of music shops on the main street (above). Mostly guitars and accessories (there's a huge choice) and a few shops for other instruments. It's walkable from Akihabara.
- Shimokitazawa's known for live music venues and there are a couple of music shops too. Hard Off has a good selection of secondhand instruments.
- There are also several stores dotted around the rest of Tokyo, including Ikebe Musical Instrument Store and Drum Station in Akihabara, Rock Inn in Shinjuku and Ishibashi Music in Shibuya.

TABLEWARE, KITCHEN STUFF AND JAPANESE KNIVES

Kappabashi is a street with all the kitchen stuff you can think of. It's interesting even if you're not really into cooking. You can walk there from Asakusa.

RECORD STORES

They're dotted around, but you'll find them in these areas - look them up on Google Maps:

- Shimokitazawa
- Shibuya (including a large branch of Tower Records)
- Shinjuku
- Koenji

HOUSEHOLD ITEMS

- Tokyu Hands is one of those huge shops you just have to visit. There's a large branch in Shinjuku, with multiple floors of all kind of things, including kitchen gadgets you never knew existed and stylish homeware.
- Loft is similar to Tokyu Hands; there are several but the most well-known is in Shibuya.
- Daiso is a 100 yen shop where everything's 100 yen. There are also 200 yen and 300 yen stores.

PRETTY MUCH EVERYTHING

Yodobashi Camera is an unbelievably huge store with multiple floors, selling basically anything you can think of. Bic Camera is very similar.

It's useful if you need batteries, headphones or memory cards - and interesting just to wander round marvelling at all the things they stock! There's also a floor or two of restaurants at the top.

There are branches all around Japan - I recommend Yodobashi Camera in Akihabara. Where else sells both Gundam model kits and grand pianos?

THINGS TO BUY IN JAPAN

Shops to Visit

SHOP

LOCATION

OPENING TIMES

NOTES

SHOP

LOCATION

OPENING TIMES

NOTES

SHOP

LOCATION

OPENING TIMES

NOTES

SHOP

LOCATION

OPENING TIMES

NOTES

SHOP

LOCATION

OPENING TIMES

NOTES

SHOP

LOCATION

OPENING TIMES

NOTES

SHOP

LOCATION

OPENING TIMES

NOTES

SHOP

LOCATION

OPENING TIMES

NOTES

SHOP

LOCATION

OPENING TIMES

NOTES

Souvenirs / Gifts

Japan has a big culture of buying souvenirs (omiyage). Whenever someone travels somewhere, they're expected to bring back gifts for their friends, family and colleagues. You'll always find beautifully-wrapped omiyage at stations and tourist attractions: often local sweets, snacks or fancy bottles of sake.

IDEAS FOR SOUVENIRS / PRESENTS

- Sweets/snacks.
- Japanese Kitkats.
- Gachapon (capsule toys).
- Good luck charms from a temple or shrine.
- Daiso is a 100 yen store with lots of unique items for cheap souvenirs.
- Don Quijote is where you'll find all the "crazy" Japanese gadgets and novelty items.

WHO TO BUY OMIYAGE FOR

TOKYO BANANA

Omiyage are often regional sweets, and Tokyo's omiyage is a banana-shaped sponge cake filled with custard cream.

What bananas have to do with Tokyo I don't know! There are lots of varieties with different flavours and limited edition patterns. I've even seen one with leopard print on the cake!

Clothes

CLOTHING SIZES
Small, medium and large are often used for clothing sizes. If you need to ask for a size, call them by their letters: "S size", "M size" etc.

The fit will be slightly smaller than western sizes. I've found that compared to the UK, you'll need a size up from what you'd normally wear.

It's quite common for clothes to be "free size", which is one size.

SHOE SIZES
Shoes are measured in centimetres. Measure from the back of your heel to the end of your toes, taking the longest measurement you can.

CHANGING ROOMS
If a shop has changing rooms and you want to try something on, hold it up and gesture towards the changing rooms, and they'll know what you mean. You could say "Daijoubu desu ka?" = Is it ok?/may I?

Remember to take off your shoes when you go into the cubicle, similar to how you'd take off your shoes when entering someone's house.

Sometimes there's a disposable face cover so you don't get make-up on the clothes.

USEFUL PHRASES

Free saizu desu ka?	*Is it one size?*
Motto ookii saizu wa arimasuka?	*Do you have a bigger size?*
Motto chisai saizu wa arimasuka?	*Do you have a smaller size?*

These are included in the pronunciation guide video: cakeswithfaces.co.uk/pronunciation

Cute Clothes Shopping in Tokyo

HARAJUKU

Kawaii capital of the world! The main shopping street is Takeshita Street. Remember to explore all the little side streets. Once you get to the end, cross the road and get lost in Urahara, the backstreets of Harajuku which are less commercial and touristy. You'll find lots of brands you recognise from fashion magazines.

If you're interested in shopping, you can easily spend all day here (and you'll probably want to come back!).

Don't go on a Sunday, it's extremely crowded - that's when all the guidebooks tell people to go! It's best to avoid the weekend altogether.

RECOMMENDED SHOPS

- ACDC Rag - Super-colourful clothes at great prices. I wear their zip-up hoodies pretty much every day!
- Closet Child - Good for secondhand lolita dresses; find prints that are no longer available.
- Wego - Cute, casual clothes.
- Paris Kids - All the accessories!
- Listen Flavor - A little more pricey but excellent quality, with unique styles and edgy designs in dark and pastel colours.

LAFORET

Harajuku

A department store very close to Takeshita Street. Head to the basement level and you'll find offical lolita brand shops. They're very expensive but it's fun to look!

SHIBUYA 109

Shibuya Station

Cross the famous scramble crossing and prepare for ten floors of cute fashion. The style is more pastel and feminine here: everyday cute fashion and slightly more mainstream than Harajuku.

Look out for Punyus, a shop that sells cute plus size clothes. It's a sister brand of Wego.

SPANK!

Nakano Broadway

Extra cute and pastel shop with vintage and handmade clothes, plushies and kawaii 80s style accessories. While Nakano Broadway isn't really about fashion, it's certainly alternative. There are lots of interesting shops, especially if you collect anime figures, or any kind of figures or vintage toys. Look out for Bar Zingaro, with artist Takashi Murakami's smiling flowers. And giant rainbow ice creams in the basement!

MARUI 0101

Shinjuku

A department store with 7 floors of alternative fashion. For me it seems incongruous seeing these types of clothes in an otherwise mainstream department store. You'll find big lolita brands, the Kera shop and lots more.

There are several Marui department stores (you can spot them by the big 0101 sign). Only one of them's for alternative fashion; the others are normal department stores. There's some conflicting information online because it changed locations, but Marui Annex is the one you want.

CLOSET CHILD

Harajuku, Shinjuku, Shibuya, Ikebukuro

Secondhand clothing store that stocks lolita, gothic and punk fashion. A great place to find brand clothing at lower prices than buying it new - and in excellent condition.

KOENJI

Koenji Station

Home of thrift shopping and vintage clothes shops. Head for Look Street. The most pastel and cute is KIKI2, with secondhand clothes from cute brands There are also lots of cute little independent cafes.

Memories

Use this section to record your memories, list your favs and make a note of all the little things you might otherwise forget, to look back on in the future.

First Impressions

What did you notice?

What surprised you?

Is it how you expected?

Stick your boarding pass/
tickets / photos /mementos
here to keep them safe!

What You Did Each Day

DATE

WEATHER

WHAT YOU DID

HIGHLIGHTS

DATE

WEATHER

WHAT YOU DID

HIGHLIGHTS

DATE

WEATHER

WHAT YOU DID

HIGHLIGHTS

DATE

WEATHER

WHAT YOU DID

HIGHLIGHTS

DATE

WEATHER

WHAT YOU DID

HIGHLIGHTS

DATE

WEATHER

WHAT YOU DID

HIGHLIGHTS

DATE

WEATHER

WHAT YOU DID

HIGHLIGHTS

DATE

WEATHER

WHAT YOU DID

HIGHLIGHTS

DATE

WEATHER

WHAT YOU DID

HIGHLIGHTS

DATE

WEATHER

WHAT YOU DID

HIGHLIGHTS

DATE

WEATHER

WHAT YOU DID

HIGHLIGHTS

DATE

WEATHER

WHAT YOU DID

HIGHLIGHTS

Bits & Pieces

Space to keep pictures and any bits and pieces as mementos of your time in Japan eg tickets, receipts, leaflets, labels, photos, maps, paper bags, packaging, gachapon inserts.

Omiyage:
Best Purchases

Tokyo Bingo

Cross out these "only in Tokyo" things as you spot them!

How many days will it take to get a full house? The winner gets a snack of their choice from the convenience store!

Spotted someone asleep on the train	Flavoured Kitkats	English translation that makes NO SENSE	Couldn't find a bin
Made a random selection from the menu	Took the wrong train	Six or more vending machines on one street	Collected 20 1 yen coins
Rainy day	Coco Curry for breakfast (bonus points if after a late night of karaoke)	Got lost in a station	Took a photo with Hachiko, the dog statue in Shibuya
Someone asks you where you're from	Random stranger helps you find your way	Shiba inu	Tried a bizarre drink from a vending machine

At the End of your Trip

I know you're sad to be leaving! But let's take a moment to look back and reflect...

Favourite things about Japan:

What "only in Japan" things did you see?

Things you'll never forget from the trip:

Scrapbook

Now start your Japlanning list for next time...

There'll always be things you missed out, places you discover after you get back and new things to try.
My Japlanning list starts as soon as I get home!

Make a note for yourself in the future, of all the things you want to do:

PLACES TO GO

THINGS TO DO

FOODS TO TRY

"Best of" List

It's important to do new things when you go back to Japan - there's so much to explore and discover. But there'll always be things you'll want to revisit - that little hidden ramen bar, your favourite shopping district, your number one snack, an evening stroll with a gorgeous view. Make them your new tradition!

About the Author

Amy Crabtree is a designer in the UK who loves visiting Japan.

Cakes with Faces is my brand of colourful clothing, homeware and gifts, featuring my designs. I love creating cute characters and fun designs to brighten up everyday life.

It started as a hobby, and my website was an online gallery of my drawings. I wanted to do more with my artwork and in 2011 I started the online shop with an initial range of five t-shirts and prints. To start with I ran my business in the evenings and weekends, then in 2014 it became my full time job. Cakes with Faces has been featured in The Guardian, BBC radio and the first Small Business Saturday 100 in the UK.

You can get my designs on cakeswithfaces.co.uk (worldwide shipping). All items are 100% original and not available anywhere else.

I make videos about Japan on YouTube, to share my experiences and help other people plan their trips. There were so many things I wanted to know before I first went, and so many things I was nervous about - and that's also why I wrote this book!

I've also written two recipe comic books (one's about making sushi!), published by Ice House Books.

Thank you to everyone who joined in by pledging on Kickstarter to help get this book printed!

Thank you to Phil, without whose constant support and encouragement I would have given up long ago.

And thank you to everyone who supports Cakes with Faces for all the comments, orders and lovely messages. I wouldn't be able to carry on doing this without you.

CAKES WITH FACES ON YOUTUBE

Watch videos of lots of places in the book, and if you have any questions you can always ask in the comments

Subscribe for travel vlogs, round-ups and trip-planning tips.

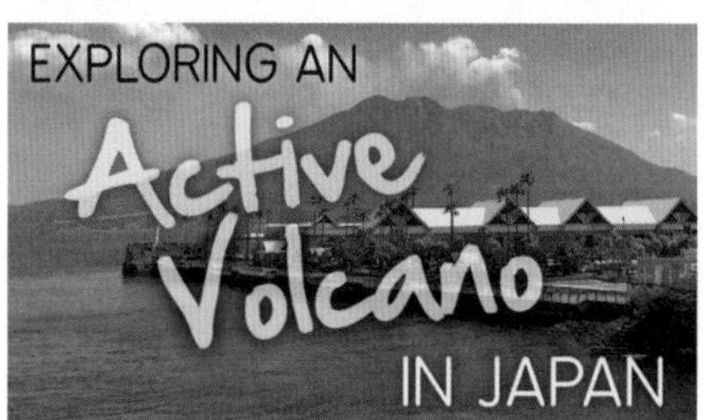

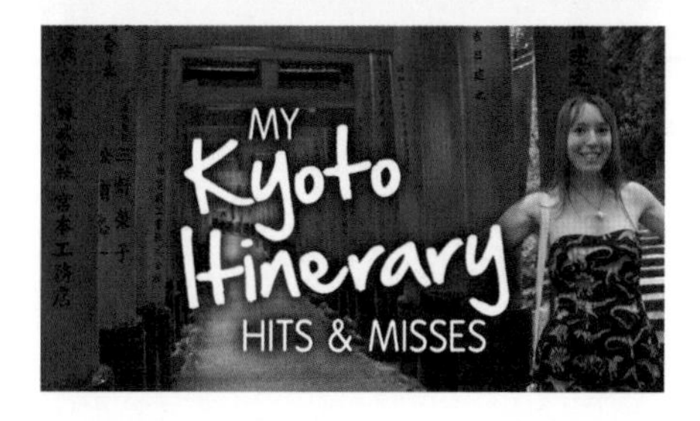

HOW DID IT GO?

I'd love to hear how your trip went - let me know on Twitter, Instagram, Facebook, or in the YouTube comments. Tag me in your pics - I always love seeing them!

And if you take this Japlanning guide with you, take a picture in Japan and send it to me!

 @cakeswithfaces

 @cakeswithfaces

 youtube.com/cakeswithfaces

 facebook.com/cakeswithfaces

NOTES